Rites, Rituals
& Religions

Dedication

With professional and personal appreciation and thanks for your knowledge and participation to all twenty collaborators and colleagues on the the eight-book series, whose total number of chapters and/or essays is in parentheses following their names in alphabetical order: John F. Burke (4); Eduardo Cerdán (6); Jorge Chavarro (5); Elizabeth White Coscio (6); Mary Jane DeLaRosa Burke (1); Lauren M.P. Derby (4); Gwen Díaz-Ridgeway (4); Montse Feu (4); Patricia González Gomes-Cásseres; (4); Jeanne Gillespie (6); Kimberly Habegger (5); Enrique Mallén (11); Luis Meneses (1); Stephen J. Miller (6); Norma Mouton (2); Jason Payton (1); Rose Mary Salum (6); Michelle Sharp (3); Juanita Sena Pfaff (2); Haiqing Sun (5); not to mention the long-suffering Sussex editor on all eight, Anthony Grahame, over the last nearly nine years—and my own content chapters (25). It has been a fascinating odyssey during which I learned so much and enjoyed working with you friends! Thank you, a safe journey onward to all.

Rites, Rituals & Religions

Amerindian, Spanish, Latin American & Latino Worlds

Edited by Debra D. Andrist

LIVERPOOL UNIVERSITY PRESS

Copyright © Liverpool University Press 2023; Introductions and editorial organization of this volume copyright © Debra D. Andrist, 2023.

The right of Debra D. Andrist to be identified as Editor of this work has been asserted in accordance with the Copyright, Designs and Patents Act 1988.

First published 2023 by
Liverpool University Press
4 Cambridge Street
Liverpool L69 7ZU

All rights reserved. Except for the quotation of short passages for the purposes of criticism and review, no part of this publication may be reproduced, stored in a retrieval system, or transmitted, in any form or by any means, electronic, mechanical, photocopying, recording or otherwise, without the prior permission of the publisher.

British Library Cataloguing-in-Publication data
A British Library CIP record is available

Paperback ISBN 978-1-78976-195-5

Typeset & designed by Sussex Academic Press, Brighton & Eastbourne.
Printed and bound by CPI Group (UK) Ltd, Croydon CR0 4YY.

Contents

Preface	viii
Acknowledgments	xii
Indigenous & Hispanic Worlds	xiii

Part I Introduction to Rites, Rituals and "Religious" Experiences

A. MYSTICAL/MAGICAL EXPERIENCE WITH CONTROL OF (CONTEMPORARY) SENSUAL & INDIVIDUAL OR SOCIAL SPACE ASSOCIATED WITH THE PHYSICAL & PSYCHOLOGICAL SENSES & INTERACTIONS

1	Art as Reflection of the Rites and Rituals of Wine Consumption in Spain *Kimberly Habegger*	6
2	Tango: Alive on the Skin *Gwendolyn Díaz-Ridgeway*	17

B. VISUAL CONTROL OF (ARTISTIC) SPACE ASSOCIATED WITH METAPHORICAL AND/OR FICTIONALIZED CONTROL. INTELLECTUAL/ LITERARY EXCHANGE AND SOCIO-POLITICAL CHANGES.

3	Self-Exorcism Through Art: Frida Kahlo's Self-Portraits *Debra D. Andrist*	23
4	Introduction to Art as Magic & Pablo Picasso as Magician: Magic and the Menace of Death in Pablo Picasso *Enrique Mallén*	33
5	Intellectual & Literary Rituals and Reflections Gone Awry due to Socio-Political Changes: Populism and Nationalism *Rose Mary Salum*	70

Part II Introduction to Rites, Rituals & Roman Catholic Religious Experiences

A. SUPERNATURAL/RELIGIOUS CONTROL CONCERNS: RELIGIOUS AND LITERARY RITES & RITUALS. METAPHORICAL AND/OR FICTIONALIZED CONTROL. AUTHORITY-DIRECTED CONTROL THROUGH ROMAN CATHOLIC CHRISTIAN & INDIGENOUS PERSPECTIVES.

6 *Song of the Hummingbird* (1996) by Graciela Limón: An Exercise in Multi-Stable Perceptions
 Debra D. Andrist — 83

7 *Nazarín* by Pérez Galdós (1895): The Challenges to the *Imitatio Christi:* When Narrators, Characters and Readers Are Skeptical
 Stephen Miller — 93

8 Rites & Rituals of the Roman Catholic Priesthood: Holy Orders: *San Manuel Bueno.* Human Weakness in the Vocation: Saintly Martyr or Sinful Hypocrite?
 Juanita Sena Pfaff — 106

B. (CONTEMPORARY) SOCIAL CONCERNS & CONTROL. LANGUAGE MAINTENANCE, RELIGIOUS PRACTICE, ECOFEMINISM & CHURCH-RELATED ACTIVITIES.

9 Traditional Spanish Language Maintenance and the Revitalization of Culture and Faith: A Mission for the Body of Christ
 Juanita Sena Pfaff — 119

10 Re-Envisioning Latina Ministry Through Ivone Gebara's Ecofeminism
 Mary Jane DeLaRosa Burke — 136

11 The Pursuit of the Beloved Community in the 21st Century
 John Francis Burke — 150

Part III Introduction to Rites, Rituals & Indigenous Religions for Control of Physical Space, Real & Fictional

ENVIRONMENT & NATURE. MYTH & GEOGRAPHY. SACRED & SECULAR. INDIGENOUS & CONQUEROR-IMPOSED

12 Sacred Geography and Gendered Ritual Violence as Social Control in Anahuac 179
    Jeanne Gillespie

13 The Mystery in a Solution: The Rituals in *Lituma en los Andes* by Vargas Llosa 197
    Haiqing Sun

14 Mythic Consciousness and Sacred Space in the Works of the Bolivian Poet, Óscar Cerruto 212
    Elizabeth White Coscio

Conclusions 226

The Editor & Contributors 227
Overview of Content of Volumes 1–7 238
Index 244

Preface

Philosophers have contemplated the meaning of life, the who & the why, since nascent self-consciousness of the evolving hominid species. Yet practical efforts, i.e, *control* of life, have always transcended the philosophical: how to dominate what happens to the physical body itself, how to control the environment and its effects, and the interaction therefrom both. Thus are born rites, rituals & religions, attempts exert power.

A rite *can* be a prescribed religious or other solemn ceremony or act—it can be a social custom or practice, or even a mundane conventional act. A ritual *can* be the established form for a ceremony, the order of words used, for example, a ritual observance *can* be either a system of ceremonial acts or actions, or an act or series of acts regularly repeated in a set precise manner. A religion is a set of beliefs, especially when considered as the creation of a superhuman agency or agencies, usually involving devotional and ritual observances (rites and rituals). However, a religion generally encompasses a social-cultural system of designated behaviors and practices, morals, beliefs, worldviews, texts, sanctified places, prophecies, ethics, or organizations, that relate humanity to supernatural, transcendental, and spiritual elements. It entails a set of beliefs concerning the cause, nature, and purpose of the universe, especially when considered as the creation of a superhuman agency or agencies, usually involving devotional and ritual observances (rites and rituals), and often containing a moral code governing the conduct of human affairs the belief in and worship of a superhuman controlling power, especially a personal god or gods or ideas about the relationship between science and religion, a particular system of faith and worship or a pursuit or an interest to which a person or persons ascribe supreme importance.

Because it is historically recurrent to refer to the "magical" aspects of traditional rites, rituals, and religions and their relationships to control efforts, I include some clarification. As one of my own chapters in this volume emphasizes about the applicability of multi-stable perceptions of seemingly same rites, rituals or religions, characterizations of those as "magical," or something much more, power over the inexplicable/uncontrollabe has far more to do with the socialization and beliefs of each perceiver than with the rites, rituals or religions themselves. *The Cambridge Encyclopedia of Anthropology*[1]

> explores magic as a 'craft'—a set of techniques through which practitioners creatively shape their relationships with the world and their own selves. Emphasis will be given to magic's documented potential to activate the imagination . . . A plausible working definition of magic, loose enough to accommodate at least most of the nuances associated with it, may describe it as a set of activities and technologies intended to manipulate invisible or immaterial agencies and energies, not recognized by science, to an advantageous end [for the manipulator and purposes].

It bears noting that the term, "magic," is very frequently applied to rites, rituals and/or religions apart from those of the speaker/writer when referring to any rites, rituals and/or religions. The entertainment aspects of "magic," encompassing "illusion, stage magic . . . performing art in which audiences are entertained by tricks, effects, or illusions of seemingly impossible feats using natural means . . . to be distinguished from paranormal [or] supernatural" as *Wikipedia* lists also influence how and whether "magic" is a concept associated with said rites, rituals and/or religions.

Therefore, given the sacred and/or secular and/or social overlays very often associated with the terms used in the title of this collection of essays, i.e., rites, rituals and religions, not to mention the linked psychological and emotional aspects for many readers, to avoid misinterpretations, the definitions of said terms according to the applications of those terms in this collection will, hopefully, deter misunderstandings and/or false impressions about the content. These interrelated and frequently overlapping term definitions move from the most general to the most specific, in my opinion, and are gleaned from several on-line and in-print sources, along with examples from the book's chapters. As editor, I shared these specific definitions with collaborators (including myself as a chapter author) prior to the submission of the chapters. I suggested general topics for chapters according to my experience with the established academic specialties of the collaborators. Of course, not all of the appropriate topics could be detailed in these particular chapters—though they may have been with a slightly different focus in earlier volumes—but a majority are at least recognized by mention as integral to the topics of rites, rituals, and religions. Furthermore, though the usual orientation for academics is to write traditionally structured scholarly articles, as they usually have in past volumes, several more of the collaborators this time felt the choice of a more personal essay or combined style for this volume, given the psychological and emotional overlays, was a more effective approach for their chapter purposes.

In the final analysis, the entire eight-book series of *Indigenous & Hispanic Worlds* has been about control in one way or another. *The Body: Subject & Subjected* centered on physical control of the space of self and/or on the environmental and/or social forces associated with the body; *Insult to Injury: Violence* focused on control of violence, whether against someone else's body or mind and/or someone else's against oneself; *S/HE: Sex & Gender* concentrated on control based on those two concepts, very nearly always misogynistic; *Family, Friends & Foes* explored control in and around relationships with others, going both ways; *Crossroads* traced the role of timing and interactions on control issues in life; *Death & Dying* on the (lack of) control over life itself; and *Sustenance for the Body & Soul* dealt with control of the senses, physical and emotional in regards to food and drink. Control efforts mentioned in this eighth volume, whether simply highlighted or detailed in chapters, range from rites, rituals and/or religions associated with everything from prehistoric cave paintings to pre-Conquest Amerindian ceremonies, and current denominational traditions. As might be expected from the histories of the areas addressed, especially in the post-Conquest Americas, several chapters focus on Christian denominational (recognizing but not addressing the conversion successes of evangelical groups over the last few decades in the Indigenous & Hispanic Worlds) or associated classic rites and rituals like those of the ubiquitous Roman Catholic Church in Latin America, e.g., baptism, communion, Holy Orders, marriage, and extreme unction/funeral practices. Too, the "crossovers," which deal with the more socio-cultural "rites of passage" like the *quinceañera* (a girl's 15th birthday/coming-out party, which almost always includes a mass and other religious trappings), Church-associated charity efforts through organized socio-religious groups and Afro-Caribbean *Santería* syncretic rites from both Yoruba (West African) and Roman Catholic (European) traditions, like dancing, drumming, interacting with spirits, and sacrifice have certainly influenced the *Indigenous & Hispanic Worlds*, not only the content of the book series but the reality of the target areas & groups.

On the socio-cultural front, the famous Southern Cone *tango*, another syncretic (dance) rite, is no-less dictated, with set rituals when performed according to tradition—but with a more risqué past quite in contrast to that which is church-associated and with roots in African *candomblé*, Cuban *habanera* and *mambo* and *rumba*, etc., and

European-imported waltzes and polkas, as well as the Spanish *gitanos' flamenco*. Because of that especially sensual aspect, this chapter dealing with *tango* is a short story to invite the reader to "experience" it. Another artform, as it is considered by *aficionados*, decidedly *not* a sport, the *corrida* (a rite known quite inaccurately in English as the bullfight), from the entire ritualized process known as *tauromaquia*, is and has been the subject of much studio art both in the Spain and the Latin Americas. The wine-tasting/drinking rites & rituals, much like the Asian tea ceremonies, exude an almost religious devotion to the pleasures of the palate, indeed, all aspects of *vinificación*.

The premise behind this volume is to discover how and why many of these rites, rituals, and religions may be addressed in real life in these divergent societies by exploring continuing rites, rituals and religions, plus visual and literary representations of control efforts as well.

Two unique aspects of this eighth volume are three chapters, somewhat more essay-like, which address and project current concerns, politics, religion and ecology, and one essay which addresses contemporary politics tie together content from the previous seven volumes in order to emphasize how applicable the contents of each are to the others' contents and the threads that run through all aspects of existence. The topics treated in the volumes are distinctly not mutually exclusive, merely emphasized for that volume. Thus, for clarification and to avoid constant repetition, because this volume is self-referential in terms of previous chapters in the entire series, references to past volumes are by short forms highlighting the main focus of that volume, if not the title itself: *The Body; Insult; S/HE; Family et al; Crossroads; Death; and Sustenance.*

It also bears mentioning that the title of this volume is an active choice to use the traditional term, *Latino*, rather than what has become the now more common (and becoming the preferred usage in the United States, especially among up-and-coming scholars and the public), *Latinx*. For explanations and definitions of all the associated terms and their variations, see prior volumes.

Note
1 Benussi, Matteo. "Magic," in *The Cambridge Encyclopedia of Anthropology*. Oct. 25, 2019. Web.

Acknowledgments

All clip art featured on this volume's cover are from public domain sites. For identification and applicability purposes, beginning top left clockwise on the cover, the clips recognize (1) the Islamic heritage of Spain (711–1492) via minarets; (2) the South American *Cono del Sur* Argentine tango; (3) a pre-Conquest Olmec (coast of Eastern Mexico) stone head; (4) the Jewish heritage of Spain via a Passover menorah; (5) a Mexican Day of the Dead decorated *calavera* (skull); (6) a Caribbean voodoo effigy; (7) an Incan symbol according to the site but inexplicably similar to the Aztec feathered serpent god, Quetzalcoatl.

Translations are by the chapter authors themselves. However, the brief explanation of Picasso's conception of art as "magic" and himself as "magician" introducing Enrique Mallén's chapter 4 and Rose Mary Salum's entire essay, chapter 5, both in **Part I 'B'**, were translated by Debra D. Andrist, as were some quotes in other chapters by other collaborators.

References to chapters from previous books are from the *Indigenous & Hispanic Worlds* series, all of which were published by Sussex since 2014.

All references to and/or illustrations of artworks and/or literature by Picasso in the chapter by Enrique Mallén are from *The On-Line Picasso Project,* founded and edited by Mallén, authorized by the Picasso Foundation. Request a password at https://picasso.shsu.edu/

All reproductions of Aztec images in the chapter by Jeanne Gillespie are from public domain sites or the author's own photographs.

Indigenous & Hispanic Worlds

The thus-far seven-volume series of *Indigenous & Hispanic Worlds*, with this, the eighth, morphed from a single first volume published by Sussex Academic in 2016, *The Body: Subject & Subjected: The Representation of the Body Itself, Illness, Injury, Treatment & Death in Spain and Indigenous and Hispanic American Art & Literature*. More than twenty years as a university department chair whose administrative duties necessitated reduced time for publication scholarship, as well as personal & professional interests in Hispanic worlds and medical fields over-all (detailed in the *Preface* of the first volume), led to the realization that I was far more enthused about, and inspired by, collaborative work, not just for efficacy of content. Certainly, I had plenty of unpublished material for several published volumes on my own. However, my continuing professional conference participation, thus hearing—and later reading of—colleagues' work, convinced me to not only publish my own works on particular themes as chapters in books but to undertake the organization, coordination, editing, and sometimes translating, of colleagues' works in a series of collaborative volumes.

The forenamed first volume combined material from the art & literature components of many of my medical (and gender-related) Spanish classes over the years (focused on practical, almost "hands-on" medical content in Spanish with much role-play, etc., not the traditional vocabulary-acquisition type of class). Like-minded works on related topics from pre-Conquest Aztec worlds by former Baylor University colleague, Jeanne Gillespie, PhD, now at University of Mississippi; the content of the monumental *Online Picasso Project* and related works on topics from Spain by current Sam Houston State University (SHSU) colleagues, Enrique Mallén, PhD, and Montse Feu, PhD; an MFA thesis by my former graduate student at University of St. Thomas/Houston (UST), later founder and publisher of *Literal: Voces Latinoamericanas*, Rose Mary Salum, MFA; papers by my graduate students, Norma Mouton, MFA, at UST and Jorge Chavarro, MD, MA, at SHSU; and a presentation at the South Central Modern Language Association (SCMLA) conference by University of Texas graduate student, Lauren M.P. Derby, MA, fit together for broad, yet focused, insights into so many Indigenous & Hispanic worlds and the "selfies," the hominid body obsession, the metaphor I chose as the overarching theme of the first volume.

The second and third volumes, *Insult to Injury: Violence in Spanish, Hispanic American and Latino Art & Literature* (2017) and *S/HE: Sex & Gender in Hispanic Cultures* (2018), also highlighted and followed up on my scholarly interests and works on gender and related issues, as well as those of the same mind. My Argentine friend from even before a co-post-graduate Mellon fellowship at Rice University, University of St. Mary professor emerita, Gwendolyn Díaz; my former colleague at UST, Elizabeth Coscio, PhD; one of Rose Mary Salum's Mexican writer-colleagues, Eduardo Cerdán; several SCMLA colleagues: Smith College professor, Colombian Patricia González Gómes Cásseres; independent scholar, Michelle Sharp, PhD; Texas A&M professor Stephen Miller, PhD; plus my former Baylor colleague, now chair at Regis University (who happens to be my sister-in-law), Kimberly Habegger, PhD, joined several of the collaborators from *The Body* to be featured in these volumes. Patterns of focus in, and segues between, subsequent chapters submitted emerged with the continuing collaborations, leading to the next theme and the applicability of some reprints of chapters from former volumes.

The fourth and fifth volumes, *Family, Friends & Foes: Human Dynamics in Hispanic Worlds* (2019) and *Crossroads: Time & Space/Tradition & Modernity in Hispanic Worlds* (2020), followed suit. New and a few reprints of chapters by continuing collaborators were joined by chapters which added more breadth to the *Indigenous & Hispanic Worlds* series' themes. For example, political scientist working in *mestizaje*, John Francis Burke, PhD, a former UST fellow chair now at Trinity University, and Haiqing Sun, PhD, Texas Southern University professor, whose work with culturally comparative aspects, especially in film, expanded the collaborator group.

The inspiration for the next book's theme comes from the last book published and the planning and the editing process for each following book begins almost as soon as the last volume has been submitted to Sussex each year. The sixth volume, *Death & Dying: The Nexus of Religions, Cultural Traditions & the Arts in Hispanic Worlds* (2021), was well in progress when the COVID-19 pandemic changed all worlds as we knew them across cultures in early 2020. While I note in the *Preface* that this title feels somewhat inappropriate—or uncomfortable at best—in these threatening times, the address of the binary aspects of death & dying by many of the continuing collaborators "still, underlying all the arguments presented . . . provides a platform to disentangle cultural context in comparative settings. Volume seven,

Sustenance for the Body & Soul: Food & Drink in Hispanic Worlds (2022), featured appropriate reprints but much new material by the faithful cadre of collaborators on topics as varied as post-conquest culinary imports from the Americas to Spain, Spanish recipe books, Columbian black clay cookware, the relation of Cuban identity to foods as exemplified in fiction, & more!

Volume eight, *Rites, Rituals & Religions,* recognizes the applicability and interpretability of nearly all the chapters in previous books to nearly all the themes so far. Rather than reprints, however, references to the appropriate books and chapters complement the inclusion of the new-material chapters introduced in the section introductions, a "summing-up," as it were. And, in addition to many repeat collaborators, two "new" colleagues join us, both Latina, one a scholar in her own right, as well as wife to a long-time collaborator, Mary Jane DeLaRosa Burke, and the other, Juanita Sena Pfaff, one of the best students whose work I ever had the pleasure to oversee at the University of St. Thomas. Each one contributes chapters focused respectively on the rites & rituals of growing up Mexican American, on a Brazilian female theologian, on a conflicted fictional Spanish priest and on the rites and rituals of the language itself, in this case, New Mexican Spanish.

PART I

Rites, Rituals and "Religious Experiences" via the Senses

Introduction to Rites, Rituals and "Religious Experiences" via the Senses

A. Mystical/Magical Experience with Control of (Contemporary) Sensual & Individual or Social Space Associated with the Physical & Psychological Senses & Interactions

The concept of rites, rituals and "religious" experiences associated with sensual experience has always been mystical, magical, even in the contemporary age. Yet, that overlay of mystery, magic, almost ethereal experience, etc., historically associated with real-life rites, rituals and religions, formal or informal, indicates that personal and direct experience, *feeling,* the inherent sensual aspects and emotion, is essential to bridge the gap between an academic, intellectual understanding of same and actual participation, rather like reading and *experiencing* the same poetic expression intended by the poet for the reader who may well have not had that experience. Part I 'A' focuses on that aspect of "religious" esoteric experiences, not denominational as in dictated-by-authorities formal ways, but in individual reactions kinds of ways.

A multi-sense experience over-all, v*inificación* covers the entire process of winemaking. At the very least, the end experience, includes *taste, smell,* and *sight*—a much more common experience and a contemporary, at least among certain socio-economic groups' "foodies" in the western worlds, a hobby, if not profession—or, simply, a meal-enhancing beverage and/or professional/work endeavor for vast numbers of many populations, particularly in the Hispanic worlds. Yet, the sensual aspects which relate to the physical experiences, though thousands of years old throughout the globe, render those wine tasting/drinking rites and rituals and experiences, indeed, all of the associated aspects: taste characteristics, "nose/bouquet," "finish," color, body, legs, the winery facilities themselves, not to mention the bottling and labeling and marketing, etc., into almost religious experiences, something akin to the eastern worlds' esoteric tea ceremonies. Kimberly Habegger has written series of academically oriented Spanish wine-related chapters blending numerous disciplines from culinary to architectural to marketing (visual) and more. Her *Linking & Selling Sustenance & Space: Wine Labels in Spain* and *Spain's Wine Museums: Where Age-Old Oenological Tradition Intersects with Contemporary Design & Modern Technology* from *Sustenance* and now, *Art as Reflection of the Rites and Rituals of Wine Consumption in Spain* for this eighth

Introduction to Part I | 3

volume, establish the physical and scholarly appeal of all aspects wine experiences across fields of study.

Of course, earlier chapters from earlier books (whose authors may or may not have contributed to this eighth volume) also address other types of sense-based experiences—but are not included here as reprints since this book is a summarizing "composite" of sorts already. However, it bears remembering that eating and drinking other than wine, as well as cooking, both "directions," if you will, can be "religious" experiences in terms of the physical senses (taste, aroma, visual presentation), with many associated rites and rituals (recipes, dictated processes and more). Michelle Sharp's chapters, *Vitamin F: First Wave Feminist-Fueled Economics and Family Responsibilities: A Recipe for the Modern Spanish Nation* from *Sustenance* (the latter a reprint from *S/HE*) demonstrate this, as do mine from the seventh volume, *(Culinary) Counter-Conquest* and *The Kitchen & Dining Room: Cooking & Consuming*. Stephen J. Miller also focuses on like topics, though from literature, with *Real Recipes and Willed Eroticism in Isabel Allende's 'Afrodita'* from *Sustenance*, as do Jorge Chavarro in *Cultural & Culinary Symbiosis: The Art of Describing Cuban Identity in José Lezama Lima's 'Paradiso'* and Eduardo Cerdán in *Metamorphosis and Food: Adela Fernández and Leonora Carrington's Short Stories* from that volume.

Including a short story in a themed scholarly collection of chapters like this volume with represents a unique—and potentially risk-fraught—structurally hybrid innovation, not a decision taken lightly by this editor, given the traditional dedicated forms and structures acceptable to/preferred by many professionally trained academic readers to whom these themes appeal. Thus, Gwen Díaz-Ridgeway's short story, *Tango: Alive on the Skin*, in this **Part I** (translated from the Spanish by the essayist herself, an Argentine-U.S. who splits her time between the two countries and does, in fact, dance the *tango*), offers that simulated sensual, physical and emotional "touch" experience, if you will, as a possibility to those who do not and probably never will, dance a *tango*. Much like her essay, *The Passing of J.S.D.* from *Death*, brought many readers to tears remembering their own family losses and, in retrospect, the rites, rituals and, possibly, religious aspects, associated with such losses, which offered them a visceral understanding of that book's theme in this context.

B. Visual Control of (Artistic) Space Associated with Metaphorical and/or Fictionalized Control. Intellectual/Literary Exchange and Socio-Political Changes

With the usual emphasis on the aesthetic value of visual art to the viewer, the reverse, while recognized, is often not accentuated. In the case of my chapter in this **Part I 'B'** on rites, rituals and "religious" experiences via control of artistic space, *Self-Exorcism Through Art: Frida Kahlo's Self-Portraits,* Kahlo both paints and verbally explains her own metaphorical attempts at "exorcism" of her physical and psychological "demons" through her ubiquitous self-portrait works, though she never uses that term per se. She does repeatedly admit that her self-portraits are cathartic. I do refer in this chapter to my previous chapter on Kahlo, *Frida & Fruit,* from the previous book, *Sustenance,* but the chapter in that volume deals with Kahlo's end-life genre focus, still-lifes, and why. Yet, the idea of fruit and fecundity ties into her life-long struggle with fertility, a major "demon" for her, though she generally does not appear herself in those still-lifes.

The world expert on Picasso, Enrique Mallén, again writes about that artist, as he has in at least one chapter in every single volume of this series. This volume includes an introduction from an unpublished article entitled *Art as Magic & Pablo Picasso as Magician,* which gives the background for the reverse scenario in Picasso's case, à la Kahlo, instead of the usual emphasis on the aesthetic value of visual art for the reviewer, the rites, rituals and "religious," "magical" experiences via control of artistic space for Picasso himself. His chapter immediately thereafter, *Magic and the Menace of Death in Pablo Picasso,* expands those aspects, especially in terms of one of the ever-changing, real-life women in Picasso's life and how they become ritualized aspects of his magical rites. In this case, the role of several, e.g., Fernande Olivier (a.k.a Amélie Lang) and Dora Maar, in the artist's life and work is highlighted. (It bears mentioning that in this chapter, due to the general usage of time period addressed and the context of the geographic art which inspired Picasso's cubism, certain now-dated term references to ethnic groups, e.g., *Negro,* are employed. While common and considered descriptive by the user, rather than discriminatory, at the time, especially in quotes, today these would substituted with other terms.) Mallén has written prolifically (and not only in this series) about related topics: Picasso's *Body & Control via Artistic Exercise* and *The (Dead) Body as Catharsis* from *Body*; *Confrontations with the Other* from *Insult*; *Conflagration of (Gender) Identities* from *S/HE; Creation vs. Infertility* (Olga Khokholova, his first wife) from *Family et al*; *Picasso's Semantically-Complex Visual Poetry Through Modern Technology*, with Luis Meneses, from *Crossroads*; *Death as Impetus for Art & Life*, *Death & the Word*, both from *Death*; and *What's Cooking with Picasso* & *The Devouring Eye (I)* from *Sustenance*.

The essay by Rose Mary Salum, *Intellectual & Literary Rituals and Reflections Gone Awry due to Socio-Political Changes: Populism and Nationalism*, the last in this Part I, is quite different in terms of "experience," not only *not* sensory in the same sort of five physical senses way, certainly not visual or magical—and focuses on loss of the pleasure of intellectual exchange and/or control. in a topsy-turvy world. Yet, because this work deals with the senses assaulted, valued personal intellectual experience with the contemporary literary world, as affected by the dramatic socio-political shifts worldwide, it is a fitting last work in **Part I** over-all. The loss of the pleasurable sensory concepts, "feeling" confused, horrified, out-of-control due to the switch to socio-economic, political space, diverges from the previous chapters: not all "religious" experiences are enjoyable—sometimes they are wrenching, uncontrollable, lacking so-called "comfortable" rites or rituals or magic available or imaginable to mediate.

Salum's earlier works, do address traditional attempts at control, notably, e.g., the academic article, *The (Spiritual) Body Cured by Alchemy* from *Body*, and the literary space/control essay, *Space, Time, Creativity* from *Crossroads*. But perhaps the closest to the current volume's essay with a, if not exactly fear for the future, at least much anxiety about the loss-of-pleasure/control, with no hopes of magical rites or rituals to deal with what is happening/changing politically, are *The Death of the World* from *Death* and *Filminas* from *Sustenance*. Those essays also express socio-political concerns from a visceral point-of-view.

CHAPTER 1

Art as Reflection of the Rites and Rituals of Wine Consumption in Spain

Kimberly Habegger

The consumption of wine has been a significant aspect of the development of human cultures due to a wide array of its innate and symbolic functions. As seen through the history of Western civilization through sacred and classical texts, wine has been credited as "promotor de la sociabilidad, acompañante en la mesa, beneficioso para la salud cardiovascular o factor de destrucción del individual/promoter of sociability, companion at the table, beneficial for cardiovascular health or a factor of destruction of the individual" (Charro 18), in addition to its critical role in sacred rituals. In order to evaluate how wine consumption has been viewed by societies, it is useful to consider attributes of wine from three broad perspectives.

The Vital

Wine has served as nutrition, hydration, and medicine. Wine provides safe liquid and nutritional value that can be preserved over significant time periods and has been applied to wounds and ingested as medicine. Wine consumption may also can result in in temporary euphoric state; it is a powerful substance. At the same time, there is an acknowledgement that abuse of wine may result in significant physical harm to the individual and to societal relationships.

The Sacred

As gift of the gods in classical worlds and fundamental in the Christian Eucharist as originally performed in the Last Supper, the power of wine becomes sanctified. The Old Testament previously discussed viniculture often and even praises wine as in the example of Ecclesiastes (31,27): "Wine is as good as life to a man, if he be drunk moderately: what life is then to a man that is without wine? for it was made to make men glad." From a spiritual perspective, the excessive use of wine is considered evil. The negative consequences of imbibing in excess have resulted in the total prohibition of alcohol and wine in select cultures or religious traditions.

The Profane

Due to its intoxicating effects, the consumption of wine is associated with profane ceremonies as well as it provides escape from the routine, a common tool for those living according to the philosophy of *carpe diem*. Wine also allows for open self-expression allowing for artistic creativity; such expressiveness may also aid an individual in pursing romantic interests. Excessive consumption may be seen as misguided and foolish.

All three of these understandings of the attributions of wine acknowledge wine's exceptional nature which enables imbibers to physically persevere, to pursue spiritual transcendence, and to express jubilation or escape from the demands of daily life. In other words, wine affords or contributes to humanity's nourishment and health, sacred rituals, and secular celebration. At the same time, these three understandings often remind the individual of the potential of the consequences of excessive intake. Different genres of art may express these attitudes from the perspective of the artist or of the societal norms of the period produced. Within a given work of art, attitudes towards wine consumption may have roots in only one or in any combination of the biological, the sacred, and the profane understandings of wine.

Spain and subsequently, the Spanish colonies, are situated squarely in the wine culture that became formalized under the Roman domination and nourished under Christianity and the art from these locations can reflect these different attitudes towards the rites, rituals, and ceremonies of wine consumption. We will be analyzing several examples of the plastic and literary arts to determine how art may express the complex rituals of consuming and appreciating wine from the Golden Age until the present day. Clearly, the works chosen for this study are a very small sampling of the works that could be included for analysis and have been selected as they directly address the roles of wine from varying viewpoints. Historically, the consumption of wine has meant different things to different individuals and societies at unique moments in time and our exploration of select of literary texts, paintings, and structures produced in the Spain will offer some insight into the significance of wine culture.

Famous Quotes[1]

Before beginning the analysis of the specific works of art, let us take the opportunity to ponder some of the quotes that celebrated artists and intellectuals have created in connection to the role of wine in individual and social life. Such quotes succinctly and creatively express insights into human experiences. Here we have not included popular *dichos*/sayings that would provide an additional and extensive source for future study.

These first examples address the importance of moderation in the consumption of wine: two from literary works by the 17th century author of the first modern novel, *Quijote*, and more, Miguel de Cervantes de Saavedra, and one from 20th century Spanish surrealist artist, Salvador Dalí: "Sé templado en el beber, considerando que el vino demasiado ni guarda secreto ni cumple palabra/Be temperate in drinking, considering that too much wine neither keeps secret nor fulfills word," que el vino que se bebe con medida jamás fue causa de daño alguno/the wine that is drunk with measure was never a cause of any harm," and "El que sabe degustar no bebe demasiado vino, pero disfruta sus suaves secretos/The one who knows how to taste does not drink too much wine, but enjoys its soft secrets." While the Cervantes' quotes directly advise the literary character/reader on the moderation consumption of wine, Dalí's insight is a bit more nuanced. Dalí makes a distinction between *degustar* and *beber* favoring the former (the tasting or savoring) over the latter (drinking). In addition, Dalí states that he who *degusta* also enjoys wine's "soft secrets" emphasized by the use of alliteration. Here the artist suggests the more magical or mystical character of wine.

Félix Lope de Vega y Carpio, the arguably best-known 17th century Spanish dramatist, noted that "El vino, mientras más se envejece, más calor tiene: al contrario de nuestra naturaleza, que mientras más vive, más se va enfriando/Wine, the older it gets, the hotter it is: contrary to our nature, the longer it lives, the more it cools down." And the 20th century Spanish writer/philosopher, José Ortega y Gasset, touted that "El vino da brillanteza a las campiñas, exhalta los corazones, enciende las pupilas y enseña a los pies a la danza/Wine gives brilliance to the countryside, exhales the hearts, ignites the pupils and teaches the feet to the dance." In the Lope and Ortega y Gasset quotes, wine acquires a power equal to or exceeding that of human capacities. For Lope, wine develops warmth/passion/life with age while humans experience the loss of these vital impulses with the passing of time through the use of antithesis. Ortega y Gasset employs personification through verbs expressing typically human activities (to give, to praise, to enflame and to teach) to illustrate the positive powers of wine that bring humans joy and passion.

Literary Texts

While some of the previous quotes originated in celebrated literary works such as *El Quijote,* here we will include texts where the effects and characteristics of wine consumption are considered more in depth. In fact, references to wine in *El Quijote* are extensive and have been objects of study as in the article by Jerónimo Anaya Flores (Anaya Flores). And previously in medieval Spain, wine also plays an important role in works such as *Milagros de Nuestra Señora* de Gonzalo de Berceo, the first Spanish poet known by name, and *El libro de Buen Amor* by the Arcipreste de Hita, often presenting the opportunity for the believer to fall into sin (Canales).

We find an early modern example of the role of wine in the anonymously penned *Lazarillo de Tormes* (1550–1560) in the episode when Lazarillo steals wine from the container from which his cruel master (*el ciego*/the blind man) drinks. Hungry and thirsty, young Lazarillo concocts a method of drinking drops of wine through a small hole in the bottom of the vessel as this master is holding the vessel in his hands. Lazarillo's delight in drinking the wine is expressed through words such as "dulces tragos/sweet slurps," and "cara puesta hacia el Cielo/face to Heaven," so he may "mejor gustar el sabroso liquor/better enjoy the tasty liquor" (34). After *el ciego* figures out the deceit, he takes the next opportunity to slam the vessel in Lazarillo's face as the boy savors the drops of wine. The resulting wounds from the broken vessel are cleaned using the spilled wine and the master gleefully taunts "Qué te parece Lázaro? Lo que te enfermó te sana y da salud/What do you think of Lazarus? What made you sick heals you and gives you health" (36). The contrast between the great joy the wine brings as Lazarillo pilfers the drips from the vessel and the sorrow and physical pain he experiences after being cruelly beaten illustrate two extreme consequences of his actions and the speed at which the joy can turn to pain. The master's ridiculing comment regarding the dual nature of wine as a substance that can harm yet also cure may be understood as a comment on the unpredictability of life, the importance of honesty, or the need for measured consumption of wine although the many cruelties exhibited by the *ciego* render any truth he utters ironic and easily dismissed by the boy.

In the *romance* by Spanish Generation of '98 writer, Antonio Machado, "He andado muchos caminos/I've followed many paths" (*Soledades* 1903), the poetic voice praises the common people (*buena gente*) he has encountered along his life's journey. Among the different metaphors used to distinguish the *buena gente* from the *mala gente* (the self-righteous and arrogant who contaminate the society around them), the poet recurs to references to wine twice. The *mala gente* believe themselves superior because they think "que saben, porque no beben/el vino de las tabernas/they know, because they don't drink/the wine of the taverns." In vivid contrast, the *buena gente* labors intensely and celebrates life whenever and however possible: "Donde hay vino, beben vino,/donde no hay vino, agua fresca/Where there is wine, they drink wine,/where there is no wine, fresh water/" (76). In this poem, wine is associated with its popular roots as it has been historically produced and largely consumed by the rural folk who cultivate the fields of grapes and age the juice that will become the life-giving liquid; wine is not seen as a privilege of the elite. In effect, the *mala gente* rejects the wine of the taverns. In this poem, we see Machado's connection between toil and celebration that characterizes life well-lived and the symbol of wine reflects those who have lived as such.

In the brief twenty-two word, "Tren de tercera edad/Train of seniors" (*Historia de Gloria* 1980), Spanish poet Gloria Fuertes uses wine to express the attributes of old age. Aging in wine is critical as a factor in the production of a superior product and Fuertes proposes that the aging of people can also result in a deeper, more intense existence. Interestingly, the poet specifically refers to sherry (*jerez*), a quintessentially Spanish wine that benefits from many years of cellar aging. The use of the adjectives, "*olororso/fragrante* " and "*fino/exquisite* " are not merely classifications of sherry—they serve as metaphors for a substantial and meaningful life well lived. Sherry aged incorrectly would be vinegar and the poet clearly aims that her life ages well, resulting in sherry, not it's bitter byproduct. Aged sherry, as well as a full life, is described as useful (*útil*) and builds onto the tradition of wine as life sustaining substance (Fuertes).

Painting

Diego de Veláquez's *El Triunfo de Baco* (1628–29), commonly known as *Los borrachos/The drunks* is one of a number of his works whose subject matter falls into the metaphorical and legendary grouping within his expansive *œuvre* that includes religious themes, historical themes, portraiture of members of the royal court, and *costumbrista* subject matter. This work is unique as it unites the classical and idealized beauty of the gods with the gritty reality of contemporary Spanish peasants on the same canvas—all imbibing in Bacchus' gift to humanity, wine itself. The luminosity and flawless youth of Bacchus and his companion provides sharp visual contrast with the sun-toasted and weathered countenances of the laboring celebrants. The rudimentary vessels created for the storage and consumption of wine (a barrel, drinking bowls, and clay jugs) are centrally placed, thus dramatizing that the act of imbibing is currently taking place. As the *Museo del Prado* notes that while previous scholarship viewed the painting as a demystification of the classical fable, scholarship is now more inclined to view the painting "as an allegory of wine, which is not only able to cheer humans and induce non-rational space, but also to stimulate poetic creation" (Velázquez), citing the ivy crown being placed on the head of Bacchus' devotee as a symbol of poetry. In this masterpiece, Velázquez portrays the act of wine consumption as an escape from the routine and hard labor of everyday existence of the peasantry that allows them a moment of magic, joy, and creativity.

Spanish impressionist, Joaquín Sorolla y Bastida (1863–1923), is known for a range of subjects including representations of traditional Spanish lifestyles that were being lost to increasing urbanization and industrialization. The painting, *La vendimia/The Vintage* (1917), features a sun-drenched vineyard where lovely maidens collect the year's bountiful harvest of grapes. Two women occupy the foreground while a few others are discernible in the distance. One woman standing in the foreground smiles playfully at the viewer and her hair is adorned with grapes leaves; she appears as an early twentieth-century goddess of the harvest. The second woman kneels reaching for a generous cluster of grapes with an expression of intense concentration. The fashionable flowing white robes and beauty of the female subjects may remind the viewer of the Art Nouveau portraits of Czech artist, Alphonse Mucha (1860–1939), not the peasants of Velázquez. Sorolla's painting celebrates the harvest and its connections to youth, beauty, fertility, and bounty relating to the tradition of wine as a source of both sustenance and pleasure.

Pablo Picasso's *La bouteille du vin* (1925–6) is a still life fitting clearly into the cubist aesthetic. As a still life, there is no human subject depicted in relationship to the wine bottle, wine glass, assorted fruits, sheet music, and a guitar-like instrument. Nevertheless, the wine as subject seems to extend beyond a merely decorative piece of the still life due to two factors that symbolically suggest a more celebratory and engaging experience with the fruits of the vine. The color scheme is bold and festive with the primary colors standing out against strong blocks of black and white and the largest area of red is found on the wine goblet itself. In addition, while a painting lacks the ability to reproduce sounds, the sheet music and the guitar suggest that other sense promising upcoming merriment and celebration. Wine and popular spirts often appear in the Picasso's œuvre as evidenced in an exhibit entitled "Picasso, the Effervescence of Shapes," April 15 to August 28, 2022, at the Cité de Vin in Bordeaux, France. Exhibit curator, Stéphane Guégan, explores this topic through more than 80 works by Picasso and some of his contemporaries that range from representations of cafés and drinkers, variation on the glass and bottle, and evocations rooted in Catholicism or Greco-Roman mythology (La Cité). Most certainly, Picasso's portrayal of wine is extensive and varied extending far beyond the example analyzed here.

Architecture

During the last two decades, there has been a sustained effort to develop wine tourism world- wide. In Spain in particular, one of the experiences that the wine tourist can expect is to access innovative and critically acclaimed architectural design displayed in new and renovated wineries. Although largely attributed to economic development motives, the physical existence of these structures also expresses the role of wine in Spanish culture. Beyond this, a select group of structures may be understood as symbolically representing attitudes towards wine consumption through the architecture itself. The following three wineries designed by world class architects successfully house centers of wine production that also dramatically represent the nature of wine culture in Spain.

Bodegas Ysios (2001), located just outside of Laguardia, Rioja, by architect Santiago Calatrava, is an exceptional structure recognized by virtually all publications featuring the innovative recent architecture of wineries in Spain and around the world. The profile of the structure against the mountains to its rear is perhaps the trait most admired as the undulating roofline mimics the dramatic mountains. Yet an additional dramatic architectural detail is the center of the façade which is punctuated by an immense gothic-arch shaped entryway that receive visitors. The overall impression of the building is one of a sanctuary or cathedral dedicated to the production and consumption of wine itself. However, Ysio's relationship to divinity lies not only in Christianity, as the name itself is in honor of Isis and Osiris, the two Egyptian gods connected to wine. The structure is connected in another way with its wine-producing environs: from the tasting room, the expansive view of the vineyards is centered on the idyllic hilltop town of Laguardia. In addition, a reflecting pool surrounding the winery may bring to mind the tale of water to wine. Thus history, geography, and viniculture are all synthesized through the design of this structure and its relationship to its surroundings; this point is further delineated by the religious connotation of the structure as a type of modern cathedral. It serves well to remember that the heart of wine cellars that house the most valued vintages are also referred to as "cathedrals."

In neighboring Elciego, the hotel at the Bodegas Marqués de Riscal (2006) by architect Frank O. Gehry interprets the consumption of wine in yet another way. The bold and unrestrained rose-toned, silver, and gold-toned sheets of undulating steel flow in all directions in a style similar to that employed by Gehry at the Bilbao Guggenheim. The curved sheets of titanium are said to mimic flowing wine and the colors symbolize the wine, silver for the wire *malla* or mesh around the bottle and gold for the capsule. The hotel at the Bodegas Marqués de Riscal also embraces the surrounding historical architecture of the renovated section of the winery and the town of Elciego: the church tower and the Gehry design visually frame the townscape. Project architect Edwin Chan elaborates further: although the hotel has its own identity "it must also have a conversation with the surrounding historic properties" (Bold 3). Gehry's expressive structure references the pouring and flowing of abundant wine as an expression of celebration, generosity and joy. The functions of the different spaces at the Marqués de Riscal complement this interpretation with the winery, a hotel, spa, fine restaurants, tasting facilities and a visitor center, all contributing to an engaging and joyful experience to winery guests.

In the far western corner of Rioja in Haro, we find the tasting room at Bodegas R. López de Heredia by architect Zaha Hadid (2006). The other structures of the winery provide an eclectic collection of traditional architecture but Hadid's contemporary tasting room located in front of the complex stands out in dramatic contrast. Hadid's contribution seems to reference a section view of a flask or decanter and the confines of the flask define the interior of the space as well. The shape references both the tradition of wine tasting and the more recent scientific chemical evaluation and refinement of the wine performed at the winery. The flask-like shape is well illuminated on the exterior and the interior, and a clinical white dominates the interior to enable accurate assessment of the wine to be evaluated by potential customers. In the rear of the tasting room, visitors discover an art nouveau-style tasting stand of carved wood that contrasts visually with Hadid's work yet expresses the historical continuity of wine tasting in general and at R. López de Heredia in particular (Habegger). The physical context of Hadid's contribution functions as an important element in determining the meaning of the structure. The long history of López de Heredia is reflected in the surrounding older structures of the winery and in the tasting stand in the heart of Hadid's tasting room. The visual juxtaposition between the past and present or tradition and innovation highlights the importance of both in the winemaking philosophy of this winery.

Conclusions

It seems quite logical that the mysteries surrounding the creation and chemistry of wine, the temporary euphoria experienced after consuming wine, and the many physical benefits from judicious use and consumption of wine endowed the substance the potential to acquire additional significance in developing mythologies and religious traditions. The "magical" essence of the liquid has contributed to wine becoming an easily deciphered metaphor for opposing human experiences ranging from a joy to despair.

Art has the capacity to illustrate this complex metaphor in different ways. Spanish art, produced within the context of a society with historical and profound connections to wine culture, reflects intricate attitudes towards a quintessential local product that is both a creation of and a creator of Spanish civilization. Among other genres, literary texts (particularly poetry), painting, and architecture creatively reflect the roles of wine in society.

As the first artform to become accessible to a broad segment of society, literature served as a vehicle for expressing attitudes to wine consumption, though classical and sacred texts long before the Spanish language existed. In medieval Spain, texts often warn of the dangers while still acknowledging the sacred and the profane; after the modern period, wine consumption as a metaphor becomes more nuanced reflecting political ideologies and acquiring a more intimate symbolism.

The paintings selected for this study portray the beauty of the harvest (Sorolla), the enjoyment of (Velázquez), and the anticipation of (Picasso) a wine experience. These works extend beyond the depiction of a bottle of wine, alluding to a drinker's encounter with and enjoyment of the gift of the gods.

Nelson Goodman's definition of architecture is useful to differentiate the three wineries studied here from the numerous examples constructed in the last two decades also celebrated for their design. According to Goodman, a building that also has reference may be considered "architecture" (Winters 84–85). In Ysios, el Marqués de Riscal, and R. López de Heredia, the reference is to wine consumption as sacred, joyful, and historical experiences is visualized and made concrete through the design of the structures. The manner in which these three structures engage with preexisting historical buildings further emphasizes wine culture as a continuation of a well-established historical practice that is pertinent for future generations as well.

Perhaps the origins of the exacting etiquette and rituals of wine service and tasting practiced by modern-day sommeliers are not to identify and evaluate different vintages but rather the product of the privileged position that wine has held throughout history. The precision with which a bottle should be corked and poured and the thoughtful evaluation of the traits of color, clarity, aroma, viscosity, taste under varying conditions are often executed with a solemnity and grace reserved for religious ceremonies.

Notes
1 Cervantes from www. frases-celebres.com and Dalí, Lope & Ortega y Gassett from vivancoculturadelvino.es

Works Cited
Anaya Flores, Jerónimo. "Zaques de generosos vinos: (El vino en *El Quijote)*" *Revista de la CECEL*, 15, 2015. pp. 137–163. Web.
Anónimo. *Lazarillo de Tormes*. Zaragoza: Editorial Ebro, S.L., 1966. Print.
"Bold Bodegas: Top Architects Change the Face of Spanish Wine." *The Wall Street Journal*. (9 Oct. 2008): 1–4. Web. 13 July 2011. Print.
Canales, Víctor. "Vendimia Literaria: Medieval I" *Vino, carretera y manta.* September 21, 2018. www.vinocarreteraymanta.com. Web. 2 May 2022.
Cervantes. www. frases-celebres.com Web.
Charro Gorgojo, Manuel Ángel. "El Rostro del Vino." *Cervantes Virtual*. Web. May 2, 2022.
Dalí, Lope & Ortega y Gassett. vivancoculturadelvino.es Web.
Fuertes, Gloria. *Historia de Gloria: (Amor, humor y desamor)*. Editorial Cátedra, Madrid, 1980. Print.

Habegger, Kimberly. "Architecture Meets Viniculture: The Iconic Structures of Spain's Rioja and Ribera del Duero Regions." *The International Journal of Architectonic, Spatial, and Environmental Design.* Vol. 6, no. 4, 2012–2013. Print.

Kahr, Madlyn Millner. *Velázquez:The Art of Painting.* New York: Harper & Row, 1976. Print.

La Cité de Vin, Bordeaux France. www.laciteduvin.com Web. 2 May 2022.

Machado, Antonio. *Poesías completas.* Madrid: Espasa-Calpe, S.A., 1975. Print.

El Museo del Prado, Madrid, Spain. www.elmuseodelprado.es Web. 2 May 2022.

Picasso Ruíz, Pablo. *La bouteille du vin.* www.pablo-ruiz-picasso.net

Sorolla, Joaquín. *La Vendimia.* www.joaquin-sorolla-y-bastida.org

The Bible. King James Version. www.thekingjam.es Web.

Velázquez, Diego de. *El triunfo de Baco.* www.elmuseodelprado.es Web. 2 May 2022.

Winters. Edward. *Aesthetics & Architecture.* London: Continuum International Publishing Group, 2007. Print.

CHAPTER
2
Tango: Alive on the Skin

Gwendolyn Díaz-Ridgeway
FROM *Buenos Aires Noir*, 2015

It was cold when Karolyn crossed Corrientes Avenue. A gust of wind struck her in the chest, cutting between the buttons of her burgundy overcoat—not quite protecting her body. She pushed hard on the huge wood and glass door. On the ground floor of the historic café there were some couples drinking tea and a few men scattered here and there reading the newspaper, their coffees only half finished. She went towards the bathroom in the back to change her shoes. There was a strong odor of urine and tobacco.

With her patent-leather high heels, she went up the broad marble staircase circling the old elevator encased in bronze latticework—a turn-of-the-century mechanical cage, a symbol of progress that once dignified the city. She could now hear strains of music growing louder. At the ticket counter, the girl charged her one hundred pesos. As she searched her pocket for the folded bills, she began to tap her foot to the rhythm of the *milonga* that the orchestra played inside.

At a glance, she saw that the atmosphere was good that evening. She entered slowly but decisively. There were so many couples on the dance floor that it was hard for her to see who was there and where might be the best place to sit. Someone was waving to her from the back of the room. A tall woman in a black lace dress had her arm in the air, summoning her over, "Come sit with us." It was Electra, the Norwegian, sitting at a large table with several people Karolyn didn't recognize. As she moved through the room, circling the dance floor to avoid colliding with the dancing couples, Karolyn could feel the stares of men looking at her. She had a good feeling about her prospects of being asked to dance.

Only recently had she met Electra, but it was as if they'd known each other forever. They were exact opposites. But they recognized in the depths of their souls, perhaps, a certain shared essence. Electra introduced her to the group. First, Bianca, with her ex-husband, Alejandro, tall and good-looking, but with his problems stamped on his face. Then there was the Irish redhead, awfully dressed, and a pot-bellied man from Córdoba wearing a beret and cravat. Bianca seemed eager to set Karolyn up with her ex. Alejandro definitely appealed to her, in spite of the stress in his face, but he was introverted. When Bianca suggested to Alejandro that he dance with Karolyn, he was taken aback, as if surprised, so she decided not to waste time on a man so riddled with complexes, no matter how good-looking. They both pretended not to have heard Bianca's suggestion and, just at that moment, the waiter approached their table. "Good ee-evening," he intoned, announcing his presence, a fleeting presence in that café where the waiters tended to be deaf and blind until the moment of paying the check. Everyone ordered coffee. Only the Irish woman ordered beer. She laughed too much and was rather awkward, despite her slender body.

A new set of melodies began to play, all waltzes. Alejandro stood up, showing off his full height, and led Bianca to the dance floor. The Irishwoman, in violation of all protocol, asked the *cordobés* to dance. Karolyn was left at the table talking to Electra, who told her that Alejandro was a rancher, son of *estancieros*, who owned thousands of acres and herds of cattle, that he loved the Argentine land the way one does when it runs through your blood from birth. But now things were not going so well for him—the economic crisis, the fluctuating dollar and the price of soy. As Electra spoke, Karolyn watched Alejandro dance. He knew the steps, would be easy to follow, but he seemed to lack drive, desire, whereas the Irishwoman danced skillfully but it was a comical skill. She grinned from ear to ear, gracelessly pivoting her small, agile body, her movements mechanical and erect.

Karolyn lived abroad but she'd come back to Buenos Aires with a grant to lead a seminar at the University of Buenos Aries and to finish writing a book on the topic of desire in contemporary narrative. But it was proving difficult for her. In one of those ironies of fate, she had traded the university classroom for the tango hall. By day, she lectured on feminism, and by evening, she swayed to the two-four time of the tango, surrendering to the embrace of a stranger.

Electra had suggested that the best place to conduct research on desire was the tango hall. Seated side by side, the Norwegian asked how the book was going. Karolyn mentioned that it had occurred to her to include a chapter on tango as a repressive phenomenon but then she decided against it. She couldn't make up her mind. She wasn't clear on whether it was repression or voluntary submission. It was hard for her to admit but there was something seductive about letting the other take the lead so completely. Or perhaps it had to do with "the other" that psychoanalysts spent so much time discussing. Could there be some truth in the cliché of the sexual dialectic? Impossible, she thought. One thing was to surrender oneself on the dance floor, and it was another thing—completely different—to allow such a thing in one's daily life.

As they spoke, Karolyn noticed a man in a blue blazer, professional-looking, sitting alone at a table on the other side of the dance floor. He was watching her discreetly, glancing at her sideways. After a while, the man in blue stared directly into her eyes. Did he want to invite her to dance? She raised her cup to take a sip and serenely stared right back. But the man in blue was immutable, he didn't raise so much as a finger as he diverted his gaze now towards the couples on the dance floor. His eyes were wide open, observing the steps as if trying to memorize every detail. Karolyn didn't understand why he was watching her if he wasn't going to invite her to dance. Perhaps he didn't know how to dance, perhaps he only came to the *milonga* in order to observe. Too bad, she thought, he looked like an interesting person.

When Electra got up to dance with Adolfo, a well-known and famed dancer, admired by all, Karolyn took the opportunity to approach Alejandro, who had just returned and, from the other end of the table, was watching the dance floor with delight. Alejandro smiled at Karolyn, grateful for her company, and mentioned that he'd been told she was doing research for a book. This led to a conversation about writing, a shared interest. He liked to read. She hazarded a guest as to his preferences: Mallea and Echeverría. And no doubt he owned an old leather-bound copy of Martín Fierro, true enough?

She liked Alejandro, he seemed to be a nice person, but there was something tragic about him, something that went beyond his own personal problems. She imagined one of those maps of the Argentine Republic where the vast pampas were adorned with images of cows as a sign of the country's cattle wealth. Only now, that wealth was a thing of the past, Alejandro was saying. Argentine ranching was trapped in a series of problems that hindered its advancement, he explained. Like cattle caught in barbed wire, the ranchers had to deal with the cost of grain, foreign sanctions, export taxes, and a long list of statutes and regulations that had little to do with cattle or the quality of sirloin, but rather with globalization and world markets.

The pot-bellied *cordobés* and Irishwoman returned to the table. "The herds are returning from the dance floor," Karolyn whispered to Alejandro. "What?" the Irishwoman asked.

Karolyn pretended not to have heard the woman. She had no interest in talking with her. The nice thing about being older was not having to do what one didn't care to do, and, in that way, she excused her own lack of patience with the poor redhead. Could it be that she was envious of the Irishwoman's agility when executing those daring steps, the *ganchos* and *ochos milongueros?* For whatever reason, she preferred to avoid her.

Once again, she was aware of the insistent stare of the man in the blue blazer. She glanced down at her blouse to see if she might be missing a button. Suddenly, she saw Electra, in her high-heeled, knee-high boots, approaching the man in the blue blazer and sitting down beside him. Well done, Electra, like a true dominator, Karolyn thought. Electra was a sex therapist, although she preferred to work in the area of domination, so it was no problem for her to approach just about any man and ask him who he was, what he did for a living, and if he wanted to dance. They didn't get up to dance, but Karolyn watched as Electra and the man in blue blazer stood up in unison and came directly towards her table.

"Karolyn, this is Sebastián. He's a professor of philosophy in Rome and he writes, like you." Electra seated the man in the blue blazer beside Karolyn and, with no possible escape, they struck up a conversation. "Your name is Karolyn?" he asked. "Yes, but people call me Kara." Fortunately, he didn't ask her where she was from or if her name was of English or North American origin, thus, they avoided the kind of interrogation she found so tedious. Having to explain her dual nationality, her ability to speak both languages, irritated her to no end. She preferred to speak about her work. Nationalism was only good for stereotypes. And then there was the disbelieving reaction of those who viewed her as an impostor. "Stop acting like a yankee; why, you're more *porteña* than *lunfardo*!" a taxi driver once snapped at her when he heard her speaking English to her companion.

Sebastián, in contrast, started off like someone who was used to explaining that he was Argentine, that he had been living for many years in exile in Italy, that he had worked at everything in Rome—waiter, taxi-driver, actor, and eventually he became a professor and writer. Kara listened with a mixture of amusement and surprise that anyone would describe himself in such detail to a complete stranger. All his timidity seemed to have disappeared as he told his story. Little by little, Kara was entering into the mysterious world of Sebastián. But she was there to dance, and this man did nothing but lecture about his work and life in exile!

"We're all exiles... from something," she commented, interrupting his lecture.

Then she added, "Why don't you dance?" "Because I don't dare ask a woman to dance. I'm too shy, maybe... no, I don't dare,"

Sebastián stammered. They went on talking, and the conversation turned interesting. Sebastián's exile was not voluntary, as hers had been. He had been a guerrilla, hunted by the authorities. Kara was being drawn into the story of this man to the point of almost forgetting that she wanted to dance. At that moment, when they heard the first measures of a tango by Pugliese, Sebastián glanced nervously at Karolyn and, tentatively, asked: "Would you like to dance with me?" "Yes," she replied.

They walked onto the dance floor and, very slowly, he took her arm. After a few moments, he slid his other arm behind her back. He held her motionless for a few more seconds, waiting, then took the first step. He paused again, before commencing to dance slowly and deliberately. Kara could feel a current flowing from the body of the man embracing hers. This man, who was so shy at the table, was transformed on the dance floor, his demeanor seductive, so intense his emotion that she felt it herself, skin deep, alive on her skin. His movements were smooth yet pronounced; long deliberate pauses drawing out the sense of expectation. His whole face revealed repressed desire. She felt she herself swaying in a rhythmic flow, punctuated by the *bandoneon*, every measure a movement in its own right. Their bodies softly coupled, a leg against her thigh, guiding her, they spun together in a dizzying rush of agitated breath. Between each step an intoxicating interval, a calculated pause to feel the beating of one body against the other. The final measures of the tango swelled into a rhythm so intense that when the *bandoneon* struck the last chord, Kara closed her eyes, her breath taken away.

They returned to the table as if in a trance, neither one of them spoke a word. It was impossible to verbalize what had just happened. The magic of tango, Kara thought. The ineffable, hidden beneath the flow of breath. The desire to live and to feel alive together with another body. Yin and yang, all enclosed in a mandala where you and I become confused in a moment beyond time. That was desire. Perhaps now she could write.

The confines of the café came back into focus. Kara realized that their friends at the table had been watching them, astonished. The Irishwoman approached her to ask who the man was she'd been dancing with, and she answered he was a fugitive who once murdered an Irish tourist. The redhead turned away, offended, but still staring eagerly at the man in the blue blazer. Alejandro, observing them, seemed to wonder how an exile could dance the tango with such intensity while he, who had never even been abroad, had two left feet on the dance floor. Electra smiled broadly as if to say, very good, darling, very good . . . now, take him to bed.

Off the dance floor, Sebastián had once again become the quiet and timid professor. He took a sip of cold coffee and sat silently, distant and introspective. Beside him, Karolyn could feel the heat radiating from the body of her dance partner, a gentle electrical current alive on the skin. At that moment, all she cared about was losing herself again and again in the magical rhythm of that secret ritual. A secret whose mystery could not be expressed in words.

CHAPTER
3
A Self-Exorcism Through Art: Frida Kahlo's Self-Portraits

DEBRA D. ANDRIST

Out with the demons! Exorcism! "Mysterious ritualized efforts, almost always elaborate, aim to regain control of a/the body from evil in general, spirits and/or whatever external controlling entity or entities in possession via formalized religious denominational ceremonies and/or magical practices which are 'ancient and part of the belief system of many cultures and religions.'"[1] According to numerous sources, among them, Benjamin Radford on the *Live Science* website,

> The belief that demons exist and can possess people is, of course, the stuff of fiction and horror films—but it is also one of the most widely held religious beliefs in the world. Most religions claim that humans can be possessed by demonic spirits (the Bible, for example, recounts six instances of Jesus casting out demons), and offer exorcisms to remedy this threat ... many religions and belief systems accept possession by both beneficent and malevolent entities for short periods of time as uncommon—and not especially alarming—aspects of spiritual life ... To the extent that exorcisms "work," it is due to the power of suggestion and psychology: If you believe you're possessed and that an exorcism will cure you, then it just might.[2]

The body and mind of the Mexican artist, Frida Kahlo (1907–1953), were possessed by traumas of all sorts, if not external spirits, from an early age. Metaphorically, if not actually, possessed by her own body's physical and psychological demons, not to mention her resultant mental obsessions due to both those physical issues, as well as the emotional challenges in her relationships, I contend that Frida Kahlo attempted self-exorcism through her ubiquitous ritualistic self-portraits, as supported and frequently explained by her own words, too. Kahlo, though she never used the word, "exorcism," herself wrote and spoke of at least the therapeutic value of her efforts.

In her diary,[3] she admitted, "The only thing I know is that I paint because I *need* to (italics mine, Andrist)" and later she specified, "My painting carries with it the message of pain." Her self-portrait as the so-identifiable ubiquitous unibrow head and face superimposed on the body of a deer much-wounded by numerous arrows, *El venado herido*/The Wounded Deer, 1946,[4] visually exemplifies her tragedies. However, she made it clear, "I am not sick. I am broken. But I am happy to be alive as long as I can paint" (fridakahlodiario.com).

All Frida's physical and emotional demons (remembering all those arrows) included at least ten categories of dire physical and emotional issues (perhaps in this actual order): (1) childhood polio resulting in a withered leg & life-long complications, most probably including later-life post-polio syndrome; (2) total bodily impalement through the uterus via a teenage bus accident, which necessitates life-long body casts, operations, etc.; (3) accident-associated constant, continuing medical & emotional complications of all sorts; (4) her two-time erstwhile husband, Mexican muralist, Diego Rivera, and his on-going indiscretions—even with her sister (not to mention Frida's own affairs); (5) various miscarriages &therapeutic abortions due to all her other medical issues; (6) her socio-political concerns; (7) emphasizing again, constant, continuing debilitating pain with medical & emotional complications of all sorts; (8) the beginning-of-the-end final leg amputation; (9) the emotional effects of on-going, off-and-on physical sequesters in hospitals and at home—though she resisted and powered through, especially to accomplish political goals, whenever possible—throughout her life due to all her medical issues; and (10) social & professional misogyny directed toward her.

Her childhood polio with the resultant withered leg has often been cited as one of the possible reasons why Frida always wore long skirts, especially those from indigenous dress traditions (another reason for the indigenous costumes being Frida's well-known socio-political views about restoring the dignity of, and overtly representing, the socio-ethnic classes historically and forcefully blocked from equal socio-economic participation and discriminated against in every ways in post-Conquest Mexico). Though only recognized and researched after her death, post-vaccination availability after Salk's 1955 development of same, post-polio syndrome, only "typically [occurs] 15 to 40 years after an initial acute paralytic attack [the timing of which correlates to Frida's later-life additional medical issues and that she became bedridden towards the end]. Symptoms include decreasing muscular function or acute weakness with pain and fatigue."[5]

A Self Exorcism through Art | 25

As I noted in a chapter entitled "Frida & Fruit" in the seventh book of this Indigenous & Hispanic Worlds series, *Sustenance for the Body & Soul: Food & Drink,* curator Mark A. Castro, in Dallas, recognized that like symptoms had become more and more problematic for Frida towards the end of her life. Thus, he dedicated his exhibit of 2021 to

> lesser known [of Kahlo's] paintings she made later in life when her health was deteriorating, and her art changed. Still-lifes were something she touched on throughout her career . . . But in those last few years she returned to them in greater number. Her themes remain: luscious fruits, love of Mexico, animals, Diego. But there are fewer radiant or tormented self-so portraits. She told friends still-lifes sold well and were easier to do [since at this point, she was mostly bedridden]. (236)

"Painting completed my life" (fridakahlodiario.com), she said. Again, as I wrote in that earlier chapter,

> This quote from Frida is telling in more ways than one, since painting very many of the so-called "fruit" works literally did constitute and complete her work of the end of her life. An appropriate aside, too important to relegate to a footnote, is that the term in Spanish for still-life is *naturaleza muerta*/dead nature. Herrera calls attention to Frida's awareness of the irony in this term, as in 1952, she painted a work titled *Naturaleza viva/Live Nature* featuring "fruits and the way they are painted restless, even the title, written across the bottom of this painting, pulsates with life: the words are formed out of creeping tendrils". (398)

Frida's second major physical challenge related to her total impalement through the uterus via a bus accident, which necessitating life-long complete body casts at different times, at least 30 surgeries over her life, and so much more. On September 19, 1926, while recovering in the initial complete body cast at her parents' home, she, in fact, drew the not-nearly-as-gory (being in black & white) as some of her later works, of *El accidente*. A later painting, *The Bus,* timing pre-accident, carries double weight. As the website section dedicated to her painting notes, "Frida demonstrated her sympathy for the dispossessed. She painted the Indian mother as Madonna-like and the blue-eyed gringo is a representation for the capitalists [but] this painting is also a depiction of the bus accident which happened in 1925 and changed her life forever."[7] Photos document that she decorated her own cast during those months, which constituted what might be construed as her first "formal" artwork, and again decorated her own casts in her later-in-life months of recuperation, if not recovery, which eased her boredom.

Many, if not most, of her self-portraits document her medical history and suffering. The website dedicated to her describes an example, *The Broken Column* (1944), thus: "the nails are stuck into her face and whole body. A split in her torso looks like an earthquake fissure. In the background is the earth with dark ravines . . . a broken column is put in place of her spine. The column appears to be on the verge of collapsing into rubble" (fridakahlo.org).

Frida's emotional health was skewered by the later on-going indiscretions and betrayals by her twice husband, Diego Rivera. She painted numerous portraits of Diego and of herself with Diego. About the one widely considered a "wedding portrait," though two years after they married, *Diego y Frida* (1931), she said "Here you see us, me Frida Kahlo, with my dearest husband, Diego Rivera." All the while she told him "I love you more than my own skin" (fridakahlo-diario.com). Another of paintings with the same title, was intended

> as a present for . . . Diego on their 15th wedding anniversary. She later repainted another version . . . to keep for herself. The dates in the title, 1929–1944, speak for their years of marriage (excluding the brief period they were divorced in 1939–40) . . . In this double portrait, they were portrayed not as a couple, but as only one person. Both halves of faces complete each other. (fridakahlo.org)

The aforementioned divorce was occasioned by Diego's indiscretion, though one among many, with Frida's own sister, Cristina. Frida documented this emotional wound with the painting, *Two Fridas* (1930), as vividly described on the website, was

> completed shortly after the divorce [showing] Frida's two different personalities . . . the traditional Frida in Tehuana costume, with a broken heart, sitting next to an independent, modern-dressed Frida. In Frida's diary . . . she later admitted [that] it expressed her desperation and loneliness with the separation from Diego. In this painting, the two Fridas are holding hands. They both have visible hearts, and the heart of the traditional Frida is cut and torn open. The main artery, which comes from the torn heart down to the right hand of the traditional Frida, is cut off by the surgical pincers held in the lap of the traditional Frida. The blood keeps dripping on her white dress, and she is in danger of bleeding to death. The stormy sky filled with agitated clouds may reflect Frida's inner turmoil. (fridakahlo.org)

A Self Exorcism through Art | 27

In 1943 and 1949, she twice employed her frequent forehead medallion in self-portraits, which portray her obsession with Diego, whose head is literally superimposed just above her unibrow. *Diego on My Mind* (started in 1940 but not finished until 1943) shows her dressed in indigenous costume, and *Diego and I* (1949), just her head is shown, with tears in her eyes, in this case, occasioned by his affair with the film star, María Félix, her friend.

About the same time, she wrote in her diary, "much of which is a love poem to him: 'DIEGO. I am alone.' Then a few pages later: 'My Diego. I am no longer alone. You accompany me. You put me to sleep, and you revive me.' Another time she drew two faces that look like vases. 'Don't cry at me,' one of them says. The other answers: 'Yes. I'll cry at you'" (fridakahlodiario.com). At yet another point, she also wrote

> Diego: Nothing is comparable to your hands, and nothing is equal to the gold-green of your eyes. My body fills itself with you for days and days. You are the mirror of the night. The violent light of lightening. The dampness of the earth. Your armpit is my refuge. My fingertips touch your blood. All my joy is to feel your life shoot forth from you fountain-flower which mine keeps in order to fill all the paths of my nerves which belong to you. (fridakahlodiario.com)

In the final analysis, however, Frida admitted that "There have been two great accidents in my life. One was the trolley, and the other was Diego. Diego was by far the worst" (fridakahlodiario.com).

Associated with her also obsessive desire to have a child with Diego, she suffered various miscarriages & therapeutic abortions also occasioned by aftermath of the horrific accident as a teenager; "I never paint dreams or nightmares. I paint my own reality." "I lost three children and a series of other things that would have completed my horrible life. My painting took the place of all this" (fridakahlodiario.com). Two of the most graphic of her associated paintings are from the particularly dark time in so many ways that the couple spent in Detroit, Michigan, U.S.A. for Diego's mural. *Frida and the Cesarean* (1932) and *Henry Ford Hospital. The Flying Bed* (1932). The website describes her paintings that horrific year:

> In May . . . she got pregnant again . . . knowing that there were some risks with her being able to carry the pregnancy, Frida chose to stop the pregnancy with abortion, as she had the previous one . . . a local Detroit specialist gives her medication and castor oil to compel the premature birth. But all of that failed and Frida chose to carry the

pregnancy to full term [having been told that she] could carry . . . to full term and deliver through cesarean operation [but] on July 4th, she endured a horrible life-threatening miscarriage . . . and in [a second] painting she started five days later, [she] depicts herself in Henry Ford Hospital . . . naked with blood and hemorrhage . . . body twisted . . . six objects flying around her. A male fetus . . . based on a medical illustration. An orchid looks like a uterus. The stomach she holds against the red ribbons . . . like umbilical cords. The snail is the symbol of the slowness of the operation. (fridakahlo.org)

In spite of all of this trauma, as I wrote in the aforementioned earlier chapter in the earlier book, "Though Frida may not have been physically able to leave a human child to the world, she conceived her artworks and carried them to term, at the end of her life featuring fruit with seeds providing the promise of new life. Almost as if dying in childbirth, Frida birthed her iconic fruit still-lifes as allegories of her life at the end of her life" (Sustenance 243).

Almost as important as the effects of her physical & marital travails, Frida's socio/economic/political concern influenced her life and work throughout her life. As a teenager,

While attending the *Escuela Nacional Preparatoria*, Frida became a member of *Los Cachuchas*, a campus-based radical group named after the style of caps they wore in rebellion against the dress code, voraciously [reading] Lenin, Marx, Hegel, Kant, Russian literature, and Mexican fiction, [considering] herself a 'daughter of the (Mexican) Revolution" (1910–20) [she participated in] debates with her peers who came from the most elite families in the country [and in] playing pranks on conservative teachers . . . By the age of 16, she had joined the youth group of the Mexican Communist Party (PCM) . . . in her early 20s, Frida joined the PCM, even though it had become outlawed (1925–35) . . . she campaigned for peace . . . collected signatures . . . contributed financial resources.

From 1930–33 . . . Frida was living in the United States at the height of the Great Depression and Jim Crow apartheid [and] became indignant [about] widespread poverty, hunger and blatant racism. [She] raised money for the anti-fascists during the Spanish Civil War (1936–39) and aided refugees . . . (1936–39) . . . seeking asylum in Mexico . . . Eleven days before her death, Frida participated—in a wheelchair and against her doctor's order—in a July 2 protest against the United States' intervention in Guatemala. (*Liberation*)

Frida was a communist, a life-long socialist and Marxist—but in the Latin American style, much more a proponent of a more-equitable-society-type of actual socialist/Marxist than the Russian totalitarian version, in spite of publicly embracing—in one case, literally—of Russian Bolsheviks like Leon Trotsky.

> References to Communism ramped up in her works from the 1950s. As scholar Andrea Kettenmann writes in her 1999 book *Frida Kahlo, 1907–1954: Pain and Passion*, the artist became "explicit in her last productive phase." In 1950, Kahlo painted a hammer and sickle on one of the orthopedic corsets that supported her increasingly weak back, and in a diary entry from 1951, she worried that her failing health would restrict her from serving the Communist cause. (Gotthardt)

"I want to turn [my work] into something useful; until now I have managed simply an honest expression of my own self, but one which is unfortunately a long way from serving the Party," she wrote. "I must struggle with all my strength to ensure that the little positive that my health allows me to do also benefits the Revolution, the only real reason to live" (fridakahlodiario.com).

> Several years later, in 1954, Kahlo painted her most pointedly political work: *Marxism will give Health to the Sick*. (Its original title was longer-winded: *Peace on Earth so the Marxist Science may Save the Sick and Those Oppressed by Criminal Yankee Capitalism*.) The canvas metaphorically links Kahlo's physical suffering with her allegiance to Communism. At the center of the composition, she holds a red Marxist book, while large hands (another symbol of the movement) embrace and uplift her corset-sheathed body. With Marxism to bolster her, she's able to fling her crutches to the side. On one side of the painting, a dove, the universal symbol of peace, hovers above planet Earth. On the other side, a depiction of Karl Marx himself strangles a monstrous Uncle Sam/Eagle hybrid. The painting's message seems clear: If Marxism can heal Kahlo, it can heal the world. (Gotthardt)

Their political views were always an important (and later, divisive romantically due to Frida's affair with Trotsky) shared aspect of their lives together. Both Frida and Diego

> advocated for a populist government and believed political power should rest in the hands of the working class... The couple also cham-

pioned *Mexicanidad*, a post-Revolutionary movement that called for stripping the country of colonial influence and replacing it with the trappings of indigenous culture . . . By the mid-1930s, Kahlo and Rivera both considered themselves Trotskyites. They'd followed the Russian Revolution and the rise of Communism closely and knew Trotsky as a hero of the 1917 October Uprising, which cemented Vladimir Lenin and the Socialist regime's rise to dominance. But when Joseph Stalin assumed leadership in 1924, he consolidated power and demoted Trotsky, exiling him for good in 1929. As a result, the Communist party fractured into two main camps: Stalinists and Trotskyites . . . As Stalin's power grew, Trotsky's supporters dwindled, and his enemies multiplied. In 1939, Kahlo and Rivera both switched camps, becoming Stalinists. (Gotthardt)

Though she never met him, Frida painted a *Self-Portrait with Stalin* (1954). However, Trotsky was another story entirely.

Kahlo had many romantic partners over the course of her short life (she died in 1954 at 47), but few resulted in dedicated paintings—and fewer pointed explicitly to her political beliefs [as her relationship with Trotsky once he was exiled to Mexico, with Diego's influence, did]. Despite their split [the affair having been a source of some great consternation to Diego, Frida and Trotsky] remained friends for some time, and on November 7th—Trotksy's birthday *and* the anniversary of the Russian Revolution—Kahlo gifted the politician a vibrant, sensual self-portrait. In the painting, Kahlo stands between two curtains, recalling the theatrical style of traditional Mexican ex-voto panels, created for devotional purposes and often found atop Catholic church altars or makeshift home shrines. She stares resolutely at the viewer, presenting herself with self-assurance and strength in a bold peach skirt and a fringed *rebozo* shawl. Rouge swaths her lips and cheeks, and ribbons weave through her thick plaits of hair. She cradles a small but bursting bouquet while holding a letter that reads: "To Leon Trotsky, with all my love, I dedicate this painting on 7th November 1937. Frida Kahlo in Saint Angel, Mexico. [Later] an undercover agent working for Stalin killed Trotsky with an ice pick. Kahlo had met [the assassin] in Paris the previous year and was brought in for questioning by the Mexican police. She was released a day later, and soon after traveled to San Francisco, where Rivera was working on a mural . . . Despite her stint in jail, the incident didn't dissuade Kahlo from continuing to embed politics into her paintings. (Gotthardt)

The beginning-of-the-end final leg amputation and being bedridden; In the last little over a decade of her life, Frida was giving up any hope, though for so long she had maintained that "At the end of the day, we can endure much more than we think we can" and There is a skeleton (or death) which flees terrified in the face of my will to live" (fridakahlodiario.com). Before the switch to still lifes, her works had become even more obsessed with death. "Death dances around my bed at night" (fridakahlodiario.com), she mused. For example, in 1940, she painted, a skeleton stretched out on the canopy of the bed in which she was later (again, remembering the post-accident decades before) trapped; in 1943, about the time she became mostly bedridden, she painted *Thinking about Death*, a self-portrait with a circular medallion (a repeated motif) of skull and crossbones on her forehead; *Without Hope* (1945), showing a disgusting mixture of food, mixed with a skull, when she had to be force-fed by physician's orders at that point.

In comparison, the social & professional misogyny Frida endured not only in Mexico but in the world was minor. Variously known in the art world as a surrealist and/or a magical realist and/or a revisionist mythmaker stylistically, Kahlo's legacy was late in being recognized by the art world due to Rivera's fame for his social realism murals mid-20th Century. In fact, when the couple was in Detroit for Diego to paint a now-destroyed-for-political-motivations mural in the Ford building, the local newspaper article dismissed Frida, not mentioning her artworks, not even getting her name right! While now widely recognized in professional art circles as a much more innovative and talented artist in many ways than Diego, her legacy has been somewhat publicly diminished by the overwhelmingly popular culture phenomenon, *Fridamania*, occasioned by naked economic gain motivations during the second half of the 20th Century, post-Kahlo's demise.

Yet, in spite of it all—and that she obviously could not exorcise her physical and emotional trauma/demons, Frida persevered with her life's work, artistic and political.

Notes
1 *Wikipedia*.
2 I chose to quote Radford on *Live Science* from the many sites addressing exorcism due to the recognition of the personal psychological factor rather than a focus on possession by external "spirit" entities like most of the religious organization websites.
3 The quotes from Frida are taken from the three main "official" website dedicated to her, especially fridakahlo.orgfridakahlodiario.com

4   All the descriptions of Kahlo's artwork, drawings, paintings and photos of, if not by, her are taken from images on the three main "official" website dedicated to her, especially fridakahlo.org
5   National Institutes of Health.

Bibliography

Andrist, Debra D. "Frida & Fruit" *in Sustenance for the Body & Soul: Food & Drink*. Sussex, England: Sussex, 2022. Print.

"Frida and Her Paintings." Frida Kahlo: 100 Paintings Analysis, Biography, Quotes, & Art. fridakahlo.org Web.

fridakahlodiario.com Web.

Frida-kahlo-foundation.org Web.

Gotthart, Alexxa. "How Frida Kahlo's Love Affair with a Communist Revolutionary Impacted Her Art," on *Art. Three White Dots*. Apr. 30, 2019. Web.

Herrera, Hayden. *Frida Kahlo*. New York City: Harper & Rowe, 1983. Print.

Márquez, Yvonne S. "Step into Frida Kahlo's Garden at a Lush New San Antonio Exhibit," *Texas Monthly*. May 17, 2021. Step Into Frida Kahlo's Garden at a Lush New San Antonio Exhibit–Texas Monthly. Web.

Milner, Frank. *Frida Kahlo*. London: Bison Books Ltd., 1995. Print.

"Post-polio Syndrome Fact Sheet." Office of Neuroscience Communications and Engagement. National Institute of Neurological Disorders and Stroke. National Institutes of Health. Web.

Radford, Benjamin. "Exorcism: Facts & Fictions About Demonic Possession" on *Live Science*. Mar. 7, 2013. Web.

Stamberg, Susan. "5 Lesser-Known, Late-In-Life Works by Frida Kahlo Now on View in Dallas," Mar. 8, 2021. 5 Frida Kahlo Works—Lesser-Known, Made Late-In Life—Now on View in Dallas : NPR. Web.

Vernon, Diana. "Frida Mania: The Frida Kahlo Effect." Dec. 18, 2016. Fridamania: The Frida Kahlo Effect (theculturetrip.com). Web.

Yañez, Candice. "Five Things to Know About Frida Kahlo's Communism," on *Liberation: Newspaper of the Party for Socialism & Liberation*. July 19, 2019. Web.

CHAPTER
4
Art as Magic: Pablo Picasso as Magician

ENRIQUE MALLÉN

Translated by Debra D. Andrist

The magical art of Picasso is based in his known tendency to attribute an external reality to his own desires and internal fantasies. This was also a crucial aspect in his recognized proclivity for superstition. Consciously and subconsciously, he felt that his work was replete with magical agents that could intervene in his life. His artistic production was, in fact, "an offensive and defensive weapon" against them. Common sense was irrelevant in this respect, he preferred to delve into the dominion of the magical. Equally illogical was his appreciation of the work of art as something real. In this, Picasso shared the analogical conception that the surrealist, André Breton, had of the world. In accordance with this visión, everything is analogically united to everything that surrounds it. The pictorial image and what it represents turns out interconnected to the extent that everything that the artist does with the image that he has created is transmitted to the reality that this represents. This is why, the artist can, in the final analysis, dominate the "forces of nature." That is to say, Picasso does not distinguish among the images that he elaborates and the objects, beings or invisible forces that they represent. Upon removing the boundary between art and life, the painter seeks to obtain a certain control of his existence and of the unknown hostile forces that are encountered hidden within it. As he said, it gives an "almost confusion" between life and art, to the extent that everything that is done with images happens equally to that symbolized. A second meaning of the magical in Picasso has to do more with common sense. The artist is conscious at times that his concept of art—as a magical form—was only a theoretical rationalization of his personal desires. In those moments, he paid more attention to the inventive and imaginary value of the magic of his art. He understood that it was no more than a projection of his own mind, a metamorphosis of his fantasies in reality. In other works, his art gave form to his fears, exorcizing them and in that way, satisfying his own desire, even though they in themselves didn't have a direct effect on reality. His primitivist conception of art as magic could therefore be interpreted as a species of skeptical amalgamation of magic and common sense. But, in the final analysis, Picasso understood the transformative power of the art forms that one encounters outside all explanation. Magical art could in this sense perhaps control life. From this perspective, the formal elements of art were more than expressions of already existing thoughts. They had the capacity to generate new thoughts and, with them, new realities. In this sense, they are truly like magic.

Magic and the Menace of Death in Pablo Picasso

Enrique Mallén

In 1906, Picasso was already well-established in the French capital, where he had settled in 1904 after several earlier failed attempts had forced him to travel back and forth to Barcelona. Towards the end of August of that year, he met the model, Fernande Olivier (a.k.a Amélie Lang), who was friends with Benedetta, the living companion of Ricardo Canals, one of his close friends from *Els Quatre Gats* years in Barcelona, now residing at the *Bateau-Lavoir*, No. 13, rue Ravignan, the dilapidated and run-down building where Pablo also had his studio. Known among his circle as "la belle Fernande," she was the artist's first real love and would become a crucial inspiration in his work through 1910; they would definitively break up in the spring of 1912. She had been born Fernande Bellevallée—an obvious Gallicization of Schoenfeld—in Paris, to a family of Jewish craftsmen, "modest manufacturers of artificial flowers, feathers, and bushes," as she herself once put it.[1] By the time she met Picasso, she had been living for over five months on the ground floor of the *Bateau-Lavoir* with Laurent Dubienne. They occupied room number three, on the rue d'Orchamps side. In the evenings, she would sit in the square and watch the artists congregate on the doorstep in front of the dirty, ochre-painted wooden portal of the *étrange et sordide maison*.[2] She had become friendly with many of them through her sister, who was the mistress of the painter, Othon Friesz.[3]

Throughout the spring, Fernande had remained uncommitted emotionally. One day in summer, she was approached by Joaquim Sunyer, another friend of Pablo's who had exhibited at the previous *Salon d'Automne*. Soon, she became his mistress, a decision as baffling to her as any other she had yet made. Her liaison with him was predictably brief but, while it lasted, it meant her moving permanently out of Dubienne's studio.[4] By now, she seemed to have been avoiding Picasso almost as a kind of ritual, without really understanding why, but on September 3, she finally moved into his studio, as both model and mistress.[5] According to her journal, it was opium that finally brought them together, a drug that instilled in even the most reclusive of them a universal feeling of empathy and comprehension.[6] "Everything seems beautiful, bright and good," she wrote after one nightlong session. "I've discovered that at last I understand Pablo, I sense him better. It seems as if I have been waiting all my twenty-three years for him."[7]

Before the move, the studio needed to be scrubbed clean. It was the poet Apollinaire that hit upon a way of cleaning the floor. Fernande had said she would pay Picasso a visit that evening, and as he gazed about it occurred to him that the place was not as inviting as he could wish. Guillaume had the answer: they would wash it with paraffin, a powerful solvent. However, after they were done, the smell was simply unbearable. There was nothing to be done but to sprinkle the whole place with a large amount of eau de Cologne.[8] She detailed her first impression of the studio: "There was a box mattress on four legs in the corner. At the far end of the room, a little, rusty iron stove on top of which was a yellow earthen basin, which served as a washstand . . . In another corner, a beat-up little trunk, painted black, made a not-too-comfortable chair. A cane chair, easels, canvases of all sizes, paint tubes scattered on the floor with paintbrushes, oil containers, and a basin for etching fluid. There were no curtains. In a table drawer, a pet white mouse, which Picasso tenderly cared for and showed to everyone . . . A fine, white linen blouse was placed next to two Louise-Philippe vases containing artificial flowers."[9]

In the beginning of their relationship both Pablo and Fernande were ecstatically in love, and the paintings and drawings he would do of her over the next months celebrated both her beauty and their personal closeness. In spite of the squalor of the *Bateau-Lavoir*, the studio would become a popular gathering place now that she was living there, with impromptu dinners, poetry readings, and repeated drug sessions. At the back of the meager lodging, Fernande would eventually discover a small shrine, with two cerulean-blue vases of artificial flowers like the ones in Cézanne's paintings, and a white, fine silk blouse he had perhaps made in her honor. Indeed, many biographers have tended to assume the shrine was to her, although Fernande presumed it had been "erected in memory of a woman he had loved."[10] She wondered: "What inspired him to create this shrine dedicated to unrequited love? As well as nostalgia, a mocking self-irony and humor, I think it showed a kind of mysticism that Pablo must have inherited from his Italian ancestors, though he himself is Spanish. He pretends to laugh at this 'votive' chapel, but he won't allow me to touch it."[11] Some have argued that the "chapel" might have been to his dead sister Conchita, an ever-present symbol of the menace of death in his life. Unger points out that this makeshift shrine offers a profound insight into Picasso's approach to his surroundings, revealing the extent to which he believed that objects, suitably arranged, could be imbued with magical powers. This was perhaps the reason why African ritual figures would eventually appeal to him and why he would make much more profound use of them than any of his colleagues. For him, "art was not primarily a visual language but a method of manipulating unseen forces."[12]

There are different theories as to when Picasso first got acquainted with African art. His first contact with a statue from that ethnicity was reported in a conversation Max Jacob had with Roland Dorgelès:

> The historic scene took place at Matisse's studio. The doyen of Fauvism had for some time already been in possession of a black idol that he made much of. One evening, when Picasso came to dinner, he caught sight of the statue on a chest of drawers and was lost in admiration; he picked it up and held it in his hands for the duration of the evening. The following morning, when Max arrived at *Bateau-Lavoir* as usual, he surprised the Spaniard drawing the figure of a woman with only one eye in the middle of her forehead, four ears round her head, a diamond-shaped mouth, a pentagonal nose and a square neck. The floor was strewn with pieces of drawing paper on which one could recognize the same monster in various guises . . . Fascinated by the black idol, he had worked right through the night. Cubism had been born.[13]

Matisse, on the other hand, maintained that the event had taken place at the Steins' apartment. He recalled: "In rue de Rennes, I frequently passed a shop called *Le Père Sauvage* belonging to a dealer in exotic curios. And late one afternoon, I went in to buy a seated figure, a little man sticking out his tongue. Then I went to Gertrude Stein's in rue de Fleurus. Picasso arrived as I was showing her the statue. We chatted about it. It was then that Picasso noticed the Negro sculpture."[14]

Gertrude had been the orchestrator of these artistic get-togethers and she truly enjoyed her role. Seated under her famous portrait by Picasso, she handed out comments with an authoritative air, glaring angrily at anyone who dared to interrupt her. She couldn't stand the painters who weren't her faithful followers: after all, wasn't she their benefactress by providing an exhibition space for those who refused to show their work at the Salons?[15] If Matisse's recollection is right, it could be said that both the painter and the writer had a share in the artist's first encounter with these objects.

The Frenchman's growing interest in African sculpture was shared with two painters he had come to influence quite deeply: Vlaminck and Derain. The former had purchased his first African sculpture during the autumn at a shop on rue de Rennes belonging to Heymann, a dealer in exotic curiosities nicknamed "le Père Sauvage."[16] It was a nineteenth-century Vili statuette (from the Congo). He later claimed to have been captivated by Negro masks as early as 1904 and to have then gotten Derain interested in them. Indeed, the latter would acquire a Fang mask directly from him. The attention they were receiving from artists is not surprising. In fact, such masks became fairly popular, arousing the curiosity of people with a taste for the exotic. They would represent a new stimulus amidst what many considered outworn subjects in art. Such objects could be picked up for very little at plenty of dusty junk-shops at Saint-Ouen or in the rue Mouffetard, but Heymann had made a specialty of them.[17] Matisse eloquently summarized the attraction African sculpture held for the diverse group of artists and intellectuals who were then looking for inspiration outside their own culture: "Compared to European sculpture, which always took its point of departure from musculature and started from the description of the object, these Negro statues were made in terms of their material, according to invented planes and proportions."[18]

Blier has explained that the diminutive size of the Vili sculpture and its relative lightness made the very act of handling it more intimate for Picasso. The artist would have noticed how different this figure was from academic sculpture: there was no musculature defining the legs, arms, or stomach; the face also showed little resemblance to any living human, although it had all the physiognomic markers. Yet, perhaps because of these very traits, the sculpture had a unique power over him. African figures and masks, like medieval sculptures and prehistoric art all had in common one element, they were linked to supernatural forces and were imbued with an incumbent ritual aura. African tribal sculpture was often made with a specific function, namely, to propitiate supernatural forces. Their execution in itself was ritualistic, for the logic and organization that went toward giving form to these invisible entities simultaneously controlled them and gave the sculptor a sense of power. The active, tactile experience, as well as the emotional charge it held for him, reinforced the tiny sculpture's unique influence. Power objects of this sort were said to address reciprocating universal forces in an ongoing interchange between the visible world of the living and the invisible realm of the dead.[19] Salmon called him an apprentice sorcerer. Blaise Cendrars wrote that the artist's works reminded him of black magic, "they exhale a strange, unhealthy, disturbing charm: they almost literally cast a spell. They are magic mirrors, sorcerer's tables."[20] Under their spell, Picasso would follow the same practice of a primitive shaman. According to Tucker, he heard the call to a type of visionary knowledge, a call that involves a severe shock to the so-called normal conditions. Mircea Eliade explains that, through the exercise of special techniques a shaman tries to reconstitute the state of primordial man mentally transporting him to "paradisiac myths" that speak of a Holy time of original harmony and unity between mankind, the animal realm, and nature; a time when there was complete "communion" between all elements of life. African myths, in particular, speak of the fall from Paradise as a result of man's distinguishing himself from the rest of nature.[21]

The influence of African art is clearly visible in the gouache *Portrait de Max Jacob*[1] that Picasso executed early in 1907. The poet lived at the end of a courtyard, in a kind of shed tucked in between two buildings, which looked straight out on to dustbins. The simple room was tiny (like all of his former lodgings). It looked like a storage space that had been emptied out and rented at a hundred francs a year. It was an appropriate reflection of the man's extreme poverty. He wrote with a cheap pen, ate mostly rice pudding, had to borrow money to take the tram to work, and spent the greater part of his meagre earnings on fuel for the oil lamp that burned night and day since the room was so dark. The place was furnished with a mattress placed on four bricks, a table, a chair, and a trunk in which he kept his manuscripts. After much insistence, he had managed to get the owner to make an opening in the zinc roof to put a skylight there. On the largest wall, in chalk, he had drawn the signs of the zodiac. He had made a name for himself as an astrologer.[22] In his portrait of Max, there is a clear influence of the medieval frescoes.[23] One must also acknowledge the importance of "primitive" carvings (ancient Iberian, African, Oceanic, etc.). In his pursuit of these sources, he believed profoundly in the creativity of the human spirit. There was in his work the implicit idea that the artist sees deeper into reality than the realm of "mere appearances" to which the common understanding is bound. His search was for an ultimate truth, the "thing in itself" which lies behind the phenomenal world of sense as comprehended by conventional understanding. His goal was to penetrate through the outer encrustation of dross to the pure essence of things.[24]

Knowing of Pablo's interest in primitive art, his friend Derain urged him to visit the *Musée d'Ethnographie du Trocadéro*.[25] André had been one of the first to see the potential of tribal art as a catalyst. However, he was too full of doubt to do much about it for another year. By urging him to visit the museum, he was relinquishing the risk involved in pursuing that route.[26] The Spaniard later recounted the magic of that experience:

> When I went to *Trocadéro* . . . I was all alone. I wanted to leave. But I didn't go. I stayed. And I stayed. I realized it was very important: something was happening to me, right? . . . The Negroes were 'intercessors'—I've learned the French word since then. Against everything, against unknown, threatening spirits. I was still looking at the fetishes when I realized that me, too, I'm against everything. Me, too, think everything is unknown, is the enemy. Everything, but everything, not just details: women, children, animals, tobacco, toys! I understood what Negroes used their sculpture for. Why they carved like that, rather than another way. All the same, they were not Cubists! Because Cubism didn't exist. Surely some guys invented the models, and other guys imitated them—that's tradition, right? But all those fetishes were used for the same thing. They were weapons. To help people become independent, to no longer obey the spirits. Tools. If we give a form to spirits, we become independent. Spirits, the unconscious (not yet discussed much), emotion, it's all the same thing. I understood why I was a painter. All alone in this dreadful museum, with masks, redskin dolls, dusty manikins. The *Demoiselles d'Avignon* had to happen that very day, not at all because of the forms: but because it was my first canvas of exorcism, that's why!"[27]

For him, these intensely formalized works helped crystallize his kinship with archaic expression, be it Iberian, Egyptian, Etruscan, Mesopotamian, or Cycladic Greek. For centuries, Spain, geographically severed from the rest of Europe had preserved many of the effects of its African and Middle Eastern contacts and was closer to the concepts and rhythms of archaic and primitive expression than any other country on the continent. He was aware that for a primitive sculptor, who carved a ritual object, there was no schism between form and content. The object was not imitative; it embodied its message in forms that created rather than reflected, became rather than described their subject. He would later say: "They speak of naturalism in opposition to modern painting, I would like to know if anyone has ever seen a natural work of art. Nature and art, being two different things, cannot be the same thing. Through art we express our conception of what nature is not. Cubism was an experience with reality, not with abstraction ... Cubism defined reality as a psychological presence rather than as a set of external appearances."[28]

Still under the spell of his experience at the museum, he became a recluse, virtually forsaking painting for drawing through March, busy filling his notepad with studies in preparation for his masterpiece, *Les demoiselles d'Avignon*$_{[2]}$.[29] This demonstrates Picasso's primary reliance on draftsmanship as a means of creative expression. He used drawing throughout his career in order to experiment with different artistic problems: how to show volume, mass and weight; how to convey movement through gesture and other means; and how to establish monumentality and scale. His numerous sketchbooks reveal how he worked out his ideas for the different figures and the overall composition. One of them was Sketchbook 1063 which contained drawings related to brothel scenes. Pablo, who freely admitted sleeping with most of his models, was doubtless seeing other women beside Fernande. He may also have reverted to his old habit of frequenting brothels, judging from these sketches. Since his subjects usually reflected the circumstances of his daily life, this is more than likely. Basing it on Gilot's statement that Picasso had confessed to her that he had caught a sexually transmitted infection at an unspecified time before his first marriage, Rubin hazards a guess that this occurred in the course of this winter and that trepidation in regard to syphilis or gonorrhea had to play some role in the symbolism of these compositions.[30]

Like a sorcerer's apprentice who transforms elements and actions of the world at will, the distorted figures in some of the preliminary studies suggests Pablo's attempt to fight the mortal dangers surrounding him through exorcism.[31] For him, there was a dynamic interplay between the constructive and destructive principles, Freud's Eros and Thanatos. The painting he had in mind was not intended to be a brothel in the normal sense of the word. As Unger states, "it was to be the great battlefield of the human soul, an Armageddon of lust and loathing but also of liberation, the site where our conflicted nature reveals itself in all its anarchic violence."[32] The representation of these women represented a cosmic principle. While the toxic and misogynistic coloring of the figures ran parallel to a bourgeois cliché about prostitutes, his nudes surpassed their prototypes in their cruelty and ugliness; they were the avenging furies of fate. Existing outside time and somehow above society, they radiated an almost aboriginal power. Kozloff even detects a touch of irony in the sardonic marriage between Matisse's Arcadian theme of bathers in a landscape in *Le bonheur de vivre* and Picasso's tribal fetishism.[33]

The watercolor *Les demoiselles d'Avignon: nu jaune (Étude)*[4] he painted during the summer might be the first study for the important figure along the right side of the large canvas. In this case, he paid particular attention to the figure's face, focusing on the angularity and dimension of the nose which was rendered with a network of cross-hatching. The inspiration clearly comes from the geometric modeling of tribal masks and the liberties that African sculptors took with the representation of facial features.[34] He would years later confess:

> When I became interested in Negro art ... it was because at the time I was against what was called beauty in museums ... men had made those masks for a sacred purpose, a magic purpose, as a kind of mediation between themselves and the unknown hostile forces that surrounded them, in order to overcome their fear and horror by giving it a form and an image. At that moment, I realized that this was what painting was all about. Painting isn't an aesthetic operation; it's a form of magic designed as a mediator between this strange, hostile world and us, a way of seizing power by giving form to our terrors as well as to our desires.[35]

He worked on another study, *Demoiselle d'Avigon*[3] through July. In it, the face and the bust were still shaped with gentle curves which became regular and stylized, but the hair, brow and nose were done with angular hatchings, which acquired their maximum intensity in the color contrasts, the beginnings of an emblematic visual aggressiveness that would define the final canvas.[36] Picasso was struggling to find an artistic language worthy of a metamorphosing energy.[37] Meyer Schapiro has written that primitive arts at this time "acquired the special prestige of the timeless and the instinctive, on the level of spontaneous animal activity, self-contained, unreflective, private, without dates and signatures, without origins or consequences except in the emotions."[38] Thus, for Picasso, African sculpture looked "rational" because it incarnated rather than simply represented its subject. He grasped, too, that African art was the vehicle for the mimicry not of things or creatures, but of a collective emotion. In *Les demoiselles d'Avignon*[2], "he saw kinship among the most widely divergent cultures and eras, establishing the precise moment when the formalized language for which he strove could find interchangeable derivations."[39]

Daix speaks of a fantastic spectacle when imagining the stocky short artist in front of the huge picture, a canvas he had been fighting with for months, in which five disjointed women were represented. The original *memento mori* had at first been intended to make fun of the title of Matisse's *Bonheur de Vivre*. But as he continued with his sketches, the idea had changed into the exact opposite of his Arcadian pastoral. Pictorially, it was even more of a contrast. For one, the rather theatrical enclosed setting of the bordello clearly contrasted with Matisse's open scenery. Moreover, the exaggerated and increasingly violent primitivism was a veritable assault on the rhythmic, limpid *cloisonnisme* of the older artist.[40] For sure, his goal with such a magisterial work had been to measure himself against established artists. The combination of the meanest brothel scene and the loftiest style was as explosive as anyone could have wished for. True, there were still underlying references to Ingres and Cézanne;[41] but progressively, under the influence of what he had seen in the *Trocadéro*, the figures had become geometrical constructs, a confusion of shapes going every which way, reminiscent of nothing known. The bodies with their broad flesh-pink planes were not shaded by either light or chiaroscuro, but violently chiseled with unrestrained fury.[42] And yet, his shock at the museum had not been caused by the sight of something new but by the recognition of something he knew already existed. The value of seeing it so clearly lay in recognizing the twin poles of mimesis: on the one hand the ideal co-incidence of object and representation, and on the other hand the complete absence of any fixed representational value.[43]

As Flam and Deutch report, Vlaminck recognized that it was Picasso who first "understood the lessons one could learn from the sculptural conceptions of African and Oceanic art and progressively incorporated these into his painting."[44] He stretched the forms, lengthened, flattened and recomposed them on his canvas; painted them with unmodulated colors, just as the Negroes did for their idols and fetishes. In doing do, we may say he initiated Cubism, or at least Proto-Cubism. Its poetic reshaping of perception would end up having an impact on twentieth-century art with its primitivistic thrust, its longing to recapture something of the so-called primitive's experience of participation mystique.[45] Tucker maintains that modern art would henceforth be distinguished above all by the challenging quality of its own thought, its ideas about the world. Such ideas have been "embodied in" rather than "illustrated by" the materials and forms of art, developing through the artist's complete involvement in the manipulation the medium. It is this approach that gives modern art its potential to be "a truly transformative activity."[46]

In its final version, the pink or ocher bodies of the women in *Les demoiselles d'Avignon*[2], almost devoid of modeling, were arranged in a low left-to-right diagonal anchored by a squatting figure on the lower right. The three women on the left still had the Iberian mask-like faces typical of 1906; one head in profile features a full-face eye and two full-face heads show the nose in profile, as sharp as a wedge of cheese; the bodies were made up largely of straight lines and angular planes and they stood against a shallow background of varying blue, the only hint of depth being a brown curtain thrust by an upheld hand. On the right, the violence of distortion reached a new pitch: the face of the squatting figure, turned right round over her back, had its features savagely jumbled, and the woman above has a long ridge for a nose, strongly hatched to give it height, very much like Congo masks: neither of these heads was of the same nature as the other three, and in this half of the picture, all the angular planes—drapery, breasts, interstices—were sharper, much more definite.[47]

Once the changes had been implemented, the five women appeared to obey mutually contradictory principles, although they were simultaneously united by a general geometrical structure which superimposes its own laws on the natural proportions, making them merge almost completely with the background.[48] All the chopping and changing of style and technique added to the general feeling of incipient anarchy. The essential difference between Iberian statuary and African art lies in the fact that the former uses disproportion, flattening, unilateral distortions, basing its expressivity on disequilibrium and anomaly, whereas African stylization is based on regularity, symmetry and equilibrium. Whereas the former seizes on "barbaric" realistic peculiarities and exaggerates them, the Negro-African masks take their essence from pure plastic forms, make use of proportion in their symbolism and invent new signs.[49] It is the combination of the two approaches that produced the desired result. What seemed like abrupt changes of style was simply the juxtaposition, in the course of work on the large canvas, of artistic techniques. The rounded contours of the figures have been transformed into a series of hard-edged shapes (principally mandorlas and triangles) that lie flat within the picture plane.[50] Speaking with Antonina Vallentin, the artist remembered: "I had done half the painting. It felt it wasn't right. Then I did the other half. I wondered whether I should redo the whole thing. But, no, I said to myself, people will understand what I wanted to do ... Yes, I knew exactly what I was letting myself in for."[51] Resisting the initial shock, the spectator had to take an active role in the encounter of the alien mask-faces, the unrelenting confrontation of unblinking eyes.[52] If the painting was an act of intercession, nothing in the imagery should make this idea explicit. In their dynamic relationship with the figures, viewers would be forced to penetrate the picture, and in the process, they would find themselves transformed.

Les demoiselles d'Avignon[2] had ushered in an expressionistic or "exorcist" phase. where African art had served as the model for a more aggressive and "savage" form of primitivism. It was, he said, the "sorcery" element in it, not its aesthetic quality, which attracted him. His assimilation of the formal freedoms of *art nègre*, not just stylistically but as a way of thinking, made possible a real break with existing concepts. As Gertrude Stein stated, "it must never be forgotten that the reality of the twentieth century was not at all the reality of the nineteenth, and Picasso has been the only one to have felt this in painting, really the only one. The struggle to express it became increasingly intense."[53] As Schwartz points out, "the furious motion in the painting prefaces the stillness of the Cubist ideal just as the explosion of a celestial body precedes a new formation of bodies in coordinated movement."[54] In his big canvas, he had begun to see the fundamental processes and principles of art differently. It was a question of identifying himself with the formal concepts of the primitive mentality and applying them to the problems of the modern painter.[55] In a work like *Femme nue aux bras levés (La danseuse d'Avignon)*[8] from late July, the viewer was confronted by piercing stares and grotesque bodies. It has been argued that his pictures at this time were devoted to the threat and power of female sexuality. He intended to make a strong connection between seeing, desiring, and punishment, but went further, making us, as spectators, the recipients of that punishment. The chaotic or apparently unresolved visual style of the painting stands for the trauma of our immersions into the composition.[56]

Picasso knew that the reliquary figures were often associated in some way with rites for the dead and meant to provide protection against evil spirits.[57] Since the power of his primitive exemplars—what he chose to call "intercessors"—resides in their being "magic objects," he also aspired to do three-dimensional works; not conventional, Rodinesque sculptures such as he had produced in years past, but carvings whose power would be totemic rather than artistic. Lacking the facilities, the tools, the technical experience and the time to spare, he often took to doing paintings as surrogates for sculpture. To give them a tribal air, he used herringbone hatching to simulate scarification and tattooing as in *Nu à la draperie: tête de femme (Étude)*[7].[58] He had learned from labels in the *Musée d'Ethnographie* that a fetish could fortify its maker's creative power and protect him against enemies, maladies and fears. It is the belief in the magic of handiwork that endowed the African sculptures with their shamanistic force. He would never part with these "guardian figures" he created.[59]

For the Spaniard, art was, at its deepest level, a shamanistic practice concerned with managing the hidden forces that rule man's fate. The key to discovering an artistic language capable of reflecting the jarring, jagged realities of contemporary life would have to come through channeling modes that issued from the remotest past, before civilization interposed the multiple layers that alienated men from their true selves. What he was looking for in the primitives was "a means to an understanding of his own time, a key to the future."[60] As we have seen, the breakthrough came when he discovered the tools to tap into the magic that was at the savage heart of all artistic creation but that was embodied most fully in the "naïve" art of so-called "primitives."[61] Eventually, he started turning in earnest to wood carving with Figure[5] and Homme debout[6]. In these works, we detect the influence again of Gauguin. As McCully notes, "keen to understand, if not appropriate, the stylistic means by which the French artist had transformed "primitivism" in his own art. He carved and incised the material, retaining the structure, shape, and rough quality of the pieces of wood he had selected, much as the makers of the museum's African spirit figures, masks, and statues had done."[62] Les demoiselles d'Avignon[2] has been called a cathartic painting, a great cry of anguish and release—a form of black magic in which Picasso summons his demons in order to vanquish them. As he explained to André Malraux, "if we give spirits a form, we become independent."[63] He often seemed to court disaster as a means of goading his creativity.

By the end of summer, the artist set the large painting aside for good.[64] As already mentioned, in its final version the figures had replaced a self-sufficient narrative with one in which the composition remains unresolved. The five women display themselves, both alluring and horrifying at the same time; fixing those that encounter them in their accusatory stare, creating, in Steinberg's memorable phrase, "the startled consciousness of a viewer who sees himself seen."[65] The painting had ended up as a hybrid of primitive styles, with dissimilar ancient Iberian and tribal forms squaring off against each other to create a jarring, dissonant effect in need of resolution during the viewing process. The period covered by the two versions corresponds more or less to what L. Delevoy called "the dismantling of the classical image."[66] Subsequent works, with priority given to abstract form and "pure" plastic rhythms, would produce a new type of image, no longer based on the relationship with external reality, but on the formal power of expression and spatial architecture. Picasso would not hesitate in distorting the human figure, chopping it up into fragments and scattering them, representing, for example, a face in frontal view but with the nose as a flat profile.[67] The savage directness of hatching also led to the increased use of straight lines and to an aggressive, angular geometrication of the facial features.[68] In the course of the work on the large canvas, the violence inherent in the scandalous naturalist subject had been transferred to the graphic techniques. Picasso has accomplished the passage from a savagery expressed by graphics to a brutality which was contrived, deliberate, and inflicted on the painting, remaining forever inscribed in it.[69]

As Daix proclaims, the age of science had arrived, the moment when, in order to represent physical phenomena correctly, scientists and artists had to disregard physical appearances and common sense.[70] From canvas to canvas, Picasso would be reinventing human anatomy and space, taking bodies, decomposing them, and then reassembling them, and he did the same for objects. This reflects his desire to reconfigure the entire picture, making each part relate to its neighbor as a pictorial and mental entity. Previously considered only food for thought, *art nègre* had become a crucial element in restructuring painting.[71] "I paint objects as I think them, not as I see them," he explained. In the long run, it could be claimed, as Seckel does, that it was not so much a matter of influence as one of a convergence of the primitive mode of representation and his: the idea behind these African forms (to represent what is "known" about the object, rather than what is "seen"), which would be one of the main points of Cubism, was every bit as important to him as their appearance.[72]

More than any of his contemporaries, he had an intuition of the uncanny dimensions of art and how they could restore the lost sense of connection with the occult forces that govern the world. What intrigued him was the piercing insight that art was, fundamentally, not an aesthetic practice at all but a system for manipulating the hidden forces of the universe.[73] Picasso's insight that art, at its deepest level, is a form of dark magic to ward off the horrors of the night was aided by the context in which he viewed tribal artifacts. They were cast spells, cryptic incantations obeying inscrutable laws. In Unger's words, he wanted to "reclaim art's totemic status."

He would return to a magical approach to art in the mid-1920s, as I discussed in another publication.[74] During a sojourn in Monte Carlo in the spring of 1925, he shut himself up in his studio for several days and worked on the oil *Les trois danseuses (La danse)*[9]. In the background we observe behind the dancer on the right a mysterious figure whose face, much more naturalistic than the others, is silhouetted against the blue sky. He told Penrose: "While I was painting this picture an old friend of mine, Ramon Pichot, died and I have always felt that it should be called 'The Death of Pichot' rather than 'The Three Dancers.'" Towards the end of the previous year, Picasso had been summoned to Montmartre to the sickbed of his friend, who was already quite ill from the combined effects of syphilis, tuberculosis and a weak heart.[75] The tall black figure on the right, according to the artist's assertion, represents his old compatriot's ghost.

In 1900, Pichot had gone with him on his first long visit to Paris together with another young painter, Carles Casagemas. The latter had fallen in love with one of the models they had befriended, named Germaine Gargallo. She had rejected him, and the young man had committed suicide after first attempting to take her life as well. Soon after this unfortunate episode, she ended up marrying Pichot, much to Picasso's chagrin[76] As O'Brian states, although the artist often quarreled with his friends, sometimes with extreme violence, he hated to let them go entirely and he rarely or never dismissed them from his mind—that was not in his definition of a relationship. The news of the death of Pichot—who was forever marked by the instability of Picasso's early career—reached him at a time when a deep dissatisfaction with his life seems to have taken shape in his mind.[77]

The picture was begun in a much more conventional way as a straightforward representation of dance rehearsals. All three figures seem to have had very similar rounded, rather melon-shaped heads and more realistic legs and feet. Then at some point, presumably after his friend's death, he made a number of radical changes that would transform the canvas into a magical object. Not only did the stylization become much more arbitrary, but also Picasso clearly set out to make each of the dancers as significant as possible. As a result, the final picture has a hieratic grandeur and a strangeness that are entirely foreign to all his previous renderings of the ballet. Silver points out how "the figures are ruthlessly distorted, impossibly flat, and terrifyingly ugly; the colors are discordant, jarring, and subversive of normal expectations; the theme of death is neither subtly alluded to nor perspicaciously avoided, but heraldically proclaimed in the cruciform central figure and in the dark male profile silhouetted against the French windows."[78]

These so-called dancers—one, in the middle, with purplish body and long-drawn-out limbs; another all brown and white, and a third with a horribly toothy grimace prancing in front of a window overlooking the sea—are reduced to spasmodic, insubstantial phantoms, stretching across the two-dimensional surface of the canvas. Their broad, colored shapes have more to do with tearing apart than with keeping together. While Picasso might have gotten the original idea from watching classical ballet dancer doing their exercises at the bar, who often force their bodies into strained positions, here the distortion of the human body almost amounts to a sort of rape, in Jean-Louis Ferrier's opinion.[79]

Boudaille describes the canvas as "a deliberate and provocative break with the complacent bourgeois shores of the world he had landed in without realizing he would stay there for such a long time."[80] Now life seems again to be governed by sexual principles, explains the critic. The body is reimagined as a sexual landscape, with phallic forms and cavities propagating and increasing their essential activity. Organ displacement lends itself to a psychoanalytic interpretation as unfettered sexual urges. Symbolic of the life instinct, their modified configuration and position distort the hierarchy of their function and are aimed at exerting a form of magic.

Pichot's passing seemed to have aroused a chain of memories and associations in the painter that led him to transform the canvas into this extraordinary composition of distorted angular characters, harsh colors and thickly worked paint expressing violent and unpleasant emotions. What we observe is a ruthless will to deform and disfigure everyday appearances, an undermining of reality that matched the contemporaneous emphasis placed by the Surrealists on the disruptive role of the subconscious. At times, Picasso would approach the body as an agglomeration of elements to be assembled and reassembled, giving rise to a powerful sense of hallucinatory metamorphosis from inanimate to animate and back again.[81] According to Gasman, Picasso shared Breton's analogical conception of the world according to which if everything is linked with everything else, then pictorial image and the referent that it stands for are interconnected as well. As a result, whatever the artist does to the image he has created is transmitted into the reality that the image represents.[82] He was quoted as saying: "Painting isn't an aesthetic operation; it's a form of magic designed as a mediator between this strange, hostile world and us, a way of seizing the power by giving form to our terrors as well as to our desires. When I came to that realization, I knew I had found my way."[83] On another occasion, the artist argued: "[Painting is] a matter of seizing the power, taking over from nature."[84]

At the beginning of May, Picasso returned to Paris from Monte Carlo.[85] Just a couple weeks earlier, the third issue of *La Révolution surréaliste* had appeared, with Breton as its director.[86] Back in the capital, he revisited *Les trois danseuses (La danse)* [9] in what has been identified as the start of his true "surrealist period" (1925–1938).[87] An antithesis of his classical drawings of dancers of the early 1920s, the painting became more expressionistic in character. The crucified ballerina at the center is usually said to stand for Olga, symbolizing his growing irritation with his wife: her terse little dash of a mouth, her right leg as stiff as if still in plaster, clearly identify her as the former beauty, although surprisingly for someone as sexually focused as Picasso, nothing between her thighs declares her gender. The painter was exhausted, constantly nagged by his wife who had become a violent, tyrannical woman, hating everyone, accusing her husband of infidelity, seeing enemies everywhere. This affected his own mood and he fell into a deep depression, haunted by frightening ideas.[88] As a result, the canvas changed from a portrait of three dancers to a representation of women as monsters and destroyers of men, as he explained many years later.[89] What had started as a pure celebration of Matissean *joie de vivre* in fact depicted the old Spanish custom of dancing around the dead when they are laid out.[90]

It is the irrational qualities in works like these that the surrealist Breton found analogous to his theory of convulsive beauty. In the hideous grimacing and contortions of the left-hand dancer, Picasso expressed the paroxysm of physical and mental rapture with such conviction that any beholder who could bear to follow the crazy twists and turns of the contours or take in the jarring changes in color patterns would experience a similar feeling of hysteria. It was this figure that underwent the most radical changes when he reworked the canvas as the cracks in the paint evince. Originally, she was naked like her companions, her head more or less at a level with theirs. At one point, she was seen from the back, but he decided to swivel her around, clothe her in clinging drapery, and grossly accentuate her sexuality, throwing her head back and out to one side and her torso upwards so that she assumes the classic arching posture of a hysterical maenad fresh from slaying Orpheus.[91]

According to Clark the paroxysm and ecstasy in *Les trois danseuses (La danse)*[9] are indicative of a departure from all possible categorizations. Ecstasy is to be read as *ec-stasis*: being out of place, losing one's stance on the ground. Picasso lived through the crisis of Truth that characterized European culture in the early 1920s. Untruth in him is a pressure from elsewhere, producing disfigurement. It is a condition, an Other entering the mind. It is the outside coming into the room. The three women are a reflection of this outside Otherness.[92] Conceived as a form of magic, the painter intended to use his canvas as a means to overcome this hostile Otherness, fate or death. It was a medium employed to transform the external evil force into a potential ally. Such a primeval conception of art rests on the assumption that the signifier is analogical with the thing signified so one may have an effect on the other. In this he emulated the "totalizing" savage conception of the world that Lévi-Strauss explored in the ancient mystical axiom of the "All is in All." According to the French anthropologist, primitive magic art, like all other manifestations of "savage thinking," was intended to restore the unity between man and nature, to reinstate man within his natural matrix. The psychologist Carl Jung also showed that unity, a desired analogy or the *mysterium coiunctionis*, was at the crux of primordial alchemical union: its fluidity was a projection of man's need for continuity within himself and with the natural world.[93]

Kris argued that, in his role as magician, Pablo felt close to the *demiurgos*, a figure akin to the heroes of the ancient world, who could even compete with the gods as creators of real things: Prometheus, Hephaestus, or Daedalus. The artist was convinced that his work had an operative magical power, a kind of hypnotism.[94] Rubin also emphasized that "Picasso's drawing is really a way of possessing things; not just the woman he draws, but everything in his visual world. It somehow becomes part of him through being drawn."[95] The natural vitality of *Les trois danseuses (La danse)*[9] was what Breton was intent on recapturing when he wrote: "if the depths of our being harbor mysterious powers capable of strengthening our outward capabilities, and even of prevailing over them, we have every reason to take hold of these powers if we can, in order to subject them, if necessary, to the control of our minds."[96] Like the other members of the surrealist movement, Picasso felt himself struggling with an intolerable and unacceptable reality the effect of which is reflected in the three distorted figures. The way to cope with it was through the transformative power of his art. Breton and Picasso remained in contact throughout these months, and on June 9, the poet wrote sending three photographs of works he wished to reproduce in the fourth issue of *La Révolution surréaliste*. Among them were *Les demoiselles d'Avignon*[2] and *Les trois danseuses (La danse)*[9].

Another oil of his time is *Atelier avec tête et bras de plâtre*[10]. While in earlier canvases the object's main role had been to make us aware of the space around them, we are now presented with an anomalous heap of objects that do not belong to the same domain, that appear to come from places far removed from each other. What we see is an attempt at setting up a congenial spirit among elements that actually repudiate each other, that apparently have nothing in common.[97] The painting's underpinning remains formal, but aspects of its facture and color and, above all, its imagery point to a new surreal dimension in Picasso's art. The square in the middle of the composition (apparently Paulo's toy theater) destroys any pretense of a coherent relationship of objects in space and undercuts the three-dimensionality suggested by the plaster bust which appears to float rather unrealistically above the table.[98] Schapiro found a certain resemblance to the cruel emperor Caracalla;[99] and Gasman saw in it as an apocalyptic vision of a fierce philosopher-king.[100] Equally mystifying are the related broken plaster casts of arms, one clutching a classical scroll, the other clenching its fist; and the pages of the opened book containing hieroglyphs which could be references to some sort of ritual, thus hinting at a threatening underworld.[101] As he said to Gilot much later, "I want to draw the mind in a direction it's not used to and wake it up. I want to help the viewer discover something he wouldn't have discovered without me."[102]

Le baiser[11] multiplies the shock of the previous work by its intense decomposition and recomposition of the figures, which spreading over the surface of the canvas, seem to fuse together.[103] Viewers are forced to disentangle what they see.[104] The symbols combine, but are interchangeable by their very displacements: eye, mouth, sexual organs merge into each other. The flat shapes are dislocated and freely reassembled like parts of a puzzle, limbs and organs turned upside-down. [105] On the left, we can barely identify the figure of the man, his target-like eye, and his phallus-shaped nose. The mouth, which can also be read as an eye or the female sex, is shared by both figures, welded together by a pattern of horizontal bars and interpenetrating organs. The woman's head, shown both in profile and from above, is thrown back. The man clasps her with one arm around her neck and with the other pins her arms behind. Her feet seem to be lifted off the ground, the toes spread in ecstasy or in an effort to resist. As Cowling asserts, the embrace looks literally devouring, the figures are violently struggling and grappling; the interlocking of arms and hands at the center of the composition suggests ferocious biting and mauling; the toes of the naked profile foot look like giant nails driving viciously into the flesh.[106]

Still mourning the death of his friend Pichot,[107] he worked on several canvases which have been grouped as the "Magic Series," among them *Tête de bélier*[12], *Buste et palette*[13], *Nature morte au buste et à la palette*[14], and *La statuaire (La femme sculpteur)*[15], among others. Gasman argued that the series is organized according to an invariant symbolic logic. The artist, at first, creates a double of his enemy, death or fate; then he acquires the omniscience and omnipotence of his adversary through a magical representation of sacrifice; and finally, he attacks the effigy of his opponent in order to transform its malevolence into goodness. The magical "presence" of death had already become visible in *Les trois danseuses (La danse)*[9], and would continue with the ritual killing of a satanic ram in *Tête de bélier*[12], only to conclude with its defeat and conversion into the principle of

Life, in *La statuaire (La femme sculpteur)*[15].[108] With respect to *Tête de bélier*[12], Palau i Fabre noticed how the artist has accentuated the apprehensiveness of the composition by endowing the ghostly octopus and the scorpion fish with menacing eyes, while rendering those of the ram closed, dead.[109] Meanwhile, the open mouths of the fish and the spiky sea urchin resemble a *vagina dentata*. Everything looks ready to bite, cut or sting. Teeth often stood out as the most unfailingly aggressive in Picasso's pictorial symbolism. They were also connected with his pictorial imagery of ritual sacrifice, making this is the scene of an exorcism, a protection against the demons which had been acting up earlier in the year.[110] As stated earlier, Picasso took the magical-rational African sculptor as an example to follow and saw art as a medium for the reconciliation, not just with his wife, but also with an entire threatening universe. In that sense, his magical primitivism brought him back to the allegedly magic aboriginal dawn of art. The primitive magician rationally submitted external factors to his own will because his rituals and imagery were invested with a sacred force. Ancient magical-religious rites in fact relied on a belief in the harmonious link between man and his surroundings. That fundamental link allowed the act to transform an external evil threatening man into a beneficial ally.[111]

In this context, the frequent presence of open windows in his works may refer to that threatening outside world he so much feared. The artist felt that there was some kind of inexplicable correspondence between them and death/fate. Windows embodied his belief that the human condition was above all defined by man's mortality, a merging with a threatening outside. Picasso counterattacked against the windows of death/fate with the disguised symbol of the knob in *Buste et palette*[13], which stands for his own hand endowed with the power of controlling fate embodied by the window, as Gasman has explained. He once said: "I shall open windows. I shall get behind the canvas and perhaps something will happen."[112] In this still life, the vibrancy of local color and sun-drenched atmosphere is intentionally misleading. Set in an intricately paneled interior that opens onto brilliant blue skies, it displays his accustomed repertoire of guitars, mandolins, bottles and fruit bowls laid on luxurious patterned cloths. However, mixed with these familiar objects we find once again a fierce Roman bust staring directly out of the picture and with a strong contrast of light and shadow across its features. A palette stands erectly on edge, as if snapped to attention as do the set of brushes to its left. Although their dark brown handles lie on the tablecloth and parallel its diagonal stripes, their thickly painted bristles seem more three-dimensional than the flat, black shadow cast across the sculpture they lean against.

Rather than mere utensils for an artist to wield, these traditional attributes seem to be presented as defensive weapons against the threatening bust.[113] They are the means for him to confront the menace of death with the tools of the trade.

In *Nature morte au buste et à la palette*[14], the malleable black knob, symbolic of his own creativity which is also again signified by a golden palette and brushes, secures the openness of the window, between whose panels he has placed a white *compotier* confronting the dark silhouette on the right. The objects are both enveloped by the mysterious light of dusk and underlined by the artificial light that comes from inside the room. The clarity barely salvages the objects that the night would have otherwise engulfed.[114] Finally, in *La statuaire (La femme sculpteur)*[15] he attached his magic knob, this time directly on the obscure silhouette's forehead, letting it flow into the black hand that creates a dazzling positive white plaster bust.[115] The artist appears to have merged with a young woman who supports the stand holding the bust, her head seen both frontally and in profile. This is one of Picasso's clearest manifestations of the importance of the female muse in his art. It is only through this collaboration between artist and inspirational model that they are both capable of exorcising the evil force of fate represented by the otherwise fierce classical bust.

If there is a woman that clearly embodies Picasso's belief in the magical power of art, it is Dora Maar, his companion in the 1930s and 1940s, as I discussed in my book dealing with their relationship.[116] To those who knew her, one of Dora's most striking features was her dazzling, soulful gaze. Penrose referred to the "dark, passionate eyes of Dora Maar," as it was her eyes that most forcefully conveyed her great depth and artistic sensibility. Curiously, in works like *Figure de femme debout*[17], *Tête de Dora Maar*[18] and *Tête de Dora Maar*[19], the artist chose to depict her wearing a mask over her face. He had always been fascinated by masks. Discussing their use in African art, he explained to André Malraux: "The masks weren't just like any other piece of sculpture. They were magic things."[117] "Intercessors," Picasso had called them. Throughout the years they were together, Dora's persona would play the same role those African masks had played for centuries.

It was in January 1936 that he had spotted Dora at a café. She had already gotten his attention the previous year.[118] As Brassaï recalled, "It was at *Les Deux-Magots* that, one day in autumn 1935, [he] met Dora . . . On an earlier day, he had already noticed the grave, drawn face of the young woman at a nearby table, the attentive look in her light-colored eyes, sometimes disturbing in its fixity. When Picasso saw her in the same café in the company of Paul Éluard, the poet introduced her to Picasso."[119] Tinged with a seductive mix of violence and dark eroticism, this first formal introduction has attained mythical status in the story of the artist's life. It reads like a surrealist fantasy. As one biographer put it: "the young woman's serious face, lit up by pale blue eyes which looked all the paler because of her thick eyebrows; a sensitive uneasy face, with light and shade passing alternately over it. She kept driving a small penknife between her fingers into the wood of the table. Sometimes she missed and a drop of blood appeared between the roses embroidered on her black gloves."[120] Of a mysterious and feline beauty, which Man Ray had captured in the pictures he took of her, a companion of Georges Bataille, Maar was an accomplished photographer, close to the surrealist doctrine. Picasso addressed her in French, which he assumed to be her language; she replied in Spanish, which she knew to be his. The raven-haired beauty proved irresistible. Immediately beguiled by her seductive sado-masochistic ritual and her dark intensity, struck by her gaze that was said to be as powerful as his own acclaimed *mirada fuerte*,[121] he felt a sudden and violent attraction to the young and beautiful woman. Another writer recalled, "Dora Maar, radiant, with her ebony hair, her blue-green eyes, her controlled gestures, fascinated him. Behind her haughty and enigmatic attitude, you could see a spontaneity restrained, a fiery temperament ready to be carried away, mad impulses ready to be unleashed. She withstood without batting an eye Picasso's stare, and he was the one to flee."[122]

Dora was then twenty-eight, he would soon be turning fifty-five.[123] It has been suggested that the encounter was far from fortuitous, and that she deliberately placed herself in his path. She arguably began by frequenting his favorite café *Les Deux Magots*, setting up a distant siege that included deliberate avoidance. Once even showing off her knowledge of Spanish by laughing out loud at one of his jokes, making her presence felt, if remotely, "like an accomplice."[124] More than any other companion or muse, she would come to symbolize "the woman with a thousand faces," the one for whom he would track every expression and attitude, every transformation and metamorphosis. A complex character, she was a figure of contradictory facets, alternately expressing sensuality and suffering, sophistication and animality. Through his obsessive concentration on her persona during these years, Picasso would translate his fascination with the woman that had seduced him on the spot into a wide range of representations. Their intellectual and emotional complicity would closely follow the tragic events taking place during these troubled years.[125]

As they walked out of the café together, Pablo asked for her blood-stained gloves, He would proudly display them in a vitrine in his apartment as a memento of their meeting for years to come.[126] The hands that she had subjected to the dangerous game of chance would always be a particularly charged motif in their tempestuous and impassioned relationship.[127] An expert at creating an impression, Maar was renowned for her chic appearance, painting her nails in different colors according to her changing mood. She also wore dashing hats, elaborate brooches and a bold scarlet lipstick, and adopted the most up-to-date fashions from a host of leading designers. He delighted in the fact that she spoke Spanish fluently, later confessing: "I just felt finally, here was somebody I could carry on a conversation with."[128] Against the backdrop of impending war, the two began a tumultuous relationship that would carry them through some of the darkest years of European history. Despite the darkness of these turbulent and tragic times, she inspired an astounding period of creativity in Picasso, becoming his most important muse and collaborator as the 1930s waned and the 1940s dawned. As Crespelle proclaimed, "this affair, coinciding with the peak of his artistic achievement, was to light up his life with a bright flame of passion."[129]

Her "official" artistic entrance into Picasso's oeuvre was marked by the drawing *Dora Maar et figure antique*[16], executed at the beginning of August. In it, she literally opens the door and walks into the atelier, wearing a coat and scarf.[130] He evokes her arrival on mythic ground, and we see her head veiled, like the sudden vision of a Vestal coming face to face with an Antique god (Picasso) accompanied by his faithful guardian Cerberus. This parodic treatment of the tension that was operating on a subconscious level in her crossing of the studio's threshold highlights the initiatory passage that would lead them both into the inner magic circle where new images would be born.[131] Yet, as with all of Pablo's paramours, these early portraits of Dora evoked a tender, calm, sensual appreciation of her form. As their relationship progressed, however, he would adopt an increasingly angular vocabulary in his depictions of her, abstracting and attacking her form, introducing extreme distortions and stylizations, as he sought to convey the psychological depths behind her enigmatic look.[132]

As the Spanish Civil War developed in 1937, for instance, Picasso projected all his feelings of anger and perplexity on Dora in *Poupée et femme se noyant*[21]. The scene depicted is unreal. She appears immobilized like a mannequin on an upright, tripod prong aimed menacingly at her sex, while she tongue-kisses a black-masked, putrid sun (Bataille's *soleil pourri*).[133] Her dress is fashionably decorated, her feet are in high-heeled laced shoes, and she wears a chain of flowers or large pieces of jewelry around her neck. But her feet hang down passively, and she holds a triangular banner displaying two arms raised in supplication. Rays emanate from the dark sun, spreading over the landscape like a rain of fire. In the water, one can see the head and pleading arms of a drowning man calling for help in vain. This explains the banner sign which might be read as a warning of potential danger. The doll-like figure therefore is aware of the disaster that occurs in her immediate vicinity. However, standing at the edge of the water and sentenced to immobility (her feet do not reach the ground), she is unable to help the poor man.[134] This may symbolize the painter's frustration at hearing about the brutal attack near his hometown, the so-called "Málaga–Almería road massacre." Unable to do anything about the tragedy, he would project his state of mind through her once again in *Portrait de Dora Maar pensive*[20].[135] Mary Ann Caws has stated: "On [her] singularly expressive face Picasso could read every international event as in a newspaper."[136] We would add that he could also inscribe those events in the portraits he made of her.

On May 24, Picasso executed *La femme qui pleure (Étude)*[22], the first in a whole series of weeping women. As Arnheim notes, "the streaming tears have been solidified into expressive objects. They supply the immobile head with the tracks of downward movement, appropriate to the subject. They also lacerate the skin with shocking grooves."[137] With her tear-shaped eyes, the weeping woman became an emblem of the sufferings inflicted on the Spanish population,[138] an icon of these dark years that Dagen describes as a "cycle of metamorphosis of mourning."[139] If the mural he had painted for another massacre, *Guernica*[23], had taken up the challenge as a "a monument to disillusionment, despair, destruction," to quote Breton's words in 1939, these female victims, described by Barr as "postscripts," followed it as "the artist's lament."[140] Often interpreted as a cruel distortion of Dora's personality, they also reflected Pablo's own inner anguish: "[He] believes that art is the daughter of sadness and pain," Sabartés had written. "He believes that sadness forces meditation and that pain is the essence of life."[141] By concentrating on the head and generalizing it, he focused on grief as an absolute. His main means to represent it was extreme facial distortion, underpinned by brutal contrasts of tone and color. His favorite metaphors included the furrowed brow, pupils and eyelashes drawn as a crown of thorns, eyes and noses as teardrops, running tears as needles or nails, eyelids as capsizing boats spilling out tears, ears as wing nuts, noses as animal snouts, teeth as fangs, tongues as daggers, etc.[142]

On June 8, he painted another weeping woman in *La femme qui pleure*[24] with an obvious resemblance to Dora. The head conveys all the pain, anguish, and horror of the images that preceded it. The blue, yellow, green, purple and black were placed where their contrast could be most effectively highlighted and to stress their tragic force.[143] As Cabanne explains, "screaming or crying, heads thrown back . . . these women scarcely look human; their eyes are out of their heads, tears large as peas streak their cheeks, and their mouths are distorted into horrible grimaces. Maar represented what happened to Picasso, what happened to Spain—for which, he would never forgive her."[144] Her features appeared in yet another drawing, *La femme qui pleure (Étude)*[25]. This time the agony, which continued to deform her face, was particularly concentrated in her eyes. The tears—which are black—blur the outline of the pupil and the eyebrows shoot up like two innocent hands pleading for help.[145] Dora would later confess to James Lord that life with Picasso was "like living at the center of the universe, thrilling and frightening, exalting and humbling at the same time."[146] But if these "masks" represented his fear and frustration at the cruelty of war, they also were the means to exact revenge. Dora's flared nostrils recall those of an animal. More concretely, her nose and mouth resemble the snout and open beak of the two devils on the far right of the Isenheim Altarpiece, and her stare brings to mind the demonic glinting eyes that hypnotize the spectator. So, although she is terrorized like the wretched Saint Anthony, she has become as monstrous in her panic as the devils that assailed him.[147]

It was during the German occupation of Paris that Dora would serve an essential ritualistic role. Many of his friends who had stayed in the capital until now made up their mind to leave. By October 1940, he was probably feeling even more insecure and off-balance with the recent regulations imposed on foreigners. After all, he discovered his emotions through what he saw in his portraits of other people, or at least what they reflected back to him through the intermediary of painting. One who certainly served as such a mirror was Dora, prone as she was to calamity. She reacted intensely to all the discriminatory regulations, followed the news closely, as a member of a relatively well-informed intellectual milieu. He had only to watch her reactions to know what his were like, although hers were even stronger and dramatized.[148]

The portraits *Tête de femme*[26] and *Tête de femme*[27] from May 1941 are characterized in general by a left/right division of the face. In the first painting, the outlines of the deranged profile, the hair, the strong jaw, mouth, collar and shoulders are all flowing curves. The paint is thinly and evenly applied, so that the bare canvas shows through.[149] During the war, Picasso worked hard to deconstruct his lover, often portraying a simultaneous view of a three-quarter profile seen from the back (*profil perdu*), and a full profile. The effigies he generated were as horrible as repulsive. The convulsed, suffering face expressed the inhumanity of the times. It has often been said that Maar, an unstable companion of these tragic years, clearly inspired these figures. One who had had the dignity of a Sphinx, often hieratic and impenetrable, and whose perfect oval face had been idealized by Man Ray, suffered here the most terrible distortions, generating numerous "hallucinating" and "pathetic" figures. Through the disturbing plasticity of her face, she best illustrated the notion of a *mater dolorosa*, subject to hysterical outbursts. In his poems and plays we find the same need to deform and metamorphose his characters. At a time when the human figure became impossible for many artists to represent, the proliferation of degenerate and comical personages, barely alive, disparage the negation of the individual perpetrated by the Nazi regime.[150]

In the second canvas, the paint was applied thickly in short, straight brushstrokes. The features were defined primarily as angular shapes. The overall effect is one of aggressive energy. The marked difference in the style and technique of the two paintings is suggestive of his desire to explore more than one plastic possibility.[151] After the thinly brushed surfaces and the grisaille tonality of the other, Picasso appears to have been eager to work in a more expressionistic manner, using a loaded brush to produce a thickly impastoed surface. The chief effect he aimed for here is that of a figure silhouetted against a light background, as if she were standing before a strong lamp radiating from behind, undergoing interrogation. He accentuated her features in strokes of brilliant yellow. Streaks of red emanate from her lower eyelids, as if her mascara were running or she were crying bloody tears. Dora had again become the mirror where he could reflect the threat they faced on a daily basis, altering and reshaping her visage to express his own distress.[152] These portraits attempted to represent stages of anxiety and helplessness, going from fear and horror to panic. As viewers observe the strong torsion of the head and the deformation of the features, they share the same feelings as the sitter.[153]

In the oil *Tête de femme*[29] from 1943, Dora's large, dark eyes stare penetratingly out of the bright white background, captivating and confronting her interrogator. With her raven-colored hair and intense expression, her visage differs from the tortured and deformed depictions that had characterized many of his depictions of her. Her long, oval face is rendered with a resounding wholeness, composed of softly curving, boldly rendered brushstrokes and contrasting planes of light and shadow, all framed by voluminous waves of luxuriant dark hair. Although there is still a look of anxiety in her eyes, she gazes at the viewer with an intense solemnity. As Léal has written, with "a temperament prone to withdrawal, to introspection; the hollowness of the cheek is most likely a sign of the mind's flight, a schizophrenic side."[154] But it could also stand for a shield. Pictured frontally, with her mouth tight-lipped and firmly set, her wide-eyed stare is desolate and disconsolate, powerfully yet silently communicating her innermost feelings to the artist, her lover. Is it with a look of resignation and acceptance that she stares from the painting or is she getting ready for the attack?[155] Allegorically speaking, she could be about to embark upon a mission Picasso has entrusted her with. Dressed in the blue color of a French uniform, she widens her eyes to face the enemy as she prepares for battle as a 20th century Jeanne d'Arc. Someone must stand up to Hitler and fascism. Her flaring nostrils and dark eyes betray her fiery personality. Yet the grotesquery of her bifurcated face signals the increasing strain as she confronts the challenge.

The stripes on the blouse the female sitter wears in the oil *Portrait de femme*[28], painted earlier in the month, relate it to the striped shirt seen in several works representing a sailor, a guise in which Picasso frequently depicted himself.[156] What began as a combined portrait of Picasso and Maar evolved into a series of self-portraits, one of which is *Buste d'homme*[30]. Together with the intensely staring eyes, the wide, exaggeratedly large nostrils and mass of dark hair, this figure becomes a paradigmatic symbol of masculinity and virility—qualities that he often sought in the cavalcade of self-referential surrogates and stand-ins through which he portrayed himself in his art. The brawny, high-spirited figure of the sailor could also be seen to relate to the epic tales of adventure.[157] "You are in every way a pure Mediterraneanist, a relative of Ulysses, terrible in cunning," Eugeni d'Ors once wrote of Picasso.[158] By depicting himself as a sailor, he was perhaps assuming the role of a modern day Odysseus; a brave and daring adventurer trapped in the confines of occupied Paris, longing to return to the idyllic southern shores and a life of freedom. "If Picasso reverted to this Mediterranean subject in the middle of war," Richardson has written, "it would have been out of a desperate yearning to be back on the shores of his native sea ... Penned up in the prison of occupied Paris in a cold, wet October, six weeks after being ordered to report to the Nazis for deportation to Germany ... Picasso would desperately have needed to raise his spirits ... [This] is surely an attempt to exorcise the hateful Germans."[159] He was once again reacting to the menace of death and resorting to the magic of his art to fight it, this time wearing a sailor's "mask."

Notes
1 Cabanne 1979, 92; O'Brian 1994, 126. Others claim that she is born as Amélie Lang (Unger 2018, 190).

2   Roe 2015, 88.
3   Cabanne 1979, 92.
4   Roe 2015, 90–91.
5   Richardson 1991, 427; Roe 2015, 114. Others date the move simply to September (Cousins & Daix 1989, 340).
6   Unger 2018, 195; Franck 2001, 59.
7   Olivier 1964, 156; also, Unger 2018, 207.
8   O'Brian 1994, 128; also, Franck 2001, 57.
9   Vallentin 1963, 51; Warnod 1972, 17.
10 Roe 2015, 115.
11 Olivier 1964, 162.
12 Unger 2018, 196.
13 Cabanne 1979, 110; Madeline 2006, 198; Blier 2019, 81–84.
14 Baldassari, et al. 2002, 363; Baldassari 2007, 334; Cousins & Elderfield 1992, 135; Roe 2015, 169; Unger 2018, 332.
15 Franck 2001, 92.
16 Franck 2001, 95.
17 Vallentin 1963, 78.
18 Mahler 2015, 52.
19 Blier 2019, 85–88.
20 Choucha 1992, 25–33.
21 Tucker 1992, 76–99.
22 Franck 2001, 37.
23 O'Brian 1994, 148–149.
24 Gray 1953, 3–20.
25 Richardson 1996, 25; Franck 2001, 96; Daemgen 2005, 19. Others date the visit more generally to spring (Baldassari, et al. 2002, 364; Roe 2015, 177); later to May (Daix 2007, 19; Mahler 2015, 54); to May or June (Fluegel 1980, 87; Dagen 2009, 484); to summer (Warncke & Walther 1991, 146; Torras 2002, 106); to the end of June or early July (Cabanne 1979, 116); or more generally to June or July (Daix cited by Richardson 1996, 25; also Mahler 2015, 54).
26 Cabanne 1979, 118; Richardson 1996, 76.
27 Picasso, quoted by Malraux, 1974; also, Gilot & Lake 1964, 248; O'Brian 1994, 153–154; Unger 2018, 329–330.
28 Schwartz 1971, 21–24.
29 Richardson 1996, 9.
30 Richardson 1996, 18.
31 Blier 2019, 123–125.
32 Unger 2018, 315–318.
33 Kozloff 1973, 78–86.
34 Sotheby's 2005, cat. no. 4, N08125.
35 Quoted in Daix 1993, 75.
36 Daix & Rosselet 1979.
37 Tucker 1992, 100–116.
38 Kozloff 1973, 18–26.

39 Idem.
40 Daix 1979, 18.
41 Daix 1979, 14–15.
42 Cabanne 1979, 113.
43 Warncke & Walther 1991, 148–153.
44 Flam and Deutch 2003, 28.
45 Tucker 1992, 27–48.
46 Tucker 1992, 49–75.
47 O'Brian 1994, 150.
48 Walther 1993, 37, 40.
49 Daix 1979, 26–28.
50 Karmel 2007, 150–151.
51 Seckel, Rubin & Cousins 1994, 224; Daix 2007, 18.
52 Cowling 2002, 160–180.
53 Vallentin 1963, 79–80.
54 Schwartz 1971, 26–30.
55 Wadley 1970, 37–45.
56 Cox 2010, 68–72.
57 Cowling 2002, 115–194.
58 Cabanne 1979, 114.
59 Richardson 1996, 40.
60 Daix 1965, 62–64.
61 Unger 2018, 263.
62 Mahler 2015, 54–55.
63 Unger 2018, 322.
64 Richardson 1996, 43. Others date the completion to early July (Fluegel 1980, 87); or to late summer (Unger 2018, 318).
65 Unger 2018, 320.
66 Daix & Rosselet 1979, 39–42.
67 Seckel 1996, 24–26.
68 Daix 1979, 23–26.
69 Daix 1993, 67–75.
70 Daix 1965, 66–68.
71 Cabanne 1979, 123.
72 Seckel 1996, 28.
73 Unger 2018, 334–339.
74 Mallen 2020.
75 Richardson 2007, 276.
76 Wilson 1991, 164.
77 O'Brian 1994, 271–272; Palau i Fabre 1999, 442–443.
78 Silver 1989, 397–398.
79 Ferrier 1996, 99.
80 Boudaille 1987, 82.
81 Cox 2010, 73–74.
82 Gasman 1981, 449–538.
83 Gilot & Lake 1964, 248.

84 Gilot & Lake 1964, 254.
85 Richardson 2007, 282, also Palau i Fabre 1999, 444. Others date the return simply to May (Cabanne 1979, 240).
86 Cousins & Seckel 1994, 185.
87 Gasman 1981, 661–756.
88 Cabanne 1979, 244.
89 McGregor-Hastie 1988, 108.
90 Warncke & Walther 1991, 366; Penrose 1981, 251.
91 Richardson 2007, 282–283; Cowling 2002, 460–469.
92 Clark 2013, 113–146.
93 Gasman 1981, 449–538.
94 Kris 1979, 53.
95 Rubin 1972, 42.
96 Cousins & Seckel 1994, 185; FitzGerald 1995, 148; Baldassari 2005, 236.
97 Palau i Fabre 1999, 448–449.
98 Rubin 1972, 120–122.
99 Cited in Gasman 1981, 768, n. 3.
100 Gasman 1981, 768.
101 Boggs 1992, 218.
102 Gilot & Lake 1964, 60.
103 Palau i Fabre 1999, 447.
104 Warncke & Walther 1991, 365–367.
105 Daix 1993, 190–194.
106 Cowling 2002, 469–482.
107 McGregor-Hastie 1988, 109.
108 Gasman 1981, 622–660; 757–870.
109 Palau i Fabre 1999, 450.
110 Gasman 1981, 661–756.
111 Gasman 1981, 449–538.
112 Penrose 1981, 352.
113 FitzGerald 2001, 116–117.
114 Palau i Fabre 1999, 446.
115 Gasman 1981, 661–756.
116 Mallen 2021.
117 Malraux 1976, 10–13.
118 Fattal 2017, 4; Freeman 1994, 167.
119 Quoted in Brassaï 1999, 51.
120 J-P. Crespelle, quoted in Caws 2000, 81–83.
121 Christie's. 2016, cat. no. 13B, 12145.
122 Gâteau, quoted in Caws 2000, 83.
123 Christie's. 2017, cat. no. 40A, 15004.
124 Baring 2017, 160.
125 Tosatto, et al. 2019, 264.
126 Cabanne 1979, 287–288.
127 Sotheby's. 2017, cat. no. 18, L17007.

128 Picasso, quoted in Gilot & Lake 1964, 236.
129 Crespelle 1969, 145.
130 Daix 1993, 244.
131 Baldassari 2006, 124.
132 Baring 2017, 35.
133 Nash 1998, 16.
134 Ullmann 1993, 73.
135 Sotheby's 2010, cat. no. 1, L10006.
136 Caws 2000, 103.
137 Arnheim 1962, 86.
138 Nash 1998, 18.
139 La Vaccara 2014, 6.
140 Tosatto, et al. 2019, 64.
141 Baring 2017, 196.
142 Cowling 2002, 589–603.
143 Palau 2011, 329.
144 Cabanne 1979, 305–306.
145 Palau 2011, 330.
146 Baring 2017, 185.
147 Cowling 2002, 589–603.
148 Baer 1998, 86.
149 Goggin 1985, 91–94.
150 Tosatto, et al. 2019, 138.
151 Goggin 1985, 93–94.
152 Christie's 2007, cat. no. 0043, 1900.
153 Ullmann 1993, 288.
154 Léal 1996, p. 395.
155 Christie's 2016, cat. no. 31B, 12145.
156 Christie's 2018, cat. no. 8A, 15971.
157 Christie's 2009, cat. no. 121, 7703.
158 d'Ors 1936, cited in Richardson 2010, 11.
159 Quoted in FitzGerald 1997, 34.

Cited Works by Pablo Picasso

[1] *Portrait de Max Jacob*. Paris. Early/1907. Gouache on paper mounted on cardboard. 62,7 x 48 cm. Museum Ludwig, Köln. (Inv ML/Z 2001/044). Schenkung 2001. OPP.07:005.

[2] *Les demoiselles d'Avignon*. Paris. [Late-March] June–July/1907. Oil on canvas. 243,9 x 233,7 cm. The Museum of Modern Art, NYC. (Inv 333.1939). Acquired through the Lillie P. Bliss Bequest. OPP.07:001.

[3] *Demoiselle d'Avigon*. Paris. [Late-Spring–July] [Summer] June–July/1907. Oil on canvas. 66 x 59 cm. Musée National d'Art Moderne, Centre Georges Pompidou, Paris. (Inv AM.4320P). Purchase 1965. OPP.07:014.

[4] *Les demoiselles d'Avignon: nu jaune (Étude)*. Paris. June–July/1907.

Watercolor, gouache & India ink on paper. 59,8 x 39,5 cm. Gretchen and John Berggruen Collection, San Francisco. OPP.07:271.
[5] *Figure*. Paris. [Summer]/1907. Carved oak with touches of oil paint. 80,5 x 24 x 20,8 cm. Musée Picasso, Paris. Dation 1979. OPP.07:376.
[6] *Homme debout*. Paris. [Summer]/1907. Carved wood, painted in yellow. 37 x 6 x 6 cm. Private collection. OPP.07:389.
[7] *Nu à la draperie: tête de femme (Étude)*. Paris. Summer–Fall/1907. Oil on canvas. 61,4 x 47,6 cm. The Museum of Modern Art, NYC. (Inv 278.83). Mr. & Mrs. John Hay Whitney Collection, 1983. OPP.07:032.
[8] *Femme nue aux bras levés (La danseuse d'Avignon)*. Paris. [Summer–] Laty-July/1907. Oil on canvas. 150 x 100 cm. Basil and Elise Goulandris Foundation, Athens. OPP.07:010.
[9] *Les trois danseuses (La danse)*. Paris–Monte Carlo. February-8-June/1925. Oil on canvas. 215,3 x 142,2 cm. Tate Modern, London. (Inv T00729). Purchased with a special Grant-in-Aid and the Florence Fox Bequest with assistance from the Friends of the Tate Gallery and the Contemporary Art Society, 1965. OPP.25:001.
[10] *Atelier avec tête et bras de plâtre*. Juan-les-Pins. Late-June/1925. Oil on canvas. 97,9 x 131,1 cm. The Museum of Modern Art, New York. (Inv 116.1964). Purchase, 1964. OPP.25:002.
[11] *Le baiser*. Juan-les-Pins. Late-June/1925. Oil on canvas. 130,5 x 97,7 cm. Musée Picasso, Paris. Dation 1979. OPP.25:003.
[12] *Tête de bélier*. Juan-les-Pins. Summer/1925. Oil on canvas. 80 x 99,1 cm. The Norton Simon Museum, Pasadena, CA. (Inv P.1978.6). Gift of Alexandre P. Rosenberg, 1978. OPP.25:024.
[13] *Buste et palette*. Paris–Monte Carlo–Juan-les-Pins. Spring–Summer/1925. Oil on canvas. 54 x 65,5 cm. Museo Nacional Centro de Arte Reina Sofia, Madrid. (Inv AS.06524). OPP.25:023.
[14] *Nature morte au buste et à la palette*. Paris–Monte Carlo–Juan-les-Pins. Spring–Summer/1925. Oil on canvas. 97 x 130 cm. Private collection, Basel. OPP.25:021.
[15] *La statuaire (La femme sculpteur)*. Juan-les-Pins. Summer/1925. Oil on canvas. 131,1 x 96,8 cm. Sotheby's. #19, New York7382, 11/10/99. OPP.25:018.
[16] *Composition: Dora Maar et figure antique*. Paris. 1-August/1936. India ink wash on paper. 34,5 x 51 cm. Private collection, Belgium. OPP.36:048.
[17] *Figure de femme debout*. Paris. 27-December/1936. Oil, gouache, pencil & watercolor on paper. 40,4 x 31,4 cm. Sotheby's. #167, L06006, 02/08/06. OPP.36:097.
[18] *Tête de Dora Maar*. Paris. 27-December/1936. Oil on paper. 40,5 x 31,5 cm. Private collection. OPP.36:199.
[19] *Tête de Dora Maar*. Paris. 27-December/1936. Oil on canvas. 55 x 46 cm. Private collection. OPP.36:200.
[20] *Portrait de Dora Maar pensive*. Paris. 28-January/1937. Pencil &

stump on paper. 31 x 40,2 cm. Sotheby's. #1, L10006, 06/22/10. OPP.37:061.
[21] *Poupée et femme se noyant.* Paris. 28-January/1937. Pencil on paper. 40,2 x 31,5 cm. Galería Gullermo de Osma, Madrid. OPP.37:224.
[22] *La femme qui pleure (Étude).* Paris. 24-May/1937. Pencil, lead pencil & gouache on paper. 29,2 x 23,2 cm. Museo Nacional Centro de Arte Reina Sofia, Madrid. OPP.37:099.
[23] *Guernica.* Paris. 11-May–4-June/1937. Oil on canvas. 349,3 x 776,6 cm. Museo Nacional Centro de Arte Reina Sofia, Madrid. (Inv DE00050).
[24] *La femme qui pleure.* Paris. 8-June/1937. Pencil, color crayon & gray gouache on white paper. 29,1 x 23,2 cm. Museo Nacional Centro de Arte Reina Sofia, Madrid. OPP.37:018.
[25] *La femme qui pleure (Étude).* Paris. 13-June/1937. Pencil, crayon & gouache on paper. 29 x 23 cm. Museo Nacional Centro de Arte Reina Sofia, Madrid. OPP.37:107.
[26] *Tête de femme.* Paris. 25-May/1941. Oil on canvas. 55 x 38 cm. Národni Galerie, Prague. (Inv O 9197). OPP.41:003.
[27] *Tête de femme.* Paris. 25-May/1941. Oil on canvas. 41 x 33,3 cm. Private collection, New York. OPP.41:226.
[28] *Portrait de femme.* Paris. 10-October/1943. Oil on canvas. 130 x 97 cm. Fundación Almine & Bernard Ruiz-Picasso para el Arte. OPP.43:235.
[29] *Tête de femme.* Paris. 18-October/1943. Oil on canvas. 64,5 x 53,2 cm. Christie's. #31B, 12145, 11/16/16. OPP.43:307.
[30] *Buste d'homme.* Paris. 24-October/1943. Pencil on light blue paper. 38,1 x 25,1 cm. Christie's. #121, 7703, 02/05/09. OPP.43:025.

Bibliography
Arnheim, Rudolf. 1962. *The Genesis of a Painting, Picasso's Guernica.* Berkely, Los Angeles, London: University of California Press.
Baer, Brigitte. 1998. "Where Do They Come From – Those Superb Paintings and Horrid Women of 'Picasso's War.'" *Picasso and the War Years: 1937–1945.* pp. 81–98. Ed. Steven A. Nash. New York: Thames & Hudson.
Baldassari, Anne, ed. 2006. *The Surrealist Picasso (Fondation Beyeler, Riehen/Basel, June 12–September 12, 2005).* New York: Random House.
——, ed. 2007. *Cubist Picasso.* Paris: Réunion des Musées Nationaux / Flammarion.
——, et al. 2002. *Matisse Picasso.* London: Tate Publishing.
Baring, Louise. 2017. *Dora Maar. Paris in the Time of Man Ray, Jean Cocteau and Picasso* New York: Rizzoli.
Blier, Suzanne Preston. 2019. *Picasso's Demoiselles: The Untold Origins of a Modern Masterpiece.* Duke University Press Books.
Boggs, Jean Sutherland, ed. 1992. *Picasso and Things.* Cleveland: Cleveland Museum of Art.

Boudaille, Georges, Marie-Laure Bernadac, & Marie-Pierre Gauthier. 1987. *Picasso*. New York: Longmeadow Press.
Brassaï. a.k.a. Gyula Halász. 1999. *Conversations with Picasso*. Chicago. University of Chicago Press.
Cabanne, Pierre. 1979. *Pablo Picasso: His Life and Times*. New York: William Morrow & Co.
Caws, Mary Ann. 2000. *Picasso's Weeping Woman: The Life and Art of Dora Maar*. New York: Bulfinch Press.
Choucha, Nadia. 1992. *Surrealism & the Occult: Shamanism, Magic, Alchemy, and the Birth of Artistic Movement*. Rochester, VT: Destiny Books.
Christie's. 2007. *Impressionist & Modern Art Evening Sale*. Auction catalogue 1900, November 6. New York.
———. 2009. *Impressionist & Modern Works on Paper*. Auction catalogue 7703, February 5. London.
———. 2016. *Impressionist & Modern Art Evening Sale*. Auction catalogue 12145, November 16. New York.
———. 2017. *Impressionist & Modern Art Evening Sale*. Auction catalogue 15004. November 13, New York.
———. 2018. *Impressionist & Modern Art Evening Sale*. Auction catalogue 15971, May 15. New York.
Clark, Timothy James. 2013. *Picasso and Truth: From Cubism to Guernica*. Princeton, NJ: Princeton University Press. 2013.
Cousins, Judith & Hélène Seckel. 1994. "Chronology." *Les Demoiselles d'Avignon*. pp.145–205 Eds. Rubin, William S. & Héléne Seckel. New York: Museum of Modern Art, Studies in Modern Art.
Cousins, Judith & John Elderfield. 1992. "Chronology." *Henri Matisse: A Retrospective*. pp. 82–421. Ed. John Elderfield. New York: The Museum of Modern Art.
Cousins, Judith & Pierre Daix. 1989. "Chronology." *Picasso and Braque: Pioneering Cubism* pp. 335–452. Ed. William S. Rubin. New York: Museum of Modern Art Graphic Society.
Cowling, Elizabeth. 2002. *Picasso: Style and Meaning*. London; New York: Phaidon.
Cox, Neil. 2010. *The Picasso Book*. London: Tate Publishing.
Crespelle, Jean-Paul. 1969. *Picasso and His Women*. New York: Coward-McCann.
Daemgen, Anke. 2005. "Picasso. Ein Leben." *Pablo. Der private Picasso: Le Musée Picasso à Berlin*. pp. 14–44. Ed. Angela Schneider & Anke Daemgen. München: Prestel.
Dagen, Philippe. 2009. "Chronology." *Picasso*. pp. 483–492. Ed. Philippe Dagen. New York: The Monacelli Press.
Daix, Pierre & Joan Rosselet. 1979. *Picasso: The Cubist Years, 1907–1916: A Catalogue Raisonné of the Paintings & Related Works*. Boston: New York Graphic Society.
Daix, Pierre. 1965. *Picasso*. New York: Preager.

―――. 1993. *Picasso: Life & Art*. New York: Icon Editions & New York: Harper-Collins.
―――. 1993. *Picasso: Life and Art*. New York: Basic Books.
―――. 2007. *Pablo Picasso*. Paris: Tallandier.
Fattal, Laura Felleman. 2017. "Dora Maar: Contextualizing Picasso's Muse." *Women in Judaism: A Multidisciplinary Journal*. Volume 14 Number 2, pp. 1–13.
Ferrier, Jean-Louis. 1996. *Picasso*. New York: Terrail.
FitzGerald, Michael C. 1995. *Making Modernism: Picasso and the Creation of the Market for Twentieth Century Art*. New York: Farrar, Straus & Giroux.
―――. 1997. *A Life of Collecting: Victor & Sally Ganz*. New York: Christie's.
―――. 2001. *Picasso: The Artist's Studio*. New Haven: Yale University Press.
Flam, Jack D. & Miriam Deutch, eds. 2003. *Primitivism and Twentieth Century Art: A Documentary History*. Berkeley, CA: University of California Press.
Fluegel, Jane. 1980. "Chronology." *Pablo Picasso. A Retrospective*. pp. 16–421. Ed. William S Rubin. New York: the Museum of Modern Art.
Franck, Dan. 2001. *Bohemian Paris: Picasso, Modigliani, Matisse, and the Birth of Modern Art* New York: Grove Press.
Freeman, Judie. 1994. *Picasso & the Weeping Women: The Years of Marie-Thérèse Walter & Dora Maar*. New York: Rizzoli.
Gasman, Lydia Csató. 1981. *Mystery, Magic & Love in Picasso, 1925-1938: Picasso & the Surrealist Poets*. Ph.D. Dissertation. Columbia University. Ann Arbor, Michigan: University Microfilms International.
Gilot, Françoise & Carlton Lake. 1964. *Life with Picasso*. New York: McGraw-Hill.
Goggin, Mary Margaret. 1985. *Picasso and his Art during the German Occupation: 1940-1944*. Ph.D. Dissertation. Stanford University. Ann Arbor, Michigan: University Microfilms International.
Gray, Christopher. 1953. *Cubist Aesthetic Theories*. Baltimore: The Johns Hopkins Press.
Karmel, Pepe. 2007. "Le Laboratoire Central." *Cubist Picasso*. pp. 149–163. Ed. Anne Baldassari. Paris: Flammarion.
Kozloff, Max. 1973. *Cubism/Futurism*. New York: Harper & Row.
Kris, Ernst y Kurz, Otto 1979. *Legend, Myth, and Magic in the Image of the Artist*. New Haven: Yale University Press.
La Vaccara, Ornella. 2014. "Dora Maar (1907–1997)." *Séminaire d'Histoire de l'art du XXe siècle. Les femmes artistes et collectionneuses dans la première moitié du XXe siècle*. pp. 1–8.
Léal, Brigitte, 1996. "'For Charming Dora': Portraits of Dora Maar." *Picasso and Portraiture: Representation and Transformation*. pp. 383–407. Ed. Rubin, William S., et al. New   York: Museum of Modern Art.
Madeline, Laurence. 2006. *Picasso and Africa*. Cape Town, Bell-Roberts Publisher.
Mahler, Luise. 2015. "Selected Exhibitions, 1910–1967." *Picasso Sculpture*.

pp. 304–311. Eds. Ann Temkin & Anne Umland. New York: The Museum of Modern Art, New York.

Mallén, Enrique. 2020. *Pablo Picasso: The Aphrodite Period (1924–1936)*. Brighton: Sussex Academic Press.

——. 2021. *Pablo Picasso and Dora Maar: A Period of Conflict (1936–1946)*. Brighton: Sussex Academic Press.

——, ed. 2021. *Online Picasso Project*. Sam Houston State University. http://picasso.shsu.edu.

Malraux, André. 1976. *Picasso's Mask*. New York: Da Capo Press.

McGregor-Hastie, Roy. 1988. *Picasso's Women*. London: Lennard Publishing.

Nash, Steven A., ed. 1998. *Picasso and the War Years: 1937–1945*. New York: Thames & Hudson.

O'Brian, Patrick. 1994. *Pablo Picasso. A Biography*. New York: W. W. Norton & Company.

Olivier, Fernande. 1964. *Picasso y sus Amigos*. Madrid: Taurus.

Palau i Fabre, Josep. 1999. *Picasso: Dels ballets al drama (1917–1926)*. Barcelona: Ediciones Polígrafa.

——. 2011. *Picasso 1927–1939. From the Minotaur to Guernica*, Barcelona: Poligrafa

Penrose, Roland. 1981. *Picasso: His Life & Work*. Berkeley: University of California Press.

Richardson, John, ed. 2010. *Picasso: The Mediterranean Years 1945–1962*. London: Gagosian Gallery.

——. 1991. *A Life of Picasso. Volume 1: The Prodigy, 1881–1906*. New York: Random House.

——. 1996. *A Life of Picasso, Volume 2: 1907–1917*. New York: Random House.

——. 2007. *A Life of Picasso, Volume 3: 1917–1932*. New York: Alfred A. Knopf.

Roe, Sue. 2015. *In Montmartre: Picasso, Matisse and Modernism in Paris 1900–1910*. New York: Penguin Press.

Rubin, William S., et al. 1972. *Picasso in the Collection of the Museum of Modern Art*. New York: Museum of Modern Art.

Schwartz, Paul Waldo. 1971. *Cubism*. New York: Praeger.

Seckel, Hélène, William S. Rubin & Judith Cousins, eds. 1994. *Les Demoiselles d'Avignon*. New York: Museum of Modern Art, Studies in Modern Art.

Seckel, Hélène. 1996. *Musée Picasso: Visitor's Guide*. Paris: Réunion des Musées Nationaux.

Silver, Kenneth Eric. 1989. *Esprit de Corps: The Art of Parisian Avant Garde and the First World War, 1914–1925*. London: Thames & Hudson, Ltd.

Sotheby's. 2005. *Impressionist & Modern Art Part I*. N08125, November 2. New York.

——. 2010. *Impressionist & Modern Art Evening Sale*. L10006, June 22. London.

———. 2017. *Actual Size: A Curated Evening Sale*. L17007, June 21. London.
Torras, Montse. 2002. "Cronología / Chronology." *Picasso joven - Young Picasso*. pp. 87–106.Ed. María Teresa Ocaña, Montse Torras, et al. A Coruña: Fundación Pedro Barrie de la Maza.
Tosatto, Guy, et al., eds. 2019. *Au coeur des ténèbres 1939–1945*. Grenoble: In Fine editions d'art.
Tucker, Michael. 1992. *Dreaming with Open Yes: The Shamanic Spirit in Twentieth Century Art and Culture*. London: Aquarian/Thorson.
Ullmann, Ludwig. 1993. *Picasso und der Krieg*. Bonn: Karl Kerber Verlag.
Unger, Miles J. 2018. *Picasso and the Painting That Shocked the World*. New York: Simon & Schuster.
Vallentin, Antonina. 1963. *Picasso*. Garden City, N. Y: Doubleday & Co.
Wadley, Nicholas. 1970. *Cubism*. New York: The Hamlyn Publishing Group.
Walther, Ingo F. 1993. *Pablo Picasso 1881–1973: Genius of the Century*. New York: Taschen.
Warncke, Carsten-Peter & Ingo F. Walther. 1991. *Pablo Picasso 1881–1973*. New York: Taschen America Ltd.
Wilson, Simon. 2008. *Tate Gallery: An Illustrated Companion*. London: Tate Gallery.

CHAPTER

5

Intellectual & Literary Rituals and Reflections Gone Awry due to Socio-Political Changes: Populism and Nationalism

ROSE MARY SALUM

Translated by Debra D. Andrist

What was going on at that moment? I asked myself upon getting on the plane that would take me to Guadalajara, that city that hosts the International Book Fair every year. More than a visit, my trip has turned into a ritual. In that place where the ideas of so many humans coexist, my participations have turned in an important part of my life. Since *Literal Publishing*, the editorial house that I founded, had begun to exist, each year I left for the Mexican city the first Monday before Thanksgiving and returned the end of the week. Everything went on more or less the same: I got in contact with new writers, I made dates with old friends and collaborators with *Literal*, I attended the presentations of the most sophisticated thinkers of the planet, and I returned home full of new projects. But that time, the ritual had been modified. The news items I saw before my departure were, frankly, disquieting. The appearance of these items, now I know, would be the beginning of a long string of adverse situations that would transform us as a society forever.

What was happening? I said to myself at that moment. The question reverberated in my brain like an interminably flashing neon sign, as if between the spaces of that movement, a response could sneak in. One day we were walking towards one direction and, the other, a technical majority imposed a dissimilar route. On the new trajectory that was announced, the systematic necessity of showing the truth wasn't important for the average type—or some power figures.

The rejection of racism had been substituted by the adoration of a white supremacy. Rigorous objectivity had been replaced by alternative facts. The redemptive figures that Richard Rorty[1] had given up for dead returned with redoubled force.

I didn't understand anything. Reality was turning alien. And that turmoil that everything provoked in me was interrupted by a flight stewardess asking, in a language foreign to my thoughts, what I wanted to drink. My mind had to take a break, stop itself and return to reality; I was making the trip to the Fair to present two publications from *Literal* and to orbit, as every year, like a ritual, in a cultural world that impassioned me but that would lose its sense if the humanistic notion, valid in the cultural world until shortly ago, ended up getting diluted into a reality show.

I ordered mineral wáter and I opted to leave off the news and my reading of Rorty, an American philosopher who had come back into circulation in the last few months thanks to a text published in the *New York Times* where one of his books, *Achieving Our Country*,[2] was reviewed. Its pages foresaw the election of a populist president given the conditions in which the average white inhabitants lived. He even warned that if the cultural left continued to ignore what he called the declinig economic condition of U.S. workers, they would become receptive again to the demagoguery of a fascist strongman who toyed with their fears and prejudices.

In another of his books, *An Ethics for Today*,[3] the American philosopher manifested his opposition to redemptive figures because history had demonstrated that the people don't want to be redeemed—but rather, to be happy. But the resurgence of populism, like a bad idea for a country which over the extent of its history had been careful to distribute power well among diverse political instances, was not exclusive to the U.S. but also to diverse nations of the European Union and the world.

At that moment, I understood what had disseminated virally, and I didn't know how to read reality, I thought while I went through Customs and after which I headed toward the hotel where I was going to spend some days as part of the delightful madness that, for me, the Fair signified. In the taxi, I revised my planned program and decided to go to a roundtable where Brexit[4] and the U.S. would be discussed. Some analists like the German political sientes, Marianne Braig,[5] and the French sociologist, Jean Rivelois,[6] would participate. I arrived at the hotel, I registered, I threw my suitcase on the bed, I stowed my passport in safe place, and I ran to the session that was just about to start.

I know that since the European Union has come to be an economic force of more than 500 million persons, its history has been plagued by crisis—the economic power that at the same time these numbers represented, the opposition to a European constitution, the crises in Greece and Spain, the reservations about the possible accession of Turkey, the lack of coordination and of proposals to confront the refugee problem and, in the last few months, the dilemma of Brexit and the nationalist inclination of its inhabitants.

The session began with a full and attentive audience. The first themes that were addressed were expressing confusion about the English/British behavior and their decision to leave the European Union. According to Jean Rivelois, the English sacrificed the integration for their own interests. The economic uncertainty had propagated a growing nationalism that, in a very clear manner, had spoken out in opposition to the Union. And that globalization had provoked a wide social breach. As Marianne Braig explained, from the decade of the nineties, the European Union had not grown more than at a degree of 1.6%, which, in economic terms, resulted in very low number compared to the European dream that aspired to a growth of 6%. In that sense, the economic austerity and the loss of buying power of so many of the citizens coincided with the political austerity and the possibility of an accelerated economic growth. Today the European institutions lacked democratic legitimacy: that is to say, and according to Braig: Europe was being run by an executive group of commissioners working in Brussels who were unknown to the majority of Europeans. They were never elected by popular vote and yet they were making decisions that were affecting all. The democratic déficit, the absence of economic and social politics in respect to the refugees, together with the deterioration of public politics, among other factors, had favored the growth of populism as much in Europe as in the U.S. The populism, Rivelois was maintaining, was anti-European and anti-globalization.

The populism in the E.U., I was thinking, was an effect of the democratic deficit: Europe didn't know how to give hope to the excluded and its political appeal had been reduced by a considerable amount. The neoliberal politics had left the development of an important percentage of the population out, which could be observed not only in that continent but in the U.S. and Mexico. The communist, socialist, social democratic parties or the parties of the center had been wiped out or were enroute to extinction, to the extent that the only way to channel the rejection to the E.U. was populism. There was a lack of political possibility. So simple. And if that absence were to continue, the populist parties would continue gaining strength in the next few years. In the end, Rivelois reiterated, it was a problem of legitimacy of the politicians who believed in progress and humanism on which the E.U. had been founded. The inhabitants, especially the youngest, had grown up in an ambience of liberty here-to-fore unimaginable: they could study and work in whichever member country of the E.U. without any obstacle whatsoever. In contrast, which we were observing now—the analyst was saying—was an effect of counter-globalization that privileged the nationalists and was leading to populism.

The dramatic part of the whole thing, I thought while I was listening attentively to them, was the hopelessness of this system that divided peoples, excluded immigrants, and set aside reason. As Marianne Braig pointed out: populism had emerged when there was a break between the promises of capitalistic democracies and reality. The power groups had been incapable of integrating their electoral base, accentuating the breach between the parties and their possible followers. It was easier fight for gays that for the minimum wage. In that sense, the intellectuals had occupied themselves with topics that didn't have to do with social or economic matters, abandoning an indispensable aspect for democracy. The changes in the electoral results that the E.U. showed were better understood but even more important yet, explained the result in the U.S. A break between government and social well-being had been produced. Entire populations had lost their jobs because the corporations had moved to other countries. However, what happened to technology? Why wasn't it mentioned in the electoral campaigns or in the intellectuals' forums as another fundamental factor that had reduced the workforce? And it wasn't necessary to bring up artificial or computer intelligence since the development of an application for cellular phone could leave entire associated work groups unemployed in a good-sized part of the world. It's enough to observe the havoc that the internet has wrought on the world economy. While the session continued, I asked myself if, in the hussle and bussle of daily life, we had the capacity to remember all those elements that had been mentioned or if, for lack of time to absorb the ever-growing amount of information available, a nation ended up opting for the simpliest, for that which was at hand, for the brief, the accesible . . . populist discourse.

Who was winning in this tug of war of dissimilar forces? The candidates that were perpetuating the labor disinformation or those that were speaking a lot and promising even more to an unemployed population with little daily time to keep up and with an excess of economic necessities? Who was favored more by a campaign of this nature than the very characters who were offering it? Human inequality was not only located, and has always been located, in buying power or in individual guarantees, but in the capacity of each human being to access the accumulated information over a lifetime and that would permit clearly seeing that which was better for his country or his democracy—I was thinking, while the audience enthusiastically applauded the panelists of that afternoon.

I left the auditorium, I mingled, as every year, with the rivers of persons who moved among the bookshelves while my phone was announcing: the president promises to reduce taxes and circumvent—on the basis of threats—the work opportunities offered by the big corporations transferring to Mexico. This seemed to be the beginning of something much larger. Ok, I said to my confused self, truly I don't understand anything . . . and there is no Richard Rorty at hand to explain to me what's going on. So, I concluded that I'd have to appeal to my imagination and take refuge in my own rituals.

Notes

1 *Wikipedia* notes that Rorty, 1931–2007, espoused *"ironism*; a state of mind where people are completely aware that their knowledge is dependent on their time and place in history and are therefore, somewhat detached from their own beliefs."

2 Peter Berkowitz's review notes that this book is "based on [Rorty's]1997 Massey lectures at Harvard, [where he] turns his attention as never before to practical politics. His aim is to encourage leftist intellectuals, once prominent in American public life, to return to the fray, 'to think of American citizenship as an opportunity for action.' What he actually accomplishes is a far different thing, however, for *Achieving Our Country* points to nothing so much as the continuing confusion in America's academic Left."

3 Rorty, Richard. *An Ethics for Today: Finding Common Ground Between Philosophy and Religion*. New York: Columbia University Press, 2010. *Colombia University Press* characterizes this as the work of "the celebrated pragmatist believed there could be no universally valid answers to moral questions, which led him to a complex view of religion rarely expressed in his writings. In this posthumous publication, Rorty, a strict secularist, finds . . . a political imagination shared by religious traditions. His intent is not to promote belief over nonbelief or to blur the distinction between religious and public domains. Rorty seeks only to locate patterns of similarity and difference so an ethics of decency and a politics of solidarity can rise."

4 Wikipedia defines Brexit as "the withdrawal of the United Kingdom (UK) from the European Union (EU) . . . on 31 January 2020. . . . The UK is the only sovereign country to have left the EU.

5 Professor of Political Science at the Institute for Latin American Studies at *Freie Universität Berlin*, whose university profile lists her "research [as] broad and focuses . . . gender segmentation in labor markets and social

and educational policy, transformation and development in Latin America, the political culture of the state and governance as well as intertwined and interdependent inequalities in the global context. She also conducts research within networks of excellence of the European Union Latin American Relations Observatory (EULARO) on gender issues, citizenship and migration."

6   A research fellow in the *Centre d'études en sciences sociales sur les mondes africains, américains et asiatiques* (CESSMA) at the *Institut de recherche pour le développement* (I.R.D.) in France, he is a member of the project Informality, Power and the Other Side of Urban Space (Inverses) Research specializing in social exclusion.

PART II

Rites, Rituals & Roman Catholic
Religious Experiences

Introduction to Rites, Rituals & Roman Catholic Religious Experiences

A. SUPERNATURAL/RELIGIOUS CONTROL CONCERNS: RELIGIOUS AND LITERARY RITES & RITUALS. METAPHORICAL AND/OR FICTIONALIZED CONTROL. AUTHORITY-DIRECTED (PRIESTLY) CONTROL THROUGH ROMAN CATHOLIC CHRISTIAN & INDIGENOUS PERSPECTIVES

Part II 'A' focuses on religion per se as represented in literature, specifically aspects of the Roman Catholic Church, mostly due to the historical dominance of that denomination in Hispanic worlds. The (notably male) authority figure, the priest, takes a central role. Choosing the literary representations of the Church and the priest in the three chapters of this section was an active decision by the editor, mostly to contrast with the real-life aspects of the three chapters of **Part II 'B'**

My initial chapter, *'Song of the Hummingbird' (1996) by Graciela Limón: An Exercise in Multi-Stable Perceptions*, addresses a fictionalized interaction between a young Spanish priest and an Aztec *anciana* in post-Conquest Mexico. Though entertaining, this novel offers the reader a comparative bridge over the real-life historical abyss between the Spanish conquerors' worldview and that of the conquered Aztecs. Limón's protagonists portray the two dramatically differing perceptions of experiences as shaped & dictated by culture, religion, imperialism, victory & vanquishment, and the beliefs and mentalities which tout superiority vs. inferiority of groups of humans. Though much less emotionally charged, the closest topical chapter I've written, *A (Culinary) Counter-Conquest* from *Sustenance*, is actually historical.

On an associated note to highlight again that there are other-than-Christianity/specifically Roman Catholicism (the Church) aspects in Hispanic worlds, it is vital to mention that, for comparative worldviews in terms of the various other religions in the Hispanic worlds, though not as conveniently combined & contrasted as Aztec beliefs and those of the Spanish Church in Limon's novel, the reader must review separate chapters from separate volumes. Jeanne Gillespie's chapters focus on indigenous religion. For example, from *Body*, her three chapter titles make the intended power of the rites, rituals and religious overlay and attempts to control same clear: *The Body and Indigenous Control of Environment. The Fluids of Life: Blood, Water, Power and Bugs à la Tlaxcalteca*; *The Body Cured by Cleansing: Washing Away the Evidence: Midwives and Ritual Cleansing in Mesoamerica and Colonial New Spain*; and *The Body Cured by*

Introduction to Part II | 79

Plants: Where have all the (Chocolate and Popcorn) Flowers Gone? Recovering Healing Botanicals in Nahuatl Poetry. For Afro-Hispanic topics, those chapters by Patricia González Gómes-Cásserez: *Creoles* from S/HE; *La Muerte* and *Death/Ikú & the Spirits in Afro-Cuban Religions* from *Death*; and *Ritual Foods in Afro-Cuban Ceremonies* from *Sustenance*, highlight the rites, rituals and religion from the African enforced-diaspora-due-to-enslavement socio-cultural aspects of Hispanic worlds.

Although not religiously oriented and considerably farther afield in socio-cultural comparisons without interactions—and more covert in highlighting differing perceptions—Haiqing Sun's chapters compare Mexican and Chinese films, *Family, Food & Fighting: A Comparative Study of the Mexican Films, 'Como agua para chocolate,' directed by Alfonso Arau, and the Chinese Film, 'Eat Drink Man Woman,' directed by Ang Lee*, first published in *Family, Friends & Foes* and reprinted in *Sustenance* and *China and 'Chinago:' Globalization of the Kung Fu Genre and the Interpretation of Hero and History* in *Crossroads*. Similarly, the chapters treating works by Lebanese Mexican author, Rose Mary Salum, e.g., my chapter from *Family et al, Life to Literature; Families Crossing and Breaking Immigrant Barriers* and Eduardo Cerdán's *Lebanese Children Against the War* from *Insult* bring in another socio-cultural group, though the Roman Catholic aspect maintains in those otherwise vastly different cultures. Numerous chapters throughout the series compare aspects of Hispanic, Anglo and Italo worlds, as in this latter case, my chapter, *Male Friendship in the Italo-Hispanic Literary Tradition* from *Family et al.*

The next two chapters in **Part II 'A'** are entirely focused on fictional Roman Catholic priest-protagonists who are complete opposites, one the "poster-boy" for a priest who really lives his vows—and suffers the Church's disdain & punishment, for same: *'Nazarín' by Pérez Galdós (1895): The Challenges to the Imitatio Christi: When Narrators, Characters and Readers Are Skeptical* by Stephen J. Miller. Miller has written several chapters for the series before, while none focused on religious aspects per se, though frequently on works by the Spanish writer, Pérez Galdós, and by the Mexican American writer, Rolando Hinojosa.

Sena Pfaff has contributed for the first time to this series, two chapters for this particular book, both chapters featuring religious (Church) orientations. Her first chapter, *Rites & Rituals of the Roman Catholic Priesthood: Holy Orders: San Manuel Bueno. Human Weakness in the Vocation: Saintly Martyr or Sinful Hypocrite,?* examines the Spanish writer Unamuno's *nivola* (1931), in which the priest-protagonist is himself, unbelievably to readers and in contrast to the titular priest in Miller's chapter, a non-believer! Sena Pfaff examines whether the priest is true to the members of his congregation, who he believes will perish if they doubt—or whether he abrogates their free will by pretending to believe. Her second chapter, which appears in **Part III**, focuses on the necessity for (Spanish) language maintenance among the members of the long-term, not recent-immigrant, Hispanic population in New Mexico and the role the Church can/must play in that maintenance.

B. (Contemporary) Social Concerns & Control. The Role of the Church. Language Maintenance, Religious Practice, Ecofeminism & Church-related Activities

Part II 'B' takes quite a different tack, though still specifically Church-oriented, by focusing on real-life social outreach and activism rather than on literary characterizations of male authority figures and offers insights into multi-stable perceptions of worldviews. The roles of women in the Church, real and projected, and society play major parts in both of the first two chapters.

Sena Pfaff's aforementioned second chapter, *Traditional Spanish Language Maintenance and the Revitalization of Culture and Faith: A Mission for the Body of Christ*, grew out of a project combining her New Mexican multi-generational, long-term residence, traditional Roman Catholic heritage and her degree in Catholic Studies at the University of St. Thomas/Houston. It bears mention that Sena Pfaff is of a distinct heritage, both cultural and linguistic, and, if you will, worldview, quite different from than the recent influx of Spanish-speaking immigrants (Mexican & Central American) to her state.

Introducing a geographic aspect of the term, *Latin American,* not overtly included before in this series due to the previous emphasis on (only) the indigenous and Hispanic aspects of Latin America, as well as on less-emphasized aspects of the Church itself, Mary Jane DeLaRosa Burke's chapter, *Re-Envisioning Latina Ministry Through Ivone Gebara's Ecofeminism,* introduces a Brazilian woman theologian (an uncommon combination in terms of country, Church, and career/calling). Further, DeLaRosa Burke takes up consideration of more active roles for women in the male-dominated Church, espouses activist awareness & concern for the environment (again, uncommon social activism for the Church, except for some Liberation Theologists[1]) and includes her own experience growing up Mexican American in Texas. Her first chapter for this series introduces not only the positive benefits and possibilities for ecofeminism, and women, and the Church, but recounts her own personal life-long Church-related activism and idealism, and her traditional multi-generation, non-immigrant, Mexican American-in-Texas (*tejana*) experience. This experience is not only very distinct from that of more recent immigrants to Texas from Mexico and Central America but also from Sena Pfaff's New Mexican experience and/or worldview of either set of generations there.

Such a crucial topic as ecological concerns in the worlds addressed by this series has been broached before, if only overtly once and in terms of eco-violence, in Jason Payton's *Violence, Trauma and Ecology in John Rollin Ridge's 'Joaquin Murieta'* from *Insult*. This is not to say that ecological concerns have been overtly neglected, but they have served more as background for other aspects of these worlds.

Author of the third chapter in **Part II 'B'**, John Francis Burke has focused his earlier chapters for this series on religion in terms of the Church, activism, and politics, almost never promoting the traditional "party-line" of the Church with its flaws—but offering the evaluation of, and best possibilities for, the Church's role in diversity, equality and fostering the best of all worlds for all. His previous chapters include '*Mestizaje*' (also the title of his first book several decades ago) *as Lateral Universality: Moving In-Between Elitist Cosmopolitanism and Populist Tribalism* from *Crossroads*; *Recasting Catholicism* from *Death*; *Eucharistic Bread & Wine: A Concrete Sacramentality That Liberates* from *Sustenance*. The chapter for this eighth book *Recasting Personalism in Light of the Beloved Community* follows that same thread. Salum's essay deals with several of the same socio-political concerns and how they affect intellectual pursuits; she clearly understands what is happening socio-politically worldwide, though she deals with the changes and results in much more personal ways (it is an essay, after all), which is why the essay appears in the book where is does. At the same time, as her friend, I know that she shares Burke's evaluation/solution which ends his chapter (very many of us do): "The ideals of the beloved community, call each of us to envision and pursue, a political community characterized by egalitarian relationships between diverse faiths, races, and ethnicities. Toward this end, we need to engage and transform prevailing unjust political socio-economic structures and relationships to enable diverse persons and groups to enrich our shared community life with their respective gifts."

Notes

1 In my (Andrist) opinion, the basic tenet of *Liberation Theology*—not only *not* espoused by the "official" Church but grounds for excommunication—is that religious authorities have the responsibility to effect socio-economic change for their constituents in this time-&-place world, not to promise them succor/relief in the next after death (*El más allá*).

CHAPTER
6

Song of Hummingbird (1996) by Graciela Limón: An Exercise in Multi-stable Perceptions

DEBRA D. ANDRIST

Sensory perception depends on the senses: sight, smell, hearing, touch and taste. Optical illusion and *trompe l'oeil* are tricks, "seeing" that which is not in actuality. Smell depends on socialization and/or physical or emotional response: the acrid odor of napalm (along with Agent Orange), horrifying smells to (and effects on) the sometimes inadvertent, so-called collateral damage, victims during the Vietnam War, which represented a "mere" tool to clear jungle foliage and create protective visual space for the U.S. military. The use of onomatopoeia in comic books or poetry, e.g., *Bam! Zap! Pop!* ties sight and/or hearing to a certain "reality" for the reader. That which is far more than simple "feel," e.g., handshakes, can covertly demonstrate equality, dominance and/or submission (Carney et al). Taste is partially socio-culturally determined, as in multi-stable perception—that which actually IS, but the interpretation of which depends on cultural perception. For example, the cricket in the U.S. is a pest; in China, it's a pet; in Thailand, it's an appetizer; and in Mexico, fried *chapulín* (frequently wrapped in chocolate) is still a treat dating from pre-Conquest times.

As writer/philosopher Anaïs Nin, herself a product of triple-cultural background,[1] noted, "We don't see things how THEY (emphasis mine—Andrist) are, we see them how WE (emphasis mine) are."[2] Several U.S. state-associated websites dealing with cultural lenses (although state entities, usually funded by the U.S. Department of Education), particularly *ITAP (Illinois)* and SPP-TAP (*California*) illuminate that quote further: "Culture is learned, shared, unconscious, dynamic, ethnocentric. Perceptions are illuminated by our 'cultural lenses.'"[3]

Chilean poet, Nicanor Segundo Parra Sandoval, 1914–2018, self-styled an "anti-poet," illustrates that concept perfectly with his poem,[4] an oppositional riff on a very recognizable, emotionally loaded for Christians, socio-religious icon:

> Our Father who art in heaven
> Full of all kinds of problems,
> Frowning
> As though you were a vulgar, an ordinary man,
> For God's sake, don't think any more about us.
> We understand that you are suffering
> Because you cannot make things better.
> We know that the Devil doesn't leave you alone
> Always undoing whatever you put together.
> He is laughing at you
> But we share your sorrow:
> Pay no heed to his diabolical laughter.
> Our Father who art where thou art
> Surrounded by disloyal angels
> I really mean it: don't put yourself out any more for us.
> You've got to realise
> That gods are not infallible
> And that we forgive everything.[5]

Though certainly not by premonition or intent, from very diverse countries and cultures and years before Limón's book, Parra alluded, quite coincidentally, to concept and salient content of *Song of the Hummingbird*, referring to "the voice of a priest in the pulpit . . . the birds [who] do the singing." Cultural mindset can lead to very specific, sometimes even unconscious, stereotyping and/or discrimination in style, logical progression and organization but there can be, even inadvertently, commonalities inherent in symbols like priests, who are religious power figures in life and fiction, and birds and flying are recognized and frequent literary symbols of freedom, especially for females in sexist societies. Although there are hundreds of examples in numerous languages, the poem, *Hombre pequeñito/Little Man*, by Argentine, Alfonsina Storni (1892–1938), is the work cited as the classic example in Latin American literature. The poem underlines the idea of gender and multi-stable perceptions appropriately, if not in socio-cultural terms of religion like *Song of the Hummingbird:*

Song of Hummingbird *(1996) by Graciela Limón* | 85

> Little man, little man,
> set free your canary that wants to fly.
> I am that canary, little little man,
> leave me to fly.
> I was in your cage, little little man,
> little little man who gave me my cage.
> I say "little" because you don't understand me
> Nor will you understand.
> Nor do I understand you, but meanwhile,
> open for me the cage from which I want to escape.
> Little little man, I loved you half an hour,
> Don't ask me again.[6]

Coincidentally, the silhouette on the front cover of the novel, is visually "interpretable," *a la* multi-stable perception, to set the stage for the contrasting life-views content.

So, why is all this particular chapter lead-in about perceptions so important to both the reading and/or the interpretation of the novel by Limón? The very concept of said novel is based on oppositional juxtapositions—of times, cultures, languages, generations by age, of the main characters (who is the protagonist and who is the antagonist is debatable, depending on the episode). Father Benito and all three *personas* of Hummingbird (English translation of the Nahuatl)/Huitzitzilin (Nahuatl)/María de Belén (Roman Catholic baptismal name) and their drastically different perceptions of the seemingly same things, confound not only the characters themselves but force the reader to confront the concept of multi-stable perceptions, especially as supported or "justified" by sociocultural and religious beliefs.

> From Aztec princess to slave and concubine, Hummingbird—or Huitzitzilin in her native Nahuatl—recounts her life during the Spanish conquest of Mexico to Father Benito, the priest who seeks to confess and convert her, to offer her an absolution she neither needs nor wants. Instead, she forces him to see the conquest, for the first time, through the eyes of the conquered". (*Good Reads*)

Sheila Rocha, in commentary on the same website, notes that this book is

> the history of the conquest of indigenous Mexico—up close as a first-person testimony. Limón takes the format of interview into an intimate dialogue between [Benito, a] Catholic priest (with his own

set of baggage) and an elder anciana, or native woman, Huitzitzlin/Hummingbird/Doña María de Belén, who lived through the full of the conquest and survived to tell her story as it affected not only her people, but her [own] womanhood. It is more fact than fiction because the value of this woman's testimony is based on the journals, chronicles and codices that recorded the holocaust of Mesoamerica during the Spanish invasion . . . This is decolonizing literature that reclaims essential history. (*Good Reads*)

Sheila Rocha and Mike Fraga go further in their PhD essay review of the book, and not only summarize the action in terms of cultures and religions but identify Huitzitzlin/Hummingbird/Doña María de Belén's specific "sins" in the eyes of the Church and thus, for Benito.

The novel, *Song of the Hummingbird* by Graciela Limon, is a book about Huitzitzilin's encounters during the Spanish conquest and the coming of Cortés. There are many themes in this novel, such as war, religion, culture, sins and the ending of an era for the Mexicas. But it does not start off [with] her telling her stories, but of a young monk named Father Benito Lara, who is called to hear her last confession, for she was very old and knew she was near the end of her long journey.

Father Benito went to listen to Huitzitzilin every day for she had much to say about her life and about her culture before and during the Spanish conquest. She told him some sins throughout their conversations, and when she did not talk about their sins, he would write down all that she was saying so he can record her side of what happened during the Conquest, for he only heard teachings of how the Spaniards had seen the conquest. The novel starts of in a convent at Coyoacán in 1583.

The concepts of the gender difference and the vastly different ages/generations/stages of life of these characters is also notable. She is old enough to at least be his grandmother and has lived what she recounts; he has to rely on only the accounts of others of his same lifeview. Thus, their interactions are skewed by not only by outlook at different stages of life and cultural but by those dramatically different socio-religious socializations, not to mention the misogyny of both cultures.

Father Benito is only 27, and Huitzitzilin is 82. As Huitzitzilin starts her story, it is spring in the year 1501 when she was born. She describes her growing up in her tribe and of her traditions and

Song of Hummingbird (1996) by Graciela Limón | 87

customs. Some of these disturbed the monk because he felt that they were devil worshipers and did not want to hear such chants for he feels the devil will try to pull him in. Huitzitzilin tried to tell him that she was not a devil-worshipper, but she has gods of her own that she did worship.

He was taught differently of her tribe and did not understand most of the things she had to say, but he still listened, for he was fascinated by most of the things she had to say about her life and about her tribe. [The author] Graciela Limón is arguing for Huitzitzilin, for the way she wrote this novel explained in detail Huitzitzilin's journey through all her hardships she had to face during the time of the Spanish conquests. Limón did not suppress how Huitzitzilin looked in any way throughout the novel. She wrote the story as if she [were] Huitzitzilin herself, and just wanted to have her story told. Huitzitzilin's character had a lot to say about her life and after every conversation, she felt better after confessing her sins, for she felt a burden was being lifted of her shoulders.

One theme of the novel is religion. Religion is a theme throughout the whole novel, for Father Benito kept referring to God and about his Christianity every time Huitzitzilin talked about her gods of about some of her traditions. "No! Don't mention the idols!" Father Benito's voice trembled, betraying the fear the god's name conjured his mind ... "No? But if you don't allow me to speak of them, how can I explain the most important part of those events?" The monk was dumbfounded. Yet he had promised Father Anselmo [the abbot] that he would not allow allusion to those demons. He bit his lip in consternation because he couldn't help thinking that it would be equally difficult to speak of his own people without the mention of Jesus Christ. He kept reminding her that it was a great thing that the Spaniards brought Christianity amongst them. She repeatedly told him that she did not believe in his ways or in God, for she only [sought] the forgiveness of Father Benito, not of God. "Will you forgive me? " "God forgives all sins if there is contrition." "But will you (emphasis mine, Andrist) forgive me?" [At] the end of the novel, he understood why she kept asking for his forgiveness, for it was not for mercy or absolution but for understanding of her life.

Another theme was sins [especially sexual], for Huitzitzilin confessed sins to Father Benito [who has taken a vow of chastity as a priest] during her conversations. Her first sin was fornication with Zintle by the lake. But the way she told her sins to him bothered him for she told them in exact detailed of the way she remembered it. Her second sin she told was abortion. She was pregnant with Zintle's child, and she went to a healer that knows about some herbs that can get rid of the unborn child. She was not sorry for that sin [about which she] and the priest argued . . . She argued she did that for the sake of her own life, for if her husband to be found out about her fornication, he would have her killed. After hearing what her husband-to-be, Tetla, did to her the night of their wedding, [Benito] began to feel sorry for her. (Rocha & Fraga)

And that is the beginning of Benito's realization (acceptance?) of multi-stable perceptions of the Conquest and its aftermath! Of course, Hummingbird has committed any number of other "sins" from the Spanish cultural and Church catechism points-of-view, e.g., what she does in revenge (a fourth sin) to Paloma and to Tetla.

Given importance of names and naming, Limón also offers insights into the less-overt aspects of the novel to those who do a bit of research about the characters' all-important names[7] and associated identities. Overtly, Limón sets the reality stage with historical figures like Moctezuma, the second-to-the-last Aztec emperor whose premonitions supposedly foretold the Conquest, and Cortés, the Spanish conqueror, who was supposedly transmogrified into a returning Quetzalcoatl, the Aztec (and previously Toltec) "feathered serpent" god. An, at least cursory, understanding of the actual history of the Conquest is essential to following the internal conflicts Benito and Doña Marina/ Huitzitzilin suffer about each other—which have roots in real-life events. For example, the real-life Spanish priest/conqueror,

> Bartolomé de las Casas, spent 50 years of his life actively fighting slavery and the colonial abuse of indigenous peoples, especially by trying to convince the Spanish court to adopt a more humane policy of colonization. Unlike some other priests who sought to destroy the indigenous peoples' native books and writings, he strictly opposed this action . . . He participated in the 1550 Valladolid debate, in which [noted scholar at the time] Juan Ginés de Sepúlveda argued that the Indians were less than human, and required Spanish masters to become civilized. Las Casas maintained that they were fully human, and that forcefully subjugating them was unjustifiable.[8]

The fictional Benito, though the novel's setting is considerably later than the initial Conquest, is still an intellectual and religious product of what was the real-life Spanish Inquisition mindset, of maintaining the Spanish goals of acquisition of not only gold but souls and the techniques of conquest, i.e., monotheism vs. polytheism, and the transmogrification of many indigenous concepts for those purposes, especially the idea of sacrifice, if the Christian one for the sins of the many rather than the sacrifice of the many per se, with control of nature aspects, of the Aztecs. Hence, Benito's confusion, conflict, etc.

Coming back to the initial reference in this chapter to multi-stable perception of napalm as a metaphor, the actual Conquest represented that same slash-and-burn, scorched-earth reality for the indigenous peoples and their cultures—but justified by almost all the Spanish due to their overarching goals of acquisition. This double reality is clearly represented by the characters of Fr. Benito and Huitzitzilin/Hummingbird/Doña María de Belén in the novel—and guarantees not only their inability to relate and interact and understand each other but their suffering as a result of those inabilities, yet growing insights into the other's life-view.

Limón's other fictional inventions purposefully include rather covert cross-cultural references: Anselmo Cano, whose name comes from the German as God's helmet; an old man, with gray hair, worthy (the visual stereotype of the Christians' God—and related to reeds. That European reference segues into the indigenous Tzintle (place, diminutive form): in or behind reeds and Tetla (place). Baltázar was one of the three Magi and myrrh relates to the death of a king (an unrelated aside, just for entertainment purposes, also to a specific size of wine bottle). Huitzizitlin's punishment of her rival, Paloma, is not only another bird by name, but specifically a dove, symbolizing peace=gentle in Christian tradition. Her own "Mary of Bethlehem" baptismal name and Benito's name, a diminutive of Benedict, carry weight in the conquerors' traditions and explain the history behind not only Limón's choice of name for him but for some of Father Benito's culturally negative reactions, especially to the more sexual of María de Belem's confessions, to him in the novel. The Church tradition of priestly chastity, as well as the history of Roman Catholic saint emphasize why he is so uncomfortable.

Benedict of Norcia (480 AD–21 March 547) traveled to Montecassino [Italy] where he established a monastery and wrote "The Rule." This simple set of guidelines for how the life of a monk should be lived has become one of the most influential works in all of Western Christendom... After attending primary schools in Norcia, Benedict went to Rome to broaden his knowledge of literature and law. However, since he was probably disgusted by the dissolute lifestyle of his peers and by Rome's difficult political situation, he retired to Affile with a group of priests, taking his old nurse with him as a servant ... After resisting a strong temptation against chastity, Benedict prepared to live through a new experience, following the example of the ancient Fathers of Christian Monasticism... He prevented a monk from leading a dissolute life through intervention . . . In autumn of 542 AD, while the Goth King Totila . . . decided to test Saint Benedict . . . As a consequence, Totila sent his squire dressed as a king to greet the monk; but Saint Benedict soon unmasked him. When he finally met Totila, he warned him with a dire prediction: "You have hurt many and you continue to do it, now stop behaving badly! And that is exactly what happened . . . Saint Benedict devoted himself to evangelizing the local population who practiced pagan worship.[9]

Too, the sometimes, if not exact, certainly, parallels, between Benito and de las Casas and St. Benedict are notable, as are those in some ways, between Mallinali/Malintzin/Doña Marina/Malinche (Cortés' translator and the mother of his child, the so-called first *mestizo*) and Hummingbird.

Doña Marina's original name means "Hummingbird('s) South" or "Hummingbird('s) Left," yet it has commonly been translated as "Southern hummingbird" or "left-handed hummingbird." The discrepancy between "left" and "south" in translation stems from the Aztec belief that the south was the left side of the world. Despite the popularity of these later interpretations, her name most probably does not mean "left-handed/southern hummingbird" considering that the Classical Nahuatl hu tzilin ("hummingbird") is the modifier of ōpōchtli ("left-hand side") in this compound rather than the reverse; there continues to be much disagreement as to the full meaning of this name.[10]

Remembering the symbolism of the bird and the multiple personas of the character, "Diego Durán provides some insight to the "huitzitzilin" bird after which the Aztec god is named. He describes what appears to be the hummingbird hibernating in a tree, somewhat like the common poorwill does. He writes, "It appears to be dead, but at the advent of spring . . . the little bird is reborn."[11] Thus, like Durán's reference which reminds us of the phoenix of European legend, Limón fictionalizes the story of one female survivor of the Conquest, Hummingbird. She perhaps did not rise from, but certainly survived in spite of, the ashes of her culture, at the same time as the reader remembers and reexamines the "Black Legend"[12] stereotype of the Spaniard via Benito's conflict-fraught journey towards the recognition of multi-stable perception.

Notes

1 There is some controversy about whether Anaïs Nin was the one who first said this and, if so, from where she was quoted but the *ITAP* website cites her as the source of the quote.
2 *Wikipedia* notes that Nin's parents were Cubans living in France where she was born and she herself later came to the U.S.
3 *ITAP*
4 Again, *Wikipedia* comments on Parra's self-characterization as an "anti-poet," as do numerous other websites.
5 I've chosen the Sean Keenan (Irish) translation from the web.
6 Alfonsina Storni's *Hombre pequeño*, translation on Poetry.com
7 Remembering that Malinche was originally Malinalli or Malintzín in her indigenous personas and later, baptized Doña Marina, before being dubbed *la Chingada* much later as interpreted by those who condemned her as a cultural sell-out, something like the contemporary epithet, *coco*, if less misogynous as it may be.
8 Bartolomeo de las Casas' biography is detailed on many websites, including extensive *Wikipedia* articles on him and on the Valladolid Debate.
9 There are websites of numerous churches named after St. Benedict and *Catholic On-line's* section on Saints & Angels and other sites about saints which tell about his life.
10 As the quote notes, there is some quibbling about the exact meaning and etymology of the word(s)/name.
11 Frey Diego Durán's biography is available in a *Wikipedia* article. He was much criticized for his multi-stable perceptions in defense of the Aztecs.
12 Although not originally or only specifically used in the context of the Conquest of the Americas, the term, *Black Legend*, has come symbolize the widely held stereotype of the worst Spanish behaviors during that Conquest.

Works Cited

California Department of Education, Special Education Division's special project, State Performance Plan Technical Assistance Project (SPP-TAP). Web.
Carney, D.R., Hal, J.A. & LeBeau, L.S. (2005) "Beliefs About Non-Verbal Expression of Social Power" in *Journal of Non-Verbal Behavior*. Web.
Catholic On-line. "Benedict" in "Saints & Angels.: Web.
Good Reads. "Song of the Hummingbird." Web.
Illinois Transparency and Accountability Portal (ITAP). Web.
Keenan, Sean, Trans. *Our Father* by Nicanor Parra | Poetry Ireland. Web.
Limón, Graciela. (1996) *Song of the Hummingbird*. Houston, TX: University of Houston, Arte Público Press. Print.
Nin, Anaïs. *Wikipedia*. Web.
Parra, Nicanor. *Nicanor Parra* | *Poetry Foundation*. Web.

Rocha, Sheila and Mike Fraga. "Song of a Hummingbird" in *PhD Essays Category Birds, Christianity, Forgiveness, God.* Web.
Saint Benedict Church. *A Life of St. Benedict.* Web.
Storni, Alfonsina. *Hombre pequeñito/Little Man* on *Poetry.com* Web.
Wood, Stephanie. "Huitzilin" & "Huitzitzilin." *Nahuatl Dictionary.* University of Oregon: 2000 Web.

CHAPTER
7
Nazarín (1895) by Benito Galdós:
Challenges to the *Imitatio Christi*:
When Narrators, Characters and
Readers are Skeptical

STEPHEN J. MILLER

Among other things, the 19th-century is famous for philosophers such as Hegel and Nietzsche proclaiming the death of God, and the former Catholic seminarian Ernst Renan, perhaps for a larger audience with his famous biography, *The Life of Jesus* (1863),[1] denying the divinity and miracles of Christ while converting him into a this-worldly, completely human, non-divine exemplar of Christian virtue. Moreover, Thomas à Kempis' early fifteenth-century classic, *The Imitation of Christ*, has never been out of print and more-or-less directly obliges/d any person thinking seriously of Christianity to consider the essentially partly mystic, partly Protestant position of creating a very personal vision of and relation with Christ in the extremely devout person's manner of living.

In his May 1895 novel, *Nazarín*, as well as its de facto October-1895 sequel, *Halma*, Benito Pérez Galdós dramatized the case of a humble Spanish priest, known variously as "Nazarín," "Zaharín," and "Nazarío," and who, in a non-assuming manner during years, tried to imitate in actions his understanding of what being a follower of Christ meant. Yet, for a series of reasons beyond his intent or control, during the few months of his life recorded in the novel, he becomes a national figure whose priestly licenses are revoked and who becomes a fugitive from civil justice. Moreover, as a direct result of living and working among the poorest and most abject creatures living in the slums of Madrid's southern reaches on the sloping land leading down to the flood plain of the Manzanares River, Nazarín is assumed guilty by association at least with the crime of his tenement apartment being set on fire by a debased woman he tried to help. Seeing all doors to him as a working priest closed in Madrid, upon leaving the city, he soon sees that he has acquired two disciples. Ándara, the fire starter, is an older, sometimes-violent and now much-degraded prostitute; the other is the younger, attractive Beatrice who simply lives the hard life of the vulnerable urban poor yet has been much impressed by Nazarín's great charity. With no direct nor indirect signs nor invitation from him, and despite his attempts to discourage them from following him, both women, known to each other, join Nazarín as he leaves Madrid by the southern Toledo Gate and across the Manzanares to begin his version of Christ on the highways and byways of areas and towns to the southwest of Madrid. He must necessarily improvise in this new life; as the circumstances and his attempt to imitate Christ determine, he acts to help those into whose lives he wanders.

This life is told by Galdós in a novel divided into five parts. These in practice function similarly to the acts in a five-act play closer in form to the Shakespearean model and tradition than to the Spanish three-act play represented in nineteenth-century Spain, most notably by Moratín's *The Maiden's Consent*,[2] and whose scenes change with the entrance and exit of any character. The denser scenes preferred by Shakespeare and this Galdós are more action than character-driven. The five subdivisions or scenes of Part/Act I are the exposition of Nazarín's obscure, hand-to-mouth priestly life just up to when he is about to become a public figure through no design of his own. The six scenes of Part/Act II are the rising action whereby the humble priest's life, because of bad luck while serving the poor, becomes the object of diocesan censure and judicial inquiry, and leads him to form the resolution of changing his life by leaving behind Madrid and, already defrocked, his life as a priest, albeit not as an imitator of Christ. The nine scenes of the Part/Act III form the climax when the priest most closely can be seen imitating the Christ characterized by his service to the downtrodden and poor, and achieving notable results. Nazarín, always efficaciously followed and aided by his two "disciples," does works of mercy which cause some in the small village from which Beatrice by chance hails, to see as a life-saving miracle and, afterwards in another, larger town, public wide recognition for his and his *disciples*' indispensable, week-long help during a smallpox outbreak. Part/Act IV, the falling action, traces how just when Nazarín and the two women, justly contented and exhausted from their labors, find in an abandoned, ruinous hilltop castle the solitude and rest from their labors they need, Madrid-based society in the form of judicial authorities catch up with them. Part/Act V, the resolution, finds

Nazarín and Ándara arrested by Civil Guards and incorporated into the bound group of detainees being herded by the Civil Guards to walk to Madrid for arraignment. Beatrice follows along out of her own will (see, for example, IV, 8: 162),[3] and during the trudge, one of the thieves who early on in their wandering robbed Nazarín and the women, also becomes a believer in Nazarín. For his part, Nazarín falls ill with a very high, self-doubt-producing fever which, once in Madrid, leads to his hospitalization. In the last paragraph of the novel (divided into two in the Spanish original), Christ himself—at least as a hallucination of the very sick Nazarín—appears to the priest and says to him:

> My son, you are still alive. You are in My holy hospital, suffering for Me. Your companions, the two women-sinners and the thief who follow your teachings, are in jail. You cannot say mass. I cannot be with you in flesh and blood, and this mass [which the hallucinating Nazarín believes he is saying] is the insane imagining of your mind. Rest, for you well deserve it. You have done something valuable for me [sic]. Do not be discontent. I know that you are to do much more. (V, 7: 200)

As many critics have indicated, there is a great amount of ambiguity as to not only this closing scene of the novel, but also as to how the reader, as is the case of many characters in the novel, are to view its titular protagonist whose very name suggests the necessity of comparison and contrast with Jesus of Nazareth, the historical figure around whose life and teachings, as interpreted over the past two millennia, have been the organizing principle of Western Civilization. Yet, as stated at the beginning of this paper, many leading thinkers and writers explored the question. By the May 1895 date when Benito Pérez Galdós (1843–1920) published *Nazarín* and its effective sequel, *Halma*, in October of that same year, questions about who Christ was had progressed to become fully part of that *fin-de-siècle* crisis of societal, religious and personal values and aspirations. For a reader such as myself, born a century after Galdós, this situation is/was not strange. From a purely Anglo-American viewpoint, the country had won the two-front World War II, but the Cold War and its constant threats of the thermonuclear end of the world never left any aware person's consciousness. During all my time as a first-year Baby Boomer, born and bred in what I fondly sometimes call my "Irish-Catholic ghetto" education with Dominican nuns in grammar school, Marianist brothers in high school, and two and one-half years in major seminary with Maryknoll Missionary priests, it had become common to ask How would Christ be received in the post-WW II America which, as I now realize, had begun to emphasize more and more the search for and confidence in secular, governmental terms the solution for so many age-old social, political and economic problems which, nonetheless remain today, if anything, seemingly more intractable? And in *Nazarín,* Galdós himself early on poses a version of the question. In conversation with Nazarín, in the exposition of Part/Act I, two characters interviewing the priest and wanting to investigate the reputation for holiness he has been acquiring among the downtrodden poor, ask him: "what do you think . . . about today's current affairs, the problems our society is facing" (I, 4: 20). And later in the climactic Part/Act III, another character, the irascible, but spiritually concerned nobleman, Don Pedro Belmonte, asks the by-now defrocked, fugitive Nazarín "about the problems we're facing in our society and religion right now" (III, 7: 104). As the conversation continues, the priest thinks it will be the Catholic pope who will become the new "Moses," which, he and Belmonte agree, society needs. Military, political, lesser-religious figures than a pope are specifically discounted. At the same time, Belmonte tells Nazarín that because of his age, semitic appearance and conversation, he may well be "the most reverend Armenian bishop, a man who has been traveling through Europe on a holy pilgrimage for the last two years" (I, 3: 109). When Nazarín expresses his surprise, Belmonte continues to assert that he is talking with no less a figure that "the patriarch of the Armenian church who has submitted to the Latin church [to the pope in Rome] and recognizes the authority of our great Pontiff, Leo XIII" (I, 8: 109). Confronted by more incredulousness by the simple priest, Don Pedro continues: "Your reverence is traveling through all the European nations on a pilgrimage, barefoot, wearing those terrible clothes. You're living from public charity so that you can fulfill the vow you made to the Lord if He would let your flock enter the great assembly of Christ" (I, 8: 109–10). Soon thereafter the conversation ends and before long, with foodstuffs supplied by Don Pedro, Nazarín returns to his two female "disciples" and their—not the Armenian's—Christian journey resumes.

Structurally, it seems the novel bears down not on anything that Nazarín and/or Don Pedro opine, but on what Nazarín does. What counts during his Christ-like wandering is that, while making no large claims nor stating any personal ambitions, he, with the aid of Ándara and Beatrice, simply continues to help and minister to the poor and suffering. Galdós stresses, then, not the theories of society and religion which interested Don Pedro Belmonte and even the reporter and narrator, but the actions themselves of his priest guided by his own *imitatio Christi.* As an ordained, orthodox Catholic priest—albeit stripped at least temporarily of his ecclesiastical licenses—it is only natural that he would, as shown in the conversation with Belmonte, look to the pope, the successor of the Apostle Peter, to be the leader of all necessary spiritual movement. But, once again, it is not a topic he concerns himself with spontaneously. Rather, he tries to follow the example of the divine Christ when he exercised his earthly ministry as demonstrated in the New Testament and through the traditions of the Catholic Church.

This is the reason why Galdós experiments with the dramatic modification of his hallmark traditional narrative presentation. In perfect accord with Aristotle's description in the *Poetics* of how tragedy works as different from epic and poetry: in drama the characters—members of their respective society—speak directly to the audience in their own voices, not through the intermediary of a narrator, nor in the private voice of the inner-life exploring lyric poet. And in *Nazarín*, Galdós not only creates an overall dramatic ordering of the action, but stresses presentations of the priest speaking in his own words. Often, in an implicit acknowledgment by his author of Plato's choice of the dialogue form to present the life and thought of Socrates, Nazarín's words are spoken mostly while conversing with others. In trying to make himself understood by them, the priest and the reader understand better the thoughts and motivations which underly Nazarín's all-important actions, i.e., his *imitatio Christi* which, of course, is action, not word-based.

Long before the 1895 publication of *Nazarín*, Galdós, who wrote some youthful plays, occasionally introduced dialogued chapters into his otherwise standardly narrated novels. But in 1889, as he entered into a period of aesthetic experimentation caused by his increased pessimism regarding the lagging socio-political modernization of Spanish society,[4] he published *Realidad. Novela en cinco jornadas* (Reality. A Novel in Five Acts). And this dialogue novel was then followed in 1892 by the dramatic version made for the stage—the first of more than twenty stage plays by the older Galdós—titled *Realidad. Drama en cinco actos* (Reality. A Drama in Five Acts). In his "'Author's Prologue' to *The Grandfather. Novel in Five Acts* (1897)," Galdós explained what we have indicated to be his Aristotelian move to dialogued narrations and, indeed, to stage plays. Galdós states of characters in the Prologue: "They make themselves, compose themselves, imitate more easily, let us say, living beings, when they manifest their moral fiber with their own words and with them, as in life, give us the more or less deep and firm relief of their actions" (Pérez Galdós, 2013, p. 90).[5]

At this juncture it may be profitable to review more scenes in which

Nazarín speaks for himself, particularly when being questioned by those who are skeptical about respecting the holiness for which he has a reputation—but which he himself never claims to have or be. And then, to compare that approach to the priest with the views of persons who have witnessed over time and in close proximity Nazarín's ministering to the poor. One issue, which in the year 2022 in the Anglo-American world may not be so clear as in 1890s Spain: how shocking it is that a man, no matter how humble his person and situation is, with the rank of Catholic priest in Spanish society would lower—and that is most certainly the word that would be used in that time and place—himself so much as to live and work in the midst of the downtrodden. While this matter of Nazarín's nominal social rank contradicted by his contrasting appearances recurs throughout the novel, its introduction and full exposition is, fittingly for its position of emphasis, the main content of Part/Act I of the novel.

The narrator of this part/act has been told about Nazarín by a reporter friend whose beat has led him to know something of the priest. The reporter first verbally introduces the narrator and the reader to the priest as they approach his tenement: "In this neighborhood, a lot of people take him for a saint, while others think he's a simpleton. Which is it? I think if we talk to him, we can find out for sure" (I, 2: 12). Now the voluminous criticism on the novel *Nazarín*, and most particularly on the evaluation of the character of its protagonist, indicates that the binary saint-simpleton stops far short of exhausting the readings/interpretations of the complex character. Or, perhaps, a character so simple that his essence escapes those whose lives are more complicated and, perhaps, filled with more contradictions.

The Exposition of Part/Act I is very valuable in this context for what Nazarín says about himself under questioning by the reporting duo. Nazarín rapidly self-identifies as an orthodox Catholic priest who has no issues nor doubts about "established Church doctrine" (I, 3: 15), and states what is true at that time: he is 1) in good standing with his hierarchical superiors (who really have no reason to occupy themselves with a priest of so low a standing, but who also causes no trouble), 2) has never been questioned nor reprimanded by them, and 3) has the paperwork that authorizes him to act as a priest of the Catholic Church in the diocese of Madrid. Not assigned to a parish, Nazarín, who shies away from preaching while preferring one-on-one conversation with those who want to speak with him, has but one source of income: the occasional mass which comes his way through his few contacts among the scant number of his priestly colleagues who bother to notice him. In fact, this unstable source of income produces an income so small that on some days Nazarín does not eat. This point is underlined when during interview with the reporter and the narrator in Part/Act I, the landlady or tenement manager appears with some food for Nazarín; she knows he has not eaten that day. Clearly the most-humble, unassuming priest with a worn cassock[6] lives, glossing Matthew, as do the birds of the air, being content to live on whatever the heavenly Father sends his way. But all the same, he often winds up sharing the little he has with neighbors he judges to be in greater need.

Following their long session with Nazarín and leaving some small change as alms with him, the reporter and narrator speak with the landlady about him and learn she views him both as a saint and a simpleton. Her observations and opinions are reinforced by an old gypsy sitting at the entrance to the tenement. Part I ends as the reporter and narrator climb back up the rise from the poor areas near the Manzanares River "to the 'high' Madrid, [their] Madrid" (I, 5: 27). While the skeptical reporter is convinced that the priest is a con man (no matter how difficult it is for the reader to understand what the "con" could be that the half-starving priest was running), his companion the narrator—an alter ego of the novelist Galdós who dramatizes himself—is of a different mind. In representation of the reader who Galdós hopes to have won over, he finds himself totally absorbed by Nazarín. And in a way not uncommon in some Galdosian stories, he makes himself the author of the remaining four parts of the book but claims not to be able to say if what follows is a true story or an invention. In any case, he will no longer be a character in the novel, and the reader will, more as if witnessing a play, have to come to "his" conclusions about Nazarín.

Part/Act II is marked by the already briefly mentioned rising action: Nazarín is accused of aiding the sometimes-violent, old prostitute Ándara to hide from the law, following a knife fight in which she is wounded and believes, incorrectly, that she has killed her opponent. Then too, he is wrongfully accused of being her accomplice in setting a fire to his apartment. This all results in the peremptory loss of his ecclesiastical licenses and, hence, his means of earning anything. Rejected by all, Nazarín decides, as seen above, to leave Madrid by its southern or Toledo gate and begin life as a poorly clad itinerant. In this part, what was learned about Nazarín from the landlady and the gypsy of Part/Act I is confirmed, but the reader sees first-hand Nazarín's interaction with the sometimes dangerous, sometimes less-than-upright poor. Also, though, in the person of the young, poor, but honest Beatrice, the reader sees the most-favorable impression Nazarín's selfless good works make on those who simply observe him, and most particularly in the case of Beatrice because she understands how poorly Ándara has treated the priest even before implicating him in her attempt to escape from the law.

The rising action of this Part/Act II ends with what is Nazarín's first vision of what could be called the post-clerical stage of the defrocked priest's life. During one of several exploratory forays into the open country south beyond the Toledo Gate before definitively abandoning the city, Nazarín sees he will "follow the life that God (*talking to his spirit* [my emphasis]) was laying out for him" (II, 6: 59). This life, expressed almost as a personal program or basis of his own personal, not doctrinal credo, means:

> He would give up all worldly interests, take up poverty, and break openly with all the trappings that make up what we call civilization. The longing for this type of life was so irresistible to him that he could hold out against it no longer. To live in Nature, far from the opulent, corrupt cities: what a delight! He thought that only in this way would he be obeying the *divine command* that was continually *revealing itself to his soul*. Only this way would he reach the highest purification possible within the human form, gather eternal blessings, and practice charity in the way he so longed for. (II, 6: 59; my emphasis)

Already Nazarín had inadvertently been calling attention to himself by the asceticism of his life as a mass-saying, albeit parish-less priest. Now, as he believes himself personally and divinely inspired, he will break with the life seen in the first two parts of the novel and begin his *imitatio Christi* by wandering the rural areas to the southwest of Madrid while doing all good that he can. This is where some critics see and stress a Quixotic dimension to his life (see Dolgin's article listed in the Bibliography). Yet, no matter the similarities—the lone quester trying to do good works—which are patent, the questions are, on one hand: to what extent does the Quijote-Nazarín comparison address the latter's origins and development within a very strong Catholic tradition of the *imitatio Christi*; and, on the other, to what extent does the early 17th-century, isolated, bored, chivalric-novels-crazed hidalgo, secularly inspired Alonso Quijano (aka Don Quijote) actually work within and respond to the Christ paradigm? Independent of all the virtues and merits of Cervantes' greatest of novels, do his character's actions have any essential or non-metaphorical relations to the claims made by—or in his name by his disciples—the world-historical, divinity-claiming Jesus of Nazareth who became nothing less the founding figure of our historico-cultural period—the perhaps now-waning Christian Era—which has lasted for two millennia.

The first paragraph of Part/Act III of *Nazarín* has the priest leaving Madrid for what he thinks will be the last time. In it, he does debate with himself if his departure is an act of rebellion against ecclesiastical authorities who want him to appear before them even though they have already defrocked him, i.e., in our Anglo-American terms, condemned him before trying him for any crimes or misdemeanors. Nonetheless, Nazarín feels justified in the classic terms that have always made the Church look askance at the faithful having an "alleged" [suspicious, highly dubious from the Church's viewpoint] personal relation with the Divinity. For the priest would have never taken his actions if "he hadn't felt the voice of the Lord and Master [i.e., Jesus Christ] in his conscience imperiously commanding him to do" what he did (III, 1: 67). At the same time, this secular priest has taken the vows of chastity and obedience (but not that of poverty which is the third one taken by priests, brothers and nuns who go into religious orders), and by custom and discipline, must consider if his failure to appear before authorities is wrong. But once again he determines it is not for the same reason. He was simply

> evading the [religious or hierarchical] superior's reprimand, and escaping the ifs, ands, and buts of a system of [civil] justice that is not justice in any sense of the word ... What did he [in direct contact with the voice of God] have in common with a [civil] judge who listened to despicable accusations [related to the fire set by Ándara—whose foul body odors could be smelled from afar—and the possibility of illicit relations between them that accounted for her "control" over him]—and from low-lives who had no conscience. It was obvious to God, who knew his inner self, that he wasn't running away because he was afraid of the vicar-general [religious] or the judge. [civil authorities] (III, 1: 67)

And this becomes the problematic of the rest of the novel. Nazarín, accompanied by the two women who become his de facto "disciples," moves from small town to small town ministering first to a little girl who's ill is never specified, but who recovers—miraculously think the locals, but not considered that way by the Nazarín himself—after ministrations by the priest. And, then after his meeting with Don Pedro Belmonte, he moves on with Ándara and Beatrice to provide nursing in Villamantilla, a village suffering from an outbreak of smallpox where "It seems like there is there's nobody [in Villamantilla] to take care of the sick, and the healthy ones are all leaving, running scared" (III, 9: 117). That is the breach into which fugitives Nazarín and Ándara, accompanied by not-sought Beatrice, step because as Nazarín sees it "The Lord is calling us. We're needed there" (III, 9: 117). In the spring-2022 writing of this study, all we veterans—beginning in mid-March or so of 2020—of the COVID pandemia have a once-in-several generations insight into what combination of nerve and faith would be required for the Christ-inspired priest and his followers—inspired by him—to run towards that from which all others, in fear of losing their lives, are fleeing.

The falling action of Part/Act IV shows Nazarín and the two women, with the latter needing special inspiration from the priest, entering Villamantilla and doing for six days the necessary and heroic work until their point of physical exhaustion coincides with the proximate arrival of "assistance from Madrid by the Organization of Charity and Health" (IV, 2: 129). This allows the three Christians, who have demonstrated their great faith through deeds done in the Lord's name, to leave the town and eventually seek rest in the ruins of a deserted castle. But because of their fame and bad luck in the form of a spurned, former boyfriend of Beatrice seeking her out, the refuge of the three becomes public knowledge and the long-arm-of-the law in the form of Civil Guards (*Guardia Civil*) simply doing their job and the local mayor (portrayed at first as a self-promoting, ambitious, sleazy politician).

Jailed overnight in this mayor's town, Nazarín is approached by the mayor for some closer conversation the purpose of which on the latter's part is to learn more about the defrocked, dressed-in-rags priest. For even the repulsive, cynical mayor, as a one-time, drop-out seminarian, actually seems finally to need to learn more about the priest and his motivations. Nazarín's most succinct response in the conversation is to affirm what the reader of the novel and God knows: he, caught up in the confused appearances and worst-possible suppositions surrounding the fire in his apartment set by Ándara, is innocent of any civil or legal wrong-doing. And then, for the last time in the novel, he, who from Part/Act I has stated to the reporter and narrator that he is a person who imitates Christ, not a person of theological interests and learning, says to the mayor:

> "I only teach the Christian doctrine, the most elementary, the simplest, to anyone who wants to learn it. I teach by word and example. I do everything that I say, and still, I don't think that makes me better than anyone else. If people [e.g., the legal system, and even the Church implicitly] put me in the same category as criminals because of this, that doesn't matter to me at all". (IV, 7: 157)

Nazarín *(1895) by Benito Galdós* | 103

The sorely tried and frequently disrespected and misunderstood Nazarín stands in the presence of only one authority he takes seriously: his Lord Jesus Christ. He has passed through the crucible of religious, secular and severe human trials without end, but without losing his faith in his Lord whom he strives to imitate. Where scholars so careful, fine and, let it be said, skeptical concerning Nazarín, as Bly and Ayo are may err is to consider the priest as a humanly moral being. But would they approach Spanish mystics so world-known as Saint Teresa of Jesus or Ávila (1515–1582) and Saint John of the Cross (1542–1591) to comport themselves simply as moral beings? What those historical mystics and the fictive Nazarín share is that they have indeed "broken on through to the other side" of Divine otherness. Their life in the world, as we see occur before our eyes in *Nazarín*, is to leave this world in life. For the rest of the novel, as well as its sequel *Halma* where the priest Nazarín is fed, dressed and housed better than ever before in his life,[7] Nazarín becomes most passive, letting those who are arresting and jailing him do their worst.

The resolution of the Part/Act V of Nazarín, in light of the foregoing, is simply stated. The priest, his disciples—now including the "good" thief who had robbed them soon after they left Madrid, but who was converted by his observation of Nazarín's way—are all tied into the troop of common criminals being led on foot by the Civil Guards to meet their justice in Madrid. Villagers along the way jeer at them all. But the priest, broken down by hard work, notable privations, and simple exhaustion develops the elevated fever and consequences of which the novel ends. Nazarín is suffering from the hallucinations that more commonly before accompanied fevers of more degrees than medicine usually tolerates today. Concretely, the priest believes he is saying mass, albeit under strange conditions. For "when he took the Host in his hands, the divine Jesus said to him:

> My son, you are still alive. You are in My holy hospital, suffering for Me. Your companions, the two women-sinners and the thief who follow your teachings, are in jail. You cannot say mass, I cannot be with you in flesh and blood, and this mass is the insane imagining of your mind. Rest, for you well deserve it. You have done something valuable for Me. Do not be discontent. I know you are to do much more. (V, 7: 199–200)

Now, Nazarín, as seen in *Halma*, will never again have any public ministry at any level. Once out of the hospital and recovered, he is superbly cared for, but his contacts with the world are so limited as to be virtually inexistent. He becomes pure passivity, waiting only until he is called to God. His *imitatio Christi* has ended, and it is up to the reader to decide 1) who and what Nazarín was, and 2) even if, as Galdós seems to have intended, his ministry, despite all, continues. Only clear is that any simple explanation will be wanting, and any very complex one may be missing the point. Like some truly exceptional and impressive person in whose life one once had a part, Nazarín will continue to fascinate and always be presenting slightly differently as the years and decades pass. But if that is to happen, is it possible to be skeptical about the priest?

Notes

1. For consideration of Renan and Nazarín, see the article by Morón Arroyo in the Bibliography.
2. See Miller, *The Maiden's Consent* for a full discussion of the play and its structure. Galdós wrote importantly and most positively about Moratín. Hence his decision to follow the Shakespearean model was very deliberate.
3. For the sake of creating a monolingual text to the extent possible, all citations from Nazarín will be taken from the 1997 Rudder-Arjona translation cited in the Bibliography.
4. I first identified this socio-aesthetic change and explained its reasons in *El mundo de Galdós* (pp. 119–43) and then expanded further on the reasons for the change in *Del realismo/naturalismo al modernismo: Galdós, Zola, Revilla y Clarín (1870–1901)* (pp. 153–83).
5. This is not the time to go into the already indicated relations between the work of the novelist/dramatist Galdós and the dramatist/poet Shakespeare. In the present context, I simply suggest to the reader that my article of 2020 in which I compare and contrast the purposes and emphases of each writer's work may give further insight into Galdós' interest in the presentation through dialogue of his characters and their world.
6. Traveling and/or living in the U.S., Mexico, Portugal and Spain has shown me how varied the cut and cloth of the cassocks worn by Catholic priests can be. Mostly they are almost invisible for their uniformity and proper appearance. But at the extremes, how different! The priests whose grades were poor in the seminary are assigned poor parishes in the country. They, often alarmingly thin, can be seen in cassocks turning greenish with age and frayed with wear. On the other end of the spectrum, many of the canons and higher figures in the hierarchy and wealthy parishes wear cassocks, which, like old insider stock trader Ivan Boesky's suits, seem always new, veritably glowing with the quality and cut of the cloth from which they are made.
7. But in *Halma*, perhaps to the disappointment of readers who have not understood the extent to which Nazarín has by his will ceased to live essentially in this world, he is physically separated from most of the world

by the hierarchy. Putting him in a luxury he never knew and never wanted, the religious authorities do not allow Nazarín contact with any but a very closed circle of people either wealthy or of position in the ecclesiastical hierarchy. His *imitatio Christi* ministry is over and he accepts his lot, for as long as he lives, as the will of God. For its part, the Church has no need of his kind and warehouses him in a golden cage.

Bibliography
Ayo, Álvaro A. "Paradigmas de imperfección: el individuo y sus espectros en *Nazarín y Halma* de Benito Pérez Galdós." *BHS* 95.1 (2018), pp. 43–59.
Bly, Peter. *Pérez Galdós."Nazarín."* London: Grant & Cutler Ltd., 1991.
Dolgin, Stacey L. "*Nazarín*: A Tribute to Galdós' Indebtedness to Cervantes." *Hispanófila* No. 97 (Septiembre 1989), 17–22. JSTOR, Url. jstor.org/stable/43808236.
Miller, Stephen. *Del realismo/naturalismo al modernismo: Galdós, Zola, Revilla y Clarín (1870–1901).* Las Palmas: Ediciones del Cabildo Insular de Gran Canaria, 1993.
———. "Galdós escritor clásico (a la luz de Shakespeare)." Galdós Centenary number of *Archiletras Científica*, 3 (verano 2020): "Galdós, genio innovador," ed. Mª· Ángeles Varela Olea, pp. 93–115.
———. "*The Maiden's Consent.*" *World Literature and Its Times: Profiles of Notable Literary Works and the Historical Events That Influenced Them.* Encyclopedia.com. 21 Apr. 2018 <http://www.encyclopedia.com>.
———. *El mundo de Galdós: teoría, tradición y evolución creativa del pensamiento socio-literario galdosiano.* Santander: Sociedad Menéndez Pelayo, 1983.
Morón Arroyo, Ciriaco. "*Nazarín y Halma*: sentido y unidad. A[nales] G[aldosianos], 2 (19670, pp. 67–81.
Pérez Galdós, Benito. "'Author's Prologue' to *The Grandfather. Novel in Five Acts* (1897)." Trans. Stephen Miller. In Stephen Miller, "The *Klail City Death Trip* as Seen through Spanish Narrative: Authors, Themes and Techniques of the Hispanic Tradition, with Special Reference to Pérez Galdós." *Rolando Hinojosa's "Klail City Death Trip Series": A Retrospective, New Directions.* Ed. Stephen Miller and José Pablo Villalobos. Houston: Arte Público Press, 2013, 89–91 [59–91].
———. *Halma.* Imprenta La Guirnalda, 1895. Edición digital basada en la de Madrid: Imprenta La Guirnalda, 1895. www.cervantesvirtual.com/obra/halma—0/.
———. *Nazarín.* Madrid: Imprenta La Guirnalda, 1895. Edición digital basada en la de Madrid: Imprenta La Guirnalda, 1895. www.cervantesvirtual.com/obra/nazarin—0/
———. *Nazarin* [sic]. Trans. Robert S. Rudder and Gloria Arjona. Pittsburgh, PA: Latin American Literary Review Press, 1997.

CHAPTER
8

Rites & Rituals of the Roman Catholic Priesthood: Holy Orders: *San Manuel Buenos*. Human Weakness in the Vocation: Saintly Martyr or Sinful Hypocrite?

JUANITA SENA PFAFF

In *San Manuel Bueno, mártir*, published shortly before his death (1936) in 1933, by the Spaniard, Miguel de Unamuno, the protagonist is a priest who struggles with his own personal faith and doubts—but he continues to lead the faith community according to the order of his vocation by making Christ visible through his actions and by giving himself in priestly service to the Church. He keeps his own struggles secret from the community rather than lead them astray or destroy their lives by filling them with doubt. Instead, he leads them as if he had an unwavering faith: "I must live for my people, die for my people."[1] This and other writings by Unamuno have been interpreted as a revelation of the personal struggles of the author through the lives of the characters. Secular criticisms and interpretations see his works as primarily psychological demonstrations of the division and fragmentation with which Unamuno struggled within himself. A common trend in criticisms on Unamuno's works is to see the works not as revealing truths within themselves but rather as finding meaning when paired with the life of the author as a revelation of Unamuno's personality or identity.

San Manuel Bueno, mártir is more than a demonstration of Unamuno's psychological state or struggles. Catholic symbolism within the work investigates and reveals the truths of the vocation of priesthood through the life of a doubting priest who struggles constantly and suffers constantly because of it. He is plagued by a deep sadness that cannot be cured because his intellect will not allow him to have faith in eternal life, even though he desires to believe with all of his being. He dedicates his life to his faith community to save himself from his doubts by living as if he had a perfect faith, and to save his community by leading and guiding them through the example of his life. By giving his life to them in service, he essentially gives them life, which *is* their faith. Don Manuel reveals the fulfillment of the vocation of holy orders despite his human weakness because as a vocation, it is dependent on God for its origin, and through his actions as an instrument of God he participates in the redemptive mission, which he is able to do by the power of the Holy Spirit, which surpasses any human power. "The communion of the priest is fulfilled above all with the Father, the ultimate origin of all his power; with the Son, in whose redemptive mission he participates; with the Holy Spirit, who gives him power for living and fulfilling that pastoral charity which qualifies him in a priestly way."[2] Don Manuel, as a priest, is united in communion with the Trinity despite and because of his weaknesses, and from this communion his vocation is fulfilled. Don Manuel is chosen through the will of God the Father, he participates actively in the redemptive mission through Jesus the Son, and he is empowered through the grace and gifts of the Holy Spirit.

According to the *Directory on the Ministry and Life of Priests*, "the ministerial priesthood renders tangible the actual work of Christ, the Head, and gives witness to the fact that Christ has not separated himself from the Church; rather He continues to vivify her through the everlasting priesthood."[3] In Pope Paul VI's decree *Presbyterorum Ordinis*, priests are the members of the community given the sacred power of orders to offer sacrifice and forgive sins; they are "heralds of the Gospel and shepherds of the Church, [who] are to spend themselves for the spiritual growth of the Body of Christ."[4] The function and goal of the priesthood is to continue the life of Christ in the world today by serving the Church community, and this is achieved through the grace of God and gifts of the Holy Spirit that empower the priest to give life to the community. The *Catechism of the Catholic Church* states that "this presence of Christ in the minister is not to be understood as if the latter were preserved from all human weaknesses."[5] While the priest is given the grace to transcend his own humanity and make Christ visible in the community of believers, he is still bound by his humanity in his struggles, temptation, sin, and error. He does not assume the perfection of Christ, but the sacraments that he performs still maintain their root in the perfection of Christ and in his sacrifice, and they cannot be distorted by the humanness of the priest. Because the priest's main purpose is to administer the sacraments and give life to the Church by serving and guiding the faithful, a priest whose faith or life is not perfect does not distort or negate his vocation, which ultimately depends on Christ, rather than on the man himself.

Don Manuel's vocation is fulfilled in communion with God the Father, who is the origin of his vocation. Holy orders is a sacrament, which is an "outward sign of inward grace, instituted by Christ for our sanctification."[6] The sacraments cause grace in the person by producing a character in the soul that consecrates him as a servant of God. "God alone is the principal cause of the sacraments. He alone authoritatively and by innate power can give to external material rites the power to confer grace on men."[7] By this definition, Don Manuel has received the sacrament of Holy Orders, which was caused and given by God. It is not by his own power or will that he is a priest. His vocation surpasses his humanity in its Divine origin. The sacrament of Holy Orders is designed and created by God, and it is ordered to the fulfillment of His will and plan.

A priest is chosen for his vocation to which he answers a "call" from God. Each person fulfills the plan of God in a particular vocation that contributes to the salvation of humanity by cooperating with God the Father in the redemption of his creation. "Certain members are called by God, in and through the Church, to a special service of the community."[8] Vocation is dependent only on this calling, in which the person is chosen by God, and on the nature of sacrament, as a cause of grace, which produces a character in man's soul. In this way, vocation goes beyond man's will and man's nature. Just as Christ chose the apostles, he has also chosen those who protect, guide, and lead his flock. Man cannot call himself to this vocation; it requires the call of God to consecration in which he gives the fullness of his being and life to God and to the Church, which is made up of men. As was stated in the definition of sacrament, which produces a certain character, the *Catechism* states, "the sacrament of Holy Orders . . . confers an *indelible spiritual character* [which is] imprinted by ordination and is forever. The vocation and mission received on the day of his ordination mark him permanently."[9] A priest, even if he is discharged from the community or from his obligations, does not erase his vocation. He cannot cease to be a priest based on human declarations or his own human weaknesses. Once he is a priest, he is consecrated to God in this special vocation forever. It is a gift given by God that essentially cannot be given back once the individual has accepted God's will and united his own with it. It is for this reason that Don Manuel's character reveals the fullness of his vocation. He has willingly accepted the vocation of holy orders despite his imperfect faith, and even though he does not understand it completely and his faith is clouded with doubts, he retains his consecrated nature, which was given to him by God and remains by the will of God.

Even though Don Manuel has many doubts about the faith to which he is ordained, he still *lives* his vocation. Although unknowingly, he recognizes God's call within him: "By his reason, man recognizes the voice of God which urges him 'to do what is good and avoid what is evil.' Everyone is obliged to follow this law, which makes itself heard in conscience and is fulfilled in the love of God and of neighbor."[10] Although Don Manuel does not recognize the depth of his faith, it is still present in his response to the call to live a moral life. His actions manifest his love of God through the love he gives to his neighbor through his vocation in which he is in complete service to his community. His reason may not comprehend this faith, but it does recognize the call to goodness, which he fulfills by giving life to his faith community. The *Catechism* also recognizes that man's life is a struggle in which he is divided within himself, as well as separated from God and from other men. For this reason, perfect faith is not possible except in Jesus Christ himself. All of humanity suffers from interior and exterior doubt, conflict, and struggle. The supreme importance placed on reason in the world enhances these sufferings by calling us away from God, as well as isolating us from ourselves and others, which is created by the emphasis on the superiority of human intellect over any other aspect of a human being. Unamuno writes, "We used to recite in unison, with one single voice, the Creed ... and upon arriving at the part – I believe in the resurrection of the body and the life everlasting—the voice of Don Manuel plunged as into a lake, into that of the whole town, and it was there that he grew quiet."[11] He cannot understand nor accept the belief in eternal life, and he constantly struggles with this fragmentation in his life between his intellect and his faith. Don Manuel suffered from involuntary doubt, which is defined in the *Catechism* as "hesitation in believing, difficulty in overcoming objections connected with the faith, or also anxiety aroused by its obscurity."[12] This is Don Manuel's plight; his life is one of anxiety, hesitation, difficulty, and struggle. He constantly desires to believe, but his own intellect does not allow him. His lack of understanding does not allow him to believe, but he lives as if he does, which is also an example of his attempt and will to believe.

Don Manuel's vocation of Holy Orders is fulfilled through his communion with God the Father, who is the origin of his power. As a sacrament, the vocation is created by God, which surpasses any human creation or order. The man who receives it has also received and accepted the call of God, who has chosen him specifically, and by being chosen he receives an indelible character, which cannot be removed by any human act or will. Although Don Manuel does not understand his faith completely, he lives it in his dedication to the community, which expresses faith in a way that he cannot comprehend, but it is still there because faith is also a gift from God. He suffers from involuntary doubt, which causes his anxiety and struggle, but God still wills him to live his vocation, and faith is still evident in his life through his character and through his response to the call to goodness.

Don Manuel also fulfills his vocation through his communion with God the Son in his participation in the redemptive mission of Christ, which is revealed primarily through Don Manuel's action. Through this participation, he performs the sacraments, leads the community, and gives his life to the community generously and selflessly in service to the Church. "The life and the ministry of the priest are a continuation of the life and the *action* of . . . Christ."[13] His vocation is a gift that is given to the *individual* for the service of *all*.

> And how he loved his people! His life was fixing broken marriages, reconciling wild sons to their fathers, or reconciling fathers to their sons . . . consoling the bitter and bored, and to help all die a good Christian death . . . So it was that he was always busy . . . He worked manually also, helping with his arms in certain labors of the town . . . He used to accompany the doctor on his rounds . . . He often went to school to help the teacher."[14]

Don Manuel is constantly dedicating himself to the life of the community, taking an active role in their individual lives. He gives his life actively by using his energy for their benefit, always at their service. His life is modeled after Christ in this sense, as the priest's life should be, because he is constantly the servant of the people who lowers himself to serve others in love. He knows the struggles of the people because he takes part in their struggles. As is written in the *Directory on the Ministry and Life of Priests*: As pastor of the community, the priest exists and lives for it; he prays, studies, works, and sacrifices himself for the community. He is disposed to give his life for it, loving it as Christ does, pouring out upon it all his love and consideration, lavishing it with all his strength and unlimited time in order to render it, in the image of the Church, Spouse of Christ, always more beautiful and worthy of the benevolence of God and the love of the Holy Spirit.[15] Don Manuel loves the Church as Christ loves, exemplifying utter selflessness. He gives his entire being to his community, to the extent that he even with his last words and breath, he offers the sacrifice of the Mass for his people. "He died preaching to the town, in the church."¹⁶ Even though Don Manuel has many doubts, his actions reveal the depth of his faith and his commitment to the people and the Church.

As well as giving himself in service to the community, he leads them in the ways of the faith by preaching the Gospel and helping them to find their happiness in God, which is the only true happiness in life. The story specifically mentions the Good Friday service in which Jesus' Passion and Death is read, and in which Don Manuel actively participates in a way that touches his community deeply. This part of Jesus' life is central to the faith because it is through the death of Christ that the resurrection and redemption is possible for the salvation of all people. It is also central to Don Manuel's struggle because he can understand the suffering and death of Christ, especially as he is left alone to die on the cross, crying out to God with words of abandonment: "My God, my God, why have you forsaken me?" This is the only prayer that Unamuno writes for Don Manuel to say. This is also essential to the character of Don Manuel, who, with all his being, cries out to God in the same prayer that was Jesus' last prayer. He is united with Jesus in this suffering and in this strong desire for union with God, to save him from the suffering and emptiness of the world. This is Don Manuel's life struggle with solitude and abandonment. He wants to feel God at his side, but his intellect does not allow him to experience this in faith. Regardless of his human weakness, which stems from his incapacity to understand the resurrection and eternal life, he leads the people according to the Gospel. He puts supreme importance on his vocation and fulfills his obligation as a shepherd by leading them according to the faith rather than according to his own reason. "His role, in fact, 'is not to teach his own wisdom but the Word of God and to issue and urgent invitation to all men to conversion and to holiness.'"¹⁷ He is faithful to the Word of God even though his reason cannot grasp it completely. "Acting *in persona Christi capitis*, the priest becomes the minister of the essential salvific actions, transmits the truths necessary for salvation and cares for the People of God, leading them towards sanctity."¹⁸ Don Manuel also tells his people to "pray, pray to Most Holy Mary, pray to Our Lord."¹⁹ By including Mary in his direction for the people, he is including the most central truth of the Incarnation, made possible through Mary's willingness to submit to God. He is proclaiming the importance of Mary by inviting the community to venerate her through prayer and to pray through her intercession, which is central in the Church as well because Mary is the Mother of the Church. By leading his community to pray to Mary he is leading them to become true followers of the Church and true Sons and Daughters of God by accepting the mystery of the Incarnation.

Don Manuel also recognizes the longing for happiness and fulfillment that is characteristic of all humanity. He does not want his people to suffer from this longing as he does. One of Unamuno's characters recognizes this struggle and says, "I understood that the imperturbable happiness of Don Manuel was the temporal and earthly form of an infinite sadness that with heroic holiness he hid from the eyes and ears of others."[20] Don Manuel understands the suffering that is caused by the emptiness of the world, and although he cannot understand it, he somehow leads the people to fill this emptiness with God through faith. The "natural desire for happiness . . . is of divine origin: God has placed it in the human heart in order to draw man to the One who alone can fulfill it: . . . God alone satisfies."[21] This is the infinite abyss of which St. Thomas Aquinas speaks, which only God can fill in his infiniteness. Don Manuel dedicates himself to leading his people to this happiness: "I have to make the souls of my parishioners live, to make them happy"[22] Don Manuel leads his community according to the Gospel and the teachings of the Church, both in which God is the ultimate good and source of happiness beyond any earthly happiness.

He also leads them toward this sanctity by administering the sacraments; specifically, Confession, the Eucharist, Anointing of the Sick, and Matrimony are mentioned in Unamuno's text. Don Manuel celebrates the Eucharist, which is the "heart and vital center" of the priestly ministry, "which is, above all, the real presence in time of the unique and eternal sacrifice of Christ."[23] By performing the sacraments, which only a priest can do, as he is specifically consecrated for this purpose, he serves as the bridge between God and man which allows for an intimate unity with the cross of Christ reaching to the resurrection and eternal life. In Reconciliation, again, only priests can administer the sacrament, and they are "invited to call sinners to conversion and bring them back to the Father by means of a merciful judgment."[24] Through the administration of the Sacrament of Reconciliation, the priest enables the reform of the relationship between the individual and God, and by acting as Christ, he also enables the healing and peace of the wounded community through mercy. Don Manuel "forgave everyone and everything. He did not want to believe in the bad intentions of anyone . . . 'Judge not lest you be judged, our Lord said.'"[25] Don Manuel reveals the mercy of Christ in the Sacrament of Reconciliation so that his people can live in relationship with God, broken by sin but repaired by mercy and pardon, granting peace and hope to the individual.

Don Manuel's doubts do not negate the fullness of the Sacraments which he administers either, because he is only an instrument of God through which Christ acts in his redemptive mission to give grace to his people and enable them to join with him in communion through the sacraments. In the *Catechism* it says, "This presence of Christ in the minister is not to be understood as if the latter were preserved from all human weaknesses . . . While this guarantee extends to the sacraments, so that even the minister's sin cannot impede the fruit of grace."[26] Don Manuel performs the sacraments, making the presence of Christ visible in the community. In this way, Don Manuel also reveals a dimension of faith that he may not even understand, in which he allows Christ to work through him without knowing it, in the greatest manifestations of the faith which is the Sacraments.

Don Manuel participates in the redemptive mission of Christ, uniting in communion with God the Son, which is essential to his identity as a priest. Through his active participation in the community, he gives his life in sacrifice to the people, as Jesus gave his life for the salvation of all. He also leads as a shepherd who cares for his sheep, by preaching the Gospel and helping his people find happiness and fulfillment in the Lord. Through the sacraments that he administers, he also unites the people to God in the most real and intimate unity that we have been given.

Through Don Manuel's communion with the Holy Spirit, he is given the power to live and fulfill his pastoral charity. The grace and gifts of the Holy Spirit are the source of Don Manuel's ability to give himself so completely, and without these graces and gifts, he could not do so. He gives himself fully to the people, and the Holy Spirit is the source of this ability, strength, and energy that enable him to maintain the unity of the community with and in God. Priests:

> Have been consecrated by God in a new manner at their ordination and made living instruments of Christ the Eternal Priest that they may be able to carry on in time his marvelous work whereby the entire family of man is again made whole by power from above. Since therefore, every priest in his own fashion acts in place of Christ himself, he is *enriched by a special grace*, so that, as he serves the flock committed to him and the entire people of God, *he may better grow in the grace of him whose tasks he performs*, because to the weakness of our flesh there is brought the holiness of him who for us was made a High Priest 'holy, guiltless, undefiled not reckoned among us sinners.'[27]

It is through the grace of the Holy Spirit that the priest can live his vocation of service as a servant to all for the good of the community. He must live as an image of Christ, constantly building up the Church and caring for the Body of Christ. Through the Holy Spirit, man is enabled to live like Christ.

Since Don Manuel's particular struggle is with doubt, he could be considered unworthy for such a vocation or for such grace. But *Presbyterorum Ordinis* also responds to this problem: "Although divine grace could use unworthy ministers to effect the work of salvation, yet for the most part God chooses, to show forth his wonders, those who are more open to the power and direction of the Holy Spirit, and who can by reason of their close union of Christ and their holiness of life say with St. Paul: 'And yet I am alive; or rather, not I; it is Christ that lives in me.'"[28] Don Manuel is open to this power and direction of the Holy Spirit that is mentioned because he longs for God and for faith with all his heart and soul, and his life and actions are driven by this desire. He may seem unworthy according to human reason, but human reason is also that which causes the doubts from which Don Manuel suffers while still living a life of faith and devoted commitment to his vocation, which is beyond his understanding. God's will and works are beyond human understanding, and therefore, the most unworthy and weakest can be made into his most profound instruments, just as the strongest and most worthy can be sacrificed on the cross, which is for a greater purpose than the human mind can fully grasp. As in the Beatitudes, the Gospel is full of irony and paradox, in which the poor are given the kingdom, the meek are given the land, the mourners are comforted, the hungry and thirsty are filled, the merciful obtain mercy, the clean of heart see God, the peacemakers are called God's children, the suffering are given the kingdom of Heaven. Those who live contrary to the ways of the world are rewarded by God because *He* is not of this world. We should not conform to the world either; we should constantly seek union with God and his will. Don Manuel is an example of this irony that is present all throughout the Bible and the lives of the saints, in which the weakest and lowliest are chosen by God for the greatest missions. The greatest example we have of this is that of Jesus Christ himself, who was born in a stable, lived the life of a carpenter, died the worst death imaginable on the cross, and by doing so redeemed the world by gaining salvation for all through his acceptance and following of the will of God. Don Manuel does not understand his mission, but God is still working through him, and he is empowered by the grace of the Holy Spirit. His understanding is not required, only his willingness to follow the will that is higher than his own, and he demonstrates this submission of his will to that of God in his actions and in his priestly service. "Priests who perform their duties sincerely and indefatigably in the Spirit of Christ arrive at holiness by this very fact."[29] Through the Spirit he is made holy. It is not through his own actions or efforts that he is holy, but only through grace. All he can do is try to unite his will with God's in everything he does. "Through this effort, today they form a living expression of that divine grace which, given freely in the moment of Ordination, continues to grant an ever-renewing strength to their ministry."[30]

It is also through the grace of the Holy Spirit that the priest is able to live the vows he takes when he receives the sacrament of Holy Orders. These vows are poverty, chastity, and obedience, which are meant to further ensure the imaging of Christ in the life of the priest, and they serve as means for uniting with God in intimate communion. Don Manuel exemplifies the vow of poverty by living with the people in every aspect of their lives: in their suffering, struggles, joys, happiness, failings, triumphs, etc. The story of Don Manuel is also set in an old Spanish village that is considered part of the "Old World" by one of the educated characters of the story who has studied in the "New World." He lives a life of tradition and simplicity with the people. More importantly, he exemplifies poverty of spirit, which is manifested in his spirit of service revealed in his active life of pastoral ministry. "St. Paul says that Jesus did not consider 'being equal to God a thing to be clung to, but emptied himself, taking the nature of a slave.' A priest could hardly be a true servant and minister of his brothers if he were excessively worried with is comfort and well-being."[31] As was acknowledged and affirmed previously, Don Manuel empties himself as a true servant to his community, and thus, lives with a spirit of poverty in which his community's well-being supersedes his own. It is also through this vow that Don Manuel is united to Christ, whose "condition of poverty . . . manifested that he had received everything from eternity from the Father and all to him is restored in a complete offering of his life."[32] Don Manuel is the image of Christ as he offers his life completely in the spirit of poverty.

The vow of chastity is fulfilled in Don Manuel's celibate life, which reveals his intimate unity with the Church when he images Christ, whose relationship with the Church is spousal, as she is the Bride of Christ. Don Manuel's chastity is also revealed in his own spousal relationship with the Church, to whom he gives himself completely, as a husband does for his wife. One of the most obvious vows in Don Manuel's life and death is his obedience to God, whose will is manifested through the Church authority. "Obedience to the Father is the very heart of the Priesthood of Christ," as Christ was obedient unto death on the Cross, and as the priest is to image Christ in the Church.[33] Priests also vow to obey their superiors and the Church authority, who are also to lead according to the will of God. By learning and practicing obedience, he "strengthens his will of submission, thus participating in the dynamics of the obedience of Christ made Servant obedient to death on the Cross."[34] Don Manuel conforms himself to Christ by humbly obeying the authority of the Church without perfect understanding. Even in his death, he guides his community saying, "Die like me ... in the bosom of the Holy Mother Catholic Apostolic Roman Church."[35] He submits his will in obedience as an example for his people even in his death. Through the grace of the Holy Spirit, Don Manuel is able to live the vows that he took when he received the sacrament of his vocation of Holy Orders. It is only through these graces that he is able to lead and guide his community and to give himself so endlessly and completely. He continuously struggles interiorly, but his actions and will are always directed toward God and in the desire for perfect faith.

"Faith is often lived in darkness and can be put to the test."[36] Perhaps it is through this immense desire for faith and through his dark struggle and imperfection that Don Manuel is able to endeavor so strongly and devote all of his being to bringing his people into union with God and to learn perfect faith for himself. He is always faithful to his people, and it is through people that we find, serve, and love God. By being faithful to them, he is faithful to God: "Fidelity to Christ cannot be separated from faithfulness to his Church."[37] Don Manuel reveals the fullness of the priesthood regardless of his doubt, which is the human weakness that Unamuno most clearly reveals in his character. Don Manuel lives and fulfills his vocation in and through communion with the Trinity. The Father is the origin of his power because He has called and chosen him to the receive the sacrament of Holy Orders which is his vocation, and even though Don Manuel struggles with doubt, his life exemplifies the call to do good. Without always knowing it, he lives the life of Christ by sacrificing himself in generous service. It is through this active service that he participates in the redemptive mission of the Son. Through this participation, he performs the sacraments as an instrument of God, he gives the fullness of his being to the community by dedicating himself to them completely, and he leads them according to the Gospel to find fulfillment and happiness in God that cannot be found in the world. Through his communion with the Holy Spirit, he is given the power to live and fulfill his pastoral charity. This power is given to him as grace, which gives him the strength to dedicate his life and energy to his community, without which he could not do as completely as he does. The grace of the Holy Spirit also enables him to fulfill the vows of his vocation, of poverty, chastity, and obedience, in order to image Christ in the Church and to unite with Christ in intimate communion by submitting his will and the entirety of his being to God. Even though Don Manuel struggles with his doubts, this suffering and

Rights & Rituals of the Roman Catholic Priesthood | 117

searching is a source of strength in his endeavors to find God and to unite his community and himself fully with God. Don Manuel's vocation is not negated by his doubt because Christ acts through him and God works through him without his complete knowledge or understanding. His communion with the Trinity reveals the fullness of his vocation, regardless of the human weaknesses from which he suffers. "In fact, 'the nature and the mission of the ministerial priesthood cannot be defined except in this multiple and rich network or relations which spring from the Blessed Trinity and is prolonged in the communion of the Church as a sign, in Christ, of the union with God and the unity of the whole human race.'"[38]

Notes
1. Unamuno, Miguel de. *Saint Manuel the Good, Martyr*. Trans. Nancy Mayberry.
2. Sánchez, 20.
3. Sánchez, José, Cardinal. *Congregation for the Clergy, Directory on the Ministry and Life of Priests*. (1994), 1.
4. Paul VI, Pope. *Presbyterorum Ordinis*. (1965), 6.
5. *Catechism of the Catholic Church*. (NY: Doubleday, 1965), 1550.
6. Kennedy, D.J. "Sacraments." *New Advent Catholic Encyclopedia*.
7. *Ibid*.
8. *Catechism*, 1142.
9. *Ibid*., 1582–1583.
10. *Catechism*, 1706.
11. Unamuno. Trans. Mayberry.
12. *Catechism*, 2088.
13. Sanchez, 3 (emphasis added).
14. Unamuno. Trans. Mayberry.
15. Sánchez, 55.
16. Unamuno. Trans. Mayberry.
17. Sánchez, 45.
18. *Ibid*., 7.
19. Unamuno. Trans. Mayberry.
20. *Ibid*.
21. *Catechism*, 1718.
22. Unamuno. Trans. Mayberry.
23. Sánchez, 48.
24. *Ibid*., 51.
25. Unamuno. Trans. Mayberry
26. *Catechism*, 1550.
27. Paul VI, Pope, 12 (emphasis added).
28. *Ibid*., 12.
29. *Ibid*., 13
30. Sánchez, 37.

31 *Ibid.*, 67.
32 *Ibid.*, 67.
33 *Ibid.*, 61.
34 *Ibid.*, 61.
35 Unamuno. Trans. Mayberry.
36 *Catechism*, 164.
37 Paul VI, Pope, 14.
38 Sánchez, 20.

Works Cited

Catechism of the Catholic Church. NY: Doubleday, 1995.
Kennedy, D.J. "Sacraments." *New Advent Catholic Encyclopedia.*
<http://www.newadvent.org/cathen/13295a.htm>
Paul VI, Pope. *Decree on the Ministry and Life of Priests: Presbyterorum Ordinis.* 1965
<http://www.vatican.va/archive/hist_councils/ii_vatican_council/documents/vatii_decree_19651207_presbyterorum-ordinis_en.html>
Sánchez, José, Cardinal. *Congregation for the Clergy, Directory on the Ministry and Life of Priests.* 1994
<http://www.vatican.va/roman_curia/congregations/cclergy/documents/rc_con_cclergy_oc_31011994_directory_en.html?GRAB_ID=29\&EXTRA_ARG=\&HOST_ID=42\&PAGE_ID=11603968>
Unamuno, Miguel de. *San Manuel Bueno, mártir. Aproximaciones al estudio de la literatura hispánica, Quinta Edición.* Ed., Edward H. Friedman and others. Boston: McGraw Hill, 2004. 96–120.
———. *Saint Manuel, the Good, Martyr.* Trans. Nancy Mayberry
<http://personal.ecu.edu/mayberryn/sanmanuel.htm>

CHAPTER
9

Traditional Spanish Language Maintenance and the Revitalization of Rites & Rituals of Culture and Faith: A Mission for the Body of Christ

JUANITA SENA PFAFF

The revitalization and maintenance of *traditional Spanish* in New Mexico is essential to the diversity of the world but also to the world as the Body of Christ in need of renewal and reordering in and through the culture of humans. Language plays a primary role in this cultural restoration because it affects and shapes one's perception of the world, reports and defines experience, is the method of communication, and is a symbol and means of group identity and solidarity. Through the revitalization of the language, the culture is also restored because language and culture *together* are based upon the reality in which one lives, but they also create and mold that reality. Through inculturation, the human person develops toward full and true humanity in the complete and perfect integration of faith and culture. The Catholic New Mexican Hispanic woman, who is integral to this mission of inculturation, participates in the enrichment and fulfillment of the Body of Christ by working for this restoration and revitalization, and her culture is purified, strengthened, and opened by the faith in return.

As a second-generation monolingual English speaker in both a Hispanic culture and a Hispanic family, I have long questioned the cultural effects of language death within my family. My grandparents and great-grandparents are bilingual Spanish and English speakers, but they did not teach my parents *traditional Spanish* because of the stigma at the time which devalued Spanish and its speakers, as an "English-only" policy was enforced in all areas of society and culture.

This Spanish is only used today by older generations, and if the younger generations do know it, "they find it very difficult and inconvenient to transmit it to their offspring."[1] My familiarity with the language has been only in hearing my grandparents speak to each other, in religious traditions such as *Semana Santa* or in prayers and songs, and in folklore written by New Mexicans. It is not a dialect that is taught or reinforced in any realm of society, whether it is school, business, Church, or family. The reasons for this shift and near death for *traditional Spanish* are many, and they can be traced back to the foundations of New Mexico.

The *traditional Spanish* of New Mexico dates to the early 17th century when the original settlers brought a rural Castilian Spanish to the people of the isolated mountains and deserts which has survived for over four hundred years. This Spanish can be described as a mixture of archaic Spanish, Mexican Indian words, indigenous Indian words, Mexican Spanish, and borrowed English which has been adapted for everyday use.[2] This dialect has been slowly dying for the past century, and within the last twenty years is quickly coming to near extinction. English is the official language of the area and even the Hispanos of this region are shifting to English as their most important method of communication.

There are two main regions in New Mexico that geographically separate the dialects of Spanish that are spoken. In the southern one-third of the state, the Spanish-speaking people are mainly derived from twentieth-century immigration from Mexico and are primarily first- or second-generation Mexican immigrants, whereas the northern two-thirds of the state is primarily *traditional Spanish* speakers deriving from Spanish immigration in the 17th, 18th, and 19th centuries. This Spanish is characterized by archaisms, anglicisms, and an impoverished vocabulary leading to the creation of new words. "New Mexico Spanish vocabulary is relatively impoverished but has made up the deficit by semantic evolution, creation of new words, and incorporation of huge numbers of English words."[3] Due to the isolated location of many Northern-New Mexican Spanish-speakers, their Spanish vocabulary has not developed along with the rapid changes in technology, business, medicine, and other advances of the modern world. Rather, the English influence has been the primary resource for any knowledge of change, growth, and development in the world. Instead of shifting completely to English, they have creatively adapted many words and added Spanish morphological elements.

In New Mexico, nearly 50% of the total population identifies as Hispanic or Latino and 28% of the total population claim Spanish as the *home* language. There is also an increasing abandonment of

Spanish among the young: 85% of the Hispanic population of 18 years and older claim Spanish as the home language; 50% of the Hispanic population between 5 and 17 years of age claim Spanish as the home language. Apart from recent immigrants, most speakers belong to the older generations and the numbers are decreasing rapidly for the younger generations as the language continues to disappear. The Spanish language maintenance is attributable mainly to the continuous heavy immigration from south of the border, and 40% or more of those who report using Spanish in the home are first-generation immigrants. This "immigrant generation and its children account for the great majority of Spanish-speakers in the Southwest region."[4] Even with the support and influence of Standard Spanish in the Southwest, the *traditional Spanish* has been shifting to English for the past century and is nearly facing language death, which "occurs in unstable bilingual or multilingual speech communities as a result of language shift from a regressive minority language to a dominant majority language."[5]

This language shift to English that is causing near death for *traditional Spanish* has been caused by and enforced both from outside and within the community. In the school system, an "English-only" policy was enforced dating back to the early 1900s, and children were punished for using Spanish in school, a personal experience of both my great-grandparents and grandparents. Socioeconomic status is also a motivation for the shift to English, as the higher level of English proficiency correlates with a higher income level. Another reason that language death is near is the attitude of the Spanish-speakers who believe that "English is good, and Spanish is not good" or that "Standard Spanish is good, and our Spanish is bad/incorrect."[6] These attitudes have developed as a result of Hispanic cultural influences as well as a result of influences of English-speakers. Encounters with Standard Spanish speakers have partially caused this attitude because they call the *traditional Spanish* dialect "Spanglish" or do not consider it to be real Spanish, and some New Mexicans have even been mocked or laughed at by other Spanish speakers for their dialect.[7] The *traditional Spanish* speakers have internalized this attitude of inferiority and devaluation for their Spanish which causes them to diminish the worth of their own language and way of speaking so that in many cases they deliberately do not pass it on to their children, as was the case in my family.

The *traditional Spanish* of New Mexico is caught between English and Standard Spanish, which are two very powerful linguistic forces, and the survival of this unique dialect is slim between them. Despite reinforcement from immigration, the Hispanic community at large faces an ongoing shift to English, which is nearly complete in most communities, especially in those with dialects that differ from Standard Spanish. Garland Bills states in his article about New Mexican Spanish, "The rapidity with which Southwest Hispanos in the last half of the twentieth century are shifting to English and abandoning Spanish rivals the loss of the ethnic mother tongue by practically any ethnic group in documented history."[8] It is a tragic process nearly coming to its completion specifically in Northern New Mexico.

Sabine Ulibarri, as quoted in the *Heritage Language Revitalization* Planning Manual for the New Mexico Public Education Department states:

> Each language is a unique vision of the world. All of the history of a people is synthesized in its language. It is the novel in which a people have deposited its laughter and its tears, its triumphs and its failures, its aspirations and disappointments, its attitudes, thoughts, prejudices and beliefs. The language is the living current that joins the individual to a culture, a history, a vital reality. The language gives the individual an identity and quality.[9]

Language is more than a system of symbols used for communication. It affects and shapes one's perception of the world, reports and defines experience, is the method of communication, and is a symbol and means of group identity and solidarity. It is used to describe both one's internal and external world, and to integrate and relate the two. Language is the most important tool by which humans create and distribute meaning. When one learns a language, s/he learns the ways of a group, its values, and its social norms. It is through language that we are bound together, with our past and our cultural heritage, with our present in which we reshape and recreate our past, and with the future in which we use our language to pass on what we have received and reshaped during our lifetime. We are bound to others vertically and horizontally, historically and presently, by our language, and it is what preserves any tie between us.[10] Virgilio Elizondo compares language to the family as the basis and foundation of society:

> Just as the family is the basic unit of the social system, so language is the basic unit of the system of thought. It is through language that we think, understand, remember, and communicate. The way that a group represents, interprets, and communicates its understanding of reality is its language. Every cohesive human group has a language,

and the specific language of the group is tied in with its identity and uniqueness.[11]

Language gives a person his identity which expresses a unique vision of the world, which is influenced by the history of a people that has shaped the language and is ever-present within the language itself and with the speakers. It embodies the intellectual wealth of a people, and it "makes possible the development, the elaboration, the transmission, and the accumulation of culture as a whole."[12] The language of a people is its soul, the living current that joins a person to his/her culture, his/her history, and his/her reality, through and by which meaning is created and distributed.

The person, a network of social relationships which are perpetuated by language, exists in a culture that is characterized by a particular way of life, standards of behavior, ways of thinking, and values. Culture and language are intimately linked, as they create and shape each other, and together they orient one in his reality:

> Language and culture together form the basic orientation toward reality of any given person or group of persons. The process of forming this orientation is circular and may be described as follows: reality creates both language and culture; language creates culture and is created by culture; and language and culture create reality.[13]

In the Hispanic Southwest specifically, the nature of the culture is rooted in the language, which, with culture, is based on the reality in which the people live, while also helping to create and shape that reality. The dynamic relationship of language, culture, and reality is indissoluble, and this relationship is also inseparable from the human. It is because culture is so fundamental to man's being and existence that the Catholic Church values culture and needs to work within it in order to bring man to his proper and full humanity.

The Pontifical Council for Culture, a department of the Roman Curia which aids the Pope in service of the universal Church and of particular Churches, defines culture as:

> the particular way in which persons and peoples cultivate their relationship with nature and their brothers and sisters, with themselves and with God, so as to attain a fully human existence. Culture only exists through man, by man, and for man. It is the whole of human activity, human intelligence and emotions, the human quest for meaning, human customs and ethics. Culture is so natural to man that human nature can only be revealed through culture.[14]

Culture is important to the Church because it is the way in which God approaches us, through a particular language and culture. Language is fundamental to the revelation of God because He reveals himself through Jesus Christ who is the Word made flesh, and in Sacred Scripture which is recorded and transmitted through language. Culture is also important to the Church because it is the way in which we think about and embrace the mystery of creation and the way that we approach God. It is the way in which man humanizes life by developing his gifts, through communication, improvements, and preservation of customs and institutions.[15]

The diversity of the Church comes from the variety of God's gifts and the diversity of the people who receive them, all of whom are gathered within the Church as the People of God and are essential to its fullness as the Body of Christ. This diversity serves to manifest the fullness of the life and love of God in the world, and therefore the culture, in its fullness, must promote the development of the human person for the good of the community and for all of creation. By embracing the cultures of man, the Church takes the culture into her care to be evangelized and renewed so that both the culture and the Church are enhanced and enriched. In this mutuality, the human grows toward his/her fullness through the integration of faith and culture, and s/he participates in the redemption of the world by properly ordering and integrating his/her culture so as to be enlightened by truth, also causing truth to shine more brightly in the world through the example and the way of his culture. Cardinal George writes, "In culture we discover what man is, as distinguished from what he has. Man expresses himself in culture and objectifies himself in it . . . A culture is adequately human only if it recognizes and fosters human rights in both the spiritual and material realms, respecting their unity in the human person."[16]

The Church seeks to know and love all cultures so that she may be enriched and also so that she may renew and enrich the cultures by implanting the seed of Christ's life and love within them. It is only through this inculturation, or "the incarnation of the Gospel in native cultures," that culture is revitalized, purified, strengthened, and renewed to bring the human to the fullness of his humanity, and the Church is able to more fully embrace creation to bring it into communion with God.[17] Culture becomes evangelized and faith becomes inculturated so that each is embodied in the other. "The effect of her work is that whatever good is found sown in the minds and hearts of men or in the rites and customs of peoples, these not only are preserved from destruction, but are purified, raised up, and perfected for the glory of God, the confusion of the devil, and the happiness of man."[18] The Church works to bring man and all of creation to God, and she does this by perfecting and completing all that is part of human existence and nature, which is only revealed in our world through culture.

Language is fundamental to culture because it is fundamental to man, and thus it is also important to the completion and fulfillment of man's humanity, which is the goal of the Church. Sabine Ulibarri reveals the integration of language, culture, and faith in her passage imitating the Gospel of John:

> In the beginning was the Word. And the Word was made flesh. It was so in the beginning, and it is so today. The Language, the Word, carries within it the history, the culture, the traditions, the very life of a people, the flesh. Language is people. We cannot even conceive of a people without a language, or a language without a language, or a language without a people. The two are one and the same. To know one is to know the other. To love one is to love the other.[19]

Language is essential to the understanding of persons and to the love for persons because it is so integral to culture, whose center is the human. Language, culture, and faith are interrelated in a way which brings them to their fullness when each is properly valued, ordered, and integrated. With faith, both language and culture become even more important and essential to our development as humans and in the love of God. "Faith becomes the connection of language and culture to the transcendent and without this bond both language and culture would be self-enclosed, atrophy and die."[20]

Cardinal George emphasizes the importance of the faith becoming a global vision of all of reality because "the full truth of Christ can become clear only in a *dialogue* which includes all people, cultures, and generations. This *dialogue* demands that believers be sensitive to their own particular culture and also to Christ, since he is the leaven, the salt and the light of history. It demands attention also to the signs of the times in which we now live."[21] This dialogue is only possible through communication and language, by which people and cultures can open up to each other and to the Church, to in turn be opened, enriched, and purified. Cardinal George teaches that language is the best expression of collective identity and subjectivity, which makes a group into a community. The human's highest goal is communion with God through union with others, and this union is achieved in communities, through culture, and by language. Just as language has the potential of being the medium of communication, unfortunately, as revealed in the Biblical Tower of Babel story, it can also impede communication through the confusion of language, causing extreme disunity. Language is essential to the purpose and end of humans because it is so fundamental to his/her existence, nature, and culture. Through inculturation, faith develops culture towards its fulfillment, and as the culture develops, so does the language because it is essential to and inseparable from culture.

This dynamic of the mutuality of faith and culture places responsibility on the people of a faith and culture to grow in and develop both. The Catholic New Mexican Hispanic woman has a very important role in this process of inculturation because her culture, through and with the language, is in a crucial state of transition. Both are in danger of being lost unless the current and future generations make serious efforts to maintain and revitalize them. The direction of the transition depends on the people within the culture to either strengthen and enrich it or lose it to the past. With this responsibility to the revitalization of language, culture and faith, the woman's roles as daughter and student, professional, and wife and mother carry great weight and importance to this mission. Cardinal George writes, "People come to full humanity only through culture, which is the sum total of natural goods and values; but culture comes to its full value only through being restored and perfected in Christ."[22] Woman's role is to participate in this restoration and perfection of culture in order to also participate in the humanization of the people of the culture. As a daughter and student, she comes to *know* the language and culture; as a professional she *heals* it; and as a wife and mother, she *preserves* it.[23] By fully participating in her culture and her faith through her unique roles, she can participate in the restoration and enrichment of both culture and faith, and it is her responsibility and mission as a Catholic Hispanic woman to do so in order to build up the Body of Christ.

The Hispanic family, as in the rest of the world, is increasingly devalued and suffers from brokenness, but still endures as the center of life and has great meaning within the culture, which is primarily characterized by the importance of the family. The family is the main source of identity as well as the means of relating with others outside one's family. For example, when I meet people or am introduced to someone by a family member, the first question I receive is "whose daughter are you?" or "who do you belong to?" When I name my parents and grandparents, they willingly accept me because a person is known by her roots. The family is the center and source of life in the Hispanic culture. Through the process of inculturation, it is the responsibility of the people to restore this importance of the family and properly value it even in a changing society that exalts autonomy and distorted freedom while denying responsibility. As a *daughter and granddaughter*, the role in this restoration of family and culture begins with learning from the parents and grandparents about the culture, the language, and the family, so as to better *know* them. This unique opportunity to learn from the parents and grandparents is also a responsibility because "Education can play an outstanding role in promoting the inculturation of the Gospel . . . It begins within the family, which is always the best context for education. Any pastoral approach to culture and any deep evangelization relies heavily on education, and has the family as its starting point, the place where the education of the person primarily takes place."[24] One first *learns* her culture from the family, and once she recognizes this as a particular mission and responsibility, she must take this opportunity to learn from them. In a culture whose language is dying, this opportunity and responsibility begins with the learning of the language, which she can begin within her own family.

While learning the language, this woman will also embrace cultural ways and practices that will enrich her life, which in my experience have been such things as prayers of the rosary that are specific to New Mexico that I learned from my great-grandmother, or participating in *La Semana Santa* (Holy Week) and *El Vía Crucis* (The Way of the Cross) which are both still practiced according to the old traditions and in the Standard Spanish of the people. A particular part of a prayer of the rosary that exemplifies the deep faith and intimate unity of the people is: "Dios te Salve, María Santísima, Hija de Dios Padre, Virgen Purísima. En tus manos *encomendamos nuestra fe* para que la ilumines" (*we* commend *our faith*).[25] The prayer continues by honoring Mary as the Mother of the Son into whose hands *we* commend *our hope* to be encouraged, and as the Spouse of the Holy Spirit into whose hands *we* commend *our charity* to be inflamed. The *people* as a union commend their *one* faith, *one* hope, and *one* charity to Mary. There is also a particular devotion to the Sacred Heart in the Hispanic culture, to which there is a version of the rosary that is said in New Mexico. By learning these traditions and the language from the Hispanic woman's family, she then carries them with her into the world and brings this richness and deep union to others by sharing her culture and its customs. By doing so, she brings the unique faith, which is deeply embedded in and inseparable from the Hispanic culture and family to the world.

As a *student*, this responsibility to *learn* the language is especially important. The Pontifical Council for Culture writes:

> Bishops, priests, men and women religious and lay people need to *develop* a sensitivity to this culture, in order to protect and promote

it in the light of Gospel values, above all when it is a minority culture. Such attention to culture can offer those who are in any way disadvantaged a way to faith and to a better quality of Christian life at the heart of the Church. Men and women who have integrated a deep faith with their education and culture are living witnesses who will help many others to rediscover the Christian roots of their culture.[26]

When the Catholic New Mexican Hispanic woman studies the Spanish language in her education, she is enhancing the education she receives from her family and growing in her knowledge of her culture, which is manifested in the language. She can then more fully know her culture and her language to further enrich her family, while also bringing her experience of culture and family to her education, which humanizes it. Through her education, she is better prepared to work in the world and to take on a particular mission, which is supported by her education that has been humanized and enriched through learning the language and culture of her heritage.

As a *professional*, this woman has the opportunity and responsibility to *heal* the language and culture of her heritage, and possibly of other heritages through her knowledge of the importance and value of culture in the world and to the Body of Christ. Her own culture then becomes an opening into other cultures, and this is a way of healing sin and division among peoples. In *Ad Gentes Divinitus* it is written:

> They must give expression to this newness of life in their own society and culture and in a manner that is in keeping with the traditions of their own land. They must be familiar with this culture, they must purify and guard it, they must develop it in accordance with present-day conditions, they must perfect it in Christ so that the faith of Christ and the life of the Church will not be something foreign to the society in which they live but will begin to transform and permeate it.[27]

As a professional, this woman *heals* her culture by restoring and revitalizing the language and the customs of the people, while also developing them within the culture through her participation in and support of their use and practice. With the knowledge that she gains from her family and her education in the language and culture of her heritage, she is better prepared to use this knowledge by maintaining cultural practices even in her work, such as the use of Spanish, the customs of respect, or the faithful way of life which is a vital part of Hispanic culture in which every act or work of the day is preceded by a prayer or is thought of as a prayer.

An example of the influence of the faith on work is that during Holy Week, no one in the family worked outside of the home because it was a time for preparation and prayer: *"Empezando el miércoles de la Semana Santa, a medio día, la gente no trabaja, afuera de hacer el trabajo dentro de la casa. Nadie, pero nadie, hacía un poco de trabajo porque pensaban que le hacían mal a Dios."*[28] (Beginning the Wednesday of Holy Week at midday, the people do not work except within the house. Nobody worked because they thought that they were doing evil against or hurting God if they did.) Another example is a custom that my great-great-grandmother practiced, which was to say a particular prayer before making bread, and she had a prayer for everything:

> Juanita, they say had been blessed with many virtues, but perhaps the greatest was her devout and uncompromising faith. No day passed without its prayers, rosaries, novenas; and even the end of a long, tiring day often returned her to Church for benediction and rosary or just to spend more time with her God. Total devotion and love of God became integral, familiar parts of every day, and Juanita's God was never far from her thoughts. There was a short-worded prayer to suit any occasion—a prayer to rise with, a prayer to retire with, even a prayer to begin a day's deed, such as the baking of bread.[29]

My great-grandfather, who built adobe houses brick by brick, built the tall pillars topped with crosses at the entrance of the cemetery where he is now buried. The Catholic faith was a guidance and inspiration to his work, even in the product created by his hands. With these influences of faith and culture, the woman has strong examples to follow. Even in her choice of work she may choose a profession that specifically aids in the restoration and development of the culture and its people, such as education. In this case, she would be aiding the mission and purpose of the family in its role as the first school of life, love, and culture, which must be reinforced in the education system in order to help the youth grow in their humanity, particularly through faith and culture.[30] *Gaudium et Spes* tells us: "We must do everything possible to make all persons aware of their right to culture and their duty to develop themselves culturally and to help their fellows . . . It is up to everyone to see to it that woman's specific and necessary participation in cultural life be acknowledged and fostered."[31] By healing her culture, she participates in its fulfillment and completion, and she responds to this call to duty to develop in her culture and bring it to the world. She also brings the richness and depth of her culture to her profession by continuing the customs of her family in her own daily life. By humanizing her profession with the influences of her culture and its customs she helps others to be aware of their culture and inspires them to develop in their culture as well.

As a *wife and mother*, the Catholic New Mexican Hispanic woman has another role which is the most important in her culture, but it is informed, supported, prepared for, and guided by the other roles. The family, which is "the cradle of life and love, [and] also the source of culture... [has the] basic role as the primary place of humanization for the person and society."[32] The woman's role in the family is as the first teacher with a certain precedence over man: "Although motherhood...depends on the man, it places an essential 'mark' on the whole personal growth process of new children . . . Motherhood in its personal-ethical sense expresses a very important creativity on the part of the woman, upon whom the very humanity of the new human being mainly depends."[33] The Pontifical Council for Culture echoes this unique role of the wife and mother stating that "women are the first artisans of a more human world."[34] This woman must make every effort to prepare for this role, and her education and participation in her own family, both guided by her culture and faith, are the foundation for this preparation and for this role. The woman, as the first teacher, is primarily the one who passes the culture and the language on to the children. The role that she played as a daughter learning from the family is now the role for which she must provide as the mother. She begins and carries on the school of life, love, and culture in the family. In this role, she *preserves* the culture and the faith so that they may continue to be enriched, renewed, perfected, completed, and integrated in future generations, so that also the Body of Christ will continue to grow in its gifts, development, fulfillment, and union. "Each part contributes its own gifts to other parts and to the whole Church, so that the whole and each of the parts are strengthened by the common sharing of all things and by the common effort to attain to fullness in unity . . . These differences do not hinder unity, but rather contribute to it."[35] The wife and mother preserves, sustains, and passes on the culture and the faith within the family so that the family, the culture, and the entire Body of Christ may be strengthened, opened, and united through these contributions.

Through these three primary roles of daughter/student, professional, and wife/mother, the Catholic New Mexican Hispanic woman has the opportunity, the responsibility, and the mission to develop and enrich her culture and her faith by integrating them fully into her life. This mutuality is especially necessary in our time and in our world of division, separation, and secularization. The Pontifical Council for Culture tells us, "The split between the Gospel and culture is without a doubt the drama of our time... Therefore, every effort must be made to ensure a full evangelization of culture... In order to do this, it is necessary to proclaim the Gospel in the *language* and *culture* of men."[36] Through the roles in this woman's life, she evangelizes the culture by working for its growth and development beginning with the family and the language, through her education within the family and within the formal system, extending to her profession, and culminating in her own family, where the process begins again. It is through her family that the faith, culture, and language will be passed on to future generations to be further evangelized, enriched, and completed. In this essential dialogue of faith and culture, or inculturation, "not only are the cultures deprived of nothing, but they are actually stimulated to open themselves to the newness of the Gospel's truth and to find in it an incentive for further development."[37] She who contributes to this development of culture in a manner which is enlightened and guided by the faith contributes greatly to the entire Church community as the Body of Christ, for which all human elements should be cultivated.

The cultivation of humanity begins with the culture, whose most fundamental element is the language. Through the revitalization of *traditional Spanish* in the Catholic New Mexican Hispanic woman's roles as daughter and student, professional, and wife and mother, her culture and language are known, healed, and preserved in a very crucial time of near language death. Through inculturation, the human person is capacitated to achieve full and true humanity in the complete and perfect integration of faith and culture. In this process, the faith, which is so integral to the Hispanic culture, is restored and renewed along with the culture and the language. This woman, through her mission and work in the restoration and revitalization of language, culture, and faith, participates in the enrichment and fulfillment of the Body of Christ, and her culture is purified, strengthened, and opened by the faith so that she can continue to enrich the world with her culture.

Notes
1. Rubén Cobos, *A Dictionary of New Mexico and Southern Colorado Spanish* (Santa Fe: Museum of NM Press, 2003) xvii.
2. Cobos ix.
3. Fernando Peñalosa, *Chicano Sociolinguistics, a brief introduction* (MA: Newbury House Publishers, 1980) 109.
4. Garland Bills, "New Mexican Spanish: Demise of the Earliest European Variety in the United States," *American Speech* 72.2 (1997): 158.
5. Frederick Newmeyer, *Language: The Socio-cultural Context* (NY: Cambridge University Press, 1988) 184.

6. Bills 169.
7. José Sena. Personal interview June 2004.
8. Bills 155.
9. Sabine Ulibarri quoted in New Mexico Public Education Department, Bilingual Multicultural Education Unit. *Heritage Language Revitalization* Planning Manual November 2003, 7.
10. Tove Skutnabb-Kangas, *Bilingualism or Not: The Education of Minorities*. Trans. Lars Malmberg and David Crane. (Sweden: Tove Skutnabb-Kangas and LiberForlag, 1981) 2.
11. Virgilio Elizondo, *Galilean Journey: The Mexican American Promise* (NY: Orbis Books, 1983) 27.
12. William Bright, *Variation and Change in Language* (CA: Stanford University Press, 1976) 4.
13. Joshua Fishman, *Language Loyalty in the United States* (NY: Arno Press, 1978) 300.
14. Pontifical Council for Culture, *Towards a Pastoral Approach to Culture* (Vatican: 23 May 1999) 2.
15. *Gaudium et Spes* (Vatican: 7 Dec. 1965) 15.
16. Francis E. George, OMI, *Inculturation and Ecclesial Communion: Culture and Church in the Teaching of Pope John Paul II* (Rome: Urbaniana University Press, 1990) 39.
17. George 83.
18. *Lumen Gentium* (Vatican: 21 Nov. 1964. *Vatican Council II: The Conciliar and Post Conciliar Documents*. Vol. 1. Austin Flannery, O.P., ed. NY: Costello Publishing Company, 1998) 17.
19. NMPED 7.
20. Sr. Paula Jean Miller, F.S.E. (Notes December 2004).
21. George 45 (emphasis added).
22. George 49.
23. George 50.
24. PCC 29.
25. Isidora Flores. Personal interviews June 2004.
26. PCC 27.
27. *Ad Gentes Divinitus* (Vatican: 7 Dec. 1965. *Vatican Council II: The Conciliar and Post Conciliar Documents*. Vol. 1. Austin Flannery, O.P., ed. NY: Costello Publishing Company, 1998) 21.
28. Compendio de Folklore Nuevo Mejicano: Conjunto de las Tradiciones, Creencias y Costumbres Populares (Santa Fe: La Sociedad Folklórica de Santa Fe, Nuevo Mejico, 1977) 122.
29. Juanita Madrid Majnik, *La Casa de Madrid* (Utah: Brigham Young University Press, 1995) 22.
30. *Gaudium et Spes* 52.
31. *Gaudium et Spes* 60.
32. PCC 14.
33. Pope John Paul II, *Mulieris Dignitatem* (Vatican: 15 Aug. 1988. 30 Nov. 2004) 14.

34 PCC 14.
35 *Lumen Gentium* 365.
36 PCC 14 (emphasis added).
37 PCC 5.

Bibliography

Ad Gentes Divinitus. Vatican: 7 Dec. 1965. *Vatican Council II: The Conciliar and Post Conciliar Documents.* Vol. 1. Austin Flannery, O.P., ed. NY: Costello Publishing Co., 1998. Pp. 813–856.

Armijo, Sheri A. *Spanish in New Mexico: Diversity of a Conquering Language.* 29 Oct. 2004 <http://www.unm.edu/~abqteach/linguistics/02-08-01.htm>.

Bills, Garland D. "New Mexican Spanish: Demise of the earliest European variety in the United States." *American Speech* 72.2 (1997): pp. 154–171. *EBSCO.* 29 Oct. 2004 <http://search.epnet.com>.

Bright, William. *Variation and Change in Language.* CA: Stanford University Press, 1976.

Catechism of the Catholic Church. New York: Doubleday, 1995.

Cobos, Rubén. *A Dictionary of New Mexico & Southern Colorado Spanish.* Revised and Expanded Edition. Santa Fe: Museum of New Mexico Press, 2003.

Compendio de Folklore Nuevo Mejicano: Conjunto de las Tradiciones, Creencias y Costumbres Populares. Santa Fe: La Sociedad Folklórica de Santa Fe, Nuevo Mejico, 1977.

Elizondo, Virgilio. *Galilean Journey: The Mexican American Promise.* NY: Orbis Books, 1983.

Fishman, Joshua A. *Language and Nationalism: Two Integrative Essays.* MA: Newbury House Publishers, Inc., 1972.

———. *Language Loyalty in the United States.* NY: Arno Press, 1978.

———. *Reversing Language Shift: Theoretical and Empirical Foundations of Assistance to Threatened Languages.* PA: Multilingual Matters Ltd., 1991.

Fitzgerald, Rev. Maurus, O.F.M. *Libro católico de oraciones: Oraciones católicas populares ordenadas para el uso diario.* NY: Catholic Book Publishing Co., 1984.

Flores, Isidora. Personal interviews June 2004.

García, Nasario, ed. *Brujas, Bultos, y Brasas: Tales of Witchcraft and the Supernatural in the Pecos Valley.* NM: Western Edge Press, 1999.

Gaudium et Spes. Vatican: 7 Dec. 1965. *Vatican Council II: The Conciliar and Post Conciliar Documents.* Vol. 1. Austin Flannery, O.P., ed. NY: Costello Publishing Company, 1998. pp. 903–1001.

George, Francis E., OMI. *Inculturation and Ecclesial Communion: Culture and Church in the Teaching of Pope John Paul II.* Rome: Urbaniana University Press, 1990.

Gumperz, John J. *Language and Social Identity.* NY: Cambridge University Press, 1982.

Hale, Ken. "Language endangerment and the human value of linguistic diversity." *Language* 68.1 (1992): 35–42. *JSTOR.* 28 Oct. 2004 <http://links.jstor.org>.

John Paul II. *The Holy Father's Addresses to the Members of the Pontifical Council for Culture.* Vatican: Jan. 1983–Nov. 1999. 30 Nov. 2004.<http://www.vatican.va/roman_curia/pontifical_councils/cultr/documents/rc_pc_cultr_doc_20000126_jp-ii_addresses-pccultr_en.html>.

——. *Mulieris Dignitatem.* Vatican: 15 Aug. 1988. 30 Nov. 2004. <http://www.vatican.va/holy_father/john_paul_ii/apost_letters/documents/hf_jp- ii_apl_15081988_mulieris-dignitatem_en.html>.

Lumen Gentium. Vatican: 21 Nov. 1964. *Vatican Council II: The Conciliar and Post Conciliar Documents.* Vol. 1. Austin Flannery, O.P., ed. NY: Costello Publishing Company, 1998. pp. 350–426.

Macaulay, Ronald. *The Social Art: Language and Its Uses.* NY: Oxford University Press, 1994.

McCarty, Teresa L. "Revitalising Indigenous Languages in Homogenising Times." *Comparative Education* 39.2 (2003): 147–163. *EBSCO.* 6 Oct. 2004 <http://search.epnet.com>.

Maffi, Luisa. "Endangered Languages, endangered knowledge." *International Social Science Journal* 54.173 (2002): 385–393. *EBSCO.* 6 Oct. 2004 <http://search.epnet.com>.

Majnik, Juanita Madrid. *La Casa de Madrid.* Utah: Brigham Young University Press, 1995.

Miller, Sr. Paula Jean, F.S.E. Class notes December 2004.

New Mexico Public Education Department, Bilingual Multicultural Education Unit. *Heritage Language Revitalization.* Planning Manual November 2003. 29 Oct. 2004 <www.ped.state.nm.us/div/learn.serv/Bilingual/dl/lang.revit/lang.revit. man. doc>.

Newmeyer, Frederick J. *Language: The Socio-cultural Context.* NY: Cambridge University Press, 1988.

Peñalosa, Fernando. *Chicano Sociolinguistics: A Brief Introduction.* MA: Newbury House Publishers, Inc., 1980.

——. *Introduction to the Sociology of Language.* MA: Newbury House Publishers, Inc., 1981.

Pontifical Council for Culture. *Towards a Pastoral Approach to Culture.* Vatican: 23 May 1999. 30 Nov. 2004 <http://www.vatican.va/roman_curia/pontifical_councils/cultr/documents/rc_pc_pc-cultr_doc_03061999_pastoral_en.html>.

Schecter, Sandra R. and Robert Bayley. *Language as Cultural Practice: Mexicanos en el Norte* NJ: Lawrence Erlbaum Associates, 2002.

Sena, José. Personal interview June 2004.

Skutnabb-Kangas, Tove. *Bilingualism or Not: The Education of Minorities.* Trans. Lars Malmberg and David Crane. Sweden: Tove Skutnabb-Kangas and LiberForlag, 1981.
Stevens, Gillian. "Nativity, Intermarriage, and Mother-Tongue Shift." *American Sociological Review* 50.1 (1985): 74–83. *JSTOR.* 29 Oct. 2004 <http://links.jstor.org/>.
Van Horne, Winston A. and Thomas V. Tonnesen, eds. *Ethnicity and Language.* WI: The University of Wisconsin System, 1987.

CHAPTER
10
Re-Envisioning Latina Ministry Through Ivone Gebara's Ecofeminism

Mary Jane DeLaRosa Burke

Our Lady of Guadalupe is known as the one who said to the Mexican Indigenous in the mid-16th century: "build my church."[1] The Church[2] and the world today face many problems. Among them is the global ecological devastation of our world. Internationally known Brazilian theologian, Sr. Ivone Gebara (1944–), while shaped by liberation theology, was disappointed that male theologians were not addressing the suffering of women, especially poor women. She responds to the call to "build my church" from the perspective of ecofeminism. For decades, Gebara, a nun, Sister of Our Lady (Canonesses of St. Augustine), lived, taught and worked with the poor in one of the poorest regions of Recife in northeastern Brazil for decades.

She focuses on ecofeminism[3] to explain how the exploitation of women connects with the exploitation of nature. She argues that women, especially poor women, hold the key to solving the impending global ecological devastation through their daily experiences, the "*Cotidiano*/daily," gifts that enrich and heal a world in crisis. But Gebara states that it is the androcentric (male) and anthrocentric (human) view of the world that gets in the way. These male-controlled hierarchies disregard other perspectives and experiences, especially of women, and obstruct the care for all nature. Despite this, Gebara believes that ecofeminism is the transformation of all. This is the message that must be heard!

I will use the account of the *Nican Mopohua*[4] of Our Lady of Guadalupe to help understand the problem of an exclusively androcentric view of the world. I will discuss three daily experiences from

Re-envisioning Latina Ministry | 137

"*Cotidiano*," highlighted by Gebara, that which poor women offer to a world in crisis: survival, dialogue, and creating.

Part I: The Procession and the Deacon

Recounting a personal event, of which many may have had a similar experience, may help to understand how androcentric thinking hinders. It was the celebration of the Feast Day of Our Lady of Guadalupe, and the procession begins! The *matachines*/dancers,[5] with their *cascabeles*/jingle bells, and drums in rhythm, come in dancing their praises to our Lady. All the Marian sodalities[6] come in with their Marian banners. The multi-cultural choir of which my husband[7] was the choir director has begun singing the story of La Guadalupana: "*Desde el cielo una Hermosa manaña . . . la guadalupana, la guadalupana*/from heaven a beautiful morning . . . [devotion] to [Our Lady of] Guadalupe." There are infinite roses from one end to the other; their fragrance fills the church. The beautiful reading, "the woman clothed with the sun" is proclaimed, and then the deacon opens his mouth to give his homily in his heavy East Texas accent, *Nuestra Señora de Guadalupe no es Dios!*/Our Lady of Guadalupe is not God."

What does Gebara tell us about this way of thinking? She would say that this way of thinking is precisely what keeps us from seeing the profoundness and beauty in the divinity and prevents us from seeing our connection to creation. What, then, is causing the interference? The deacon's way of thinking is vertical, while Gebara's is horizontal. His thinking is an example of many church leaders' hierarchical and androcentric (male-centered) thinking (Gebara, *Longing* . . . vi). Meanwhile, Gebara proposes a holistic approach which includes indigenous wisdom and all cultures, genders, and nature. This approach helps us become ourselves by including other perspectives and experiences (not just dogma). We can see through women's eyes, who then turn their experience toward caring for all nature.

Secondly, the deacon seemed to want us to think that God or the divine is something that is "out there," far and away from daily experience. At the same time, Gebara's method characterizes women's experience of theology as an internal process (*Daily Life* . . . 205). Women in poverty connect the day-to-day experience as a relationship with Jesus and Mary as they all suffered oppression. In addition, as the United Nations Framework Convention on Climate Change (UNFCCC) Executive Secretary Patricia Espinosa has said, women are at the forefront of the adverse effects of global warming and climate change; consequently, their theological perspective is particularly valuable to the methods of eco-theology. They suffer the most; in turn, nature also suffers.

Gebara writes on Guadalupe that Guadalupe "lives in God." At the time of her appearance, nature responded: the mountains amplify the birds singing, and the rainbow with multiple colors shines through the clouds. She illustrates a theophany, God's manifestation or the manifestation of the Mother of God, the Virgin Mary, [in the world that we all share] (Gebara & Bingemer 47). Gebara's approach could help the deacon see that Guadalupe illuminates the feminine characteristics of God: "I am your mother."[8]

Part II: Gifts from Poor Women to a World in Crisis

How do the daily experiences and the gifts that women offer show care for creation and protecting the environment and nature? A careful reading of Gebara's work indicates that poor women offer their daily experiences as gifts to a world in the grip of a climate crisis. For Catholics, the baptismal charge mandates that all, including women and people of color, participate in caring for creation and saving creation. We go forth with this task by using our distinct gifts and reflecting on them through our daily experiences. Affirmed are gifts, qualities, aspects, and characteristics usually identified as feminine. Although Gebara never says that men cannot display these gifts, many ecofeminists agree that these gifts are generally present in women. Quoting Darcy de Oliveira,[9] Gebara describes women as having different values than men. Women uphold family and friendships. She argues that women regard themselves as "nurturers" and connected to nature (*Longing* . . . vi). Gebara references feminist scholar, Bila Sorj,[10] when she says that women take on roles that begin in the home but lead to ecological care (*Longing* . . . 10–11). We must be careful that hierarchical groups do not separate us from being ourselves. They do not allow the use of our gifts and daily experiences and prevent us from connecting with the cosmos in love, dialogue, inclusion, service, equality, dignity, and tenderness.

The first Daily experience I want to mention is the struggle to survive: women in poverty must learn how to survive. Through Gebara's experiences in Brazil, she found that women in poverty were the poorest of all in the country and most likely to reside in the worst and dirtiest places and have the worst jobs, often cleaning for others. They were looked down by society because of their culture and dominated by their male relatives. Some of their husbands were simultaneously physically abusive. Instead of protecting them, the police ignored and abused them; "after all, they were just *muleres*/women." Women in Brazil saw the police as a coercive authority while they saw real authority in themselves (Gebara, *What* ... 7, 9).

This authority is based on friendships with other women who make common decisions and share commitments, responsibilities, and dreams on how they want to lead their families. Women find strength in one another and take action (Gebara, *What* ... 9). Gebara saw how these women, oriented towards survival, struggled to feed their families. Even if they had to resort to looking through the garbage, women in poverty demonstrated resiliency. Through their struggle, they shared hope for their families.

As women in poverty struggle, they see themselves as the hemorrhaging woman who touched Jesus' cloak; it is her faith that heals her. In Jewish society, women had to suffer as wives and mothers in order to be redeemed. However, women's suffering is not equal to men's suffering, and therefore it receives little or no attention. The agony of Jesus was very public and historic. Men's suffering has great valor: "In the patriarchal society, male persecution in the form of acts of public heroism has a redemptive role for the country, the nation, and the people." Furthermore, the sacrifice of the man saves; his blood liberates while the woman's blood is impure [and hidden] (Gebara, *Out of* ... 7). The malady of women has nothing to offer (*Out of* ... 111). Contrary to traditional admonishments, Jesus is not disgusted with her bleeding; he affirms her dignity and tells her that it is her faith that has healed her.

Gebara resolves that while Christian salvation requires sacrifice, Jesus' deliverance does not come because an imperial power oppresses us but by promoting relationships of justice, respect, and tenderness among human beings (*Out of* ... 113). It is this "utopia of a sharing of mutual recognition of men and women's values" that women encounter in the life of Jesus of Nazareth (*Out of* ... 71). They identify with Jesus. "He validates their suffering and gives meaning to their lives" (*Out of* ... 88). To them, the cross of Jesus is not just the cross of an innocent man; but of a man who stands for social justice. Gebara contends that women in poverty turn their struggle to survive, not just as a sacrifice for their family but also toward social justice for their families and community. To add to this, Gebara also argues that no cross or tribulation is less significant. Gebara reimagines the cross in light of how we save one another.

Gebara links salvation and resurrection through our own crosses (*Out of* ... 122). Resurrection is not just a once and future event but is a momentary reoccurrence, especially for women in poverty. It happens through the process of salvation, "like the breath of the Holy Spirit, who blows where it will and as it can" (*Out of* . . . 126). It is the longing to be loved and escape but is combined with strive, pain, and even death if it relieves one's distress. Resurrection comes from our everyday restoration with God, nature, and human beings; "we are one another's salvation" (*Longing* . . . 9). We need each other to survive and be saved.

Ecofeminism moves beyond the traditional church teaching of salvation: the forgiveness of sins, which comes solely from God, and the restoration of our relationship with God (*Catechism* . . . 169). Gebara says that while Jesus is the way, he never defers to the powerful. Connecting with Jesus, each other, and nature brings a more profound interpretation of salvation (*Longing* . . . 174–9).

Daily experience two, dialogue: women in poverty must speak out about their daily experiences. They bear witness to their survival and commitment. Our Lady of Guadalupe, as quoted in the Ni sees the poor; she says, "You who are my messenger, in you I place my absolute trust." I have no lack of servants, of messengers." The Church needs to hear you speak in your own voice, to tell your story in your own language, and not interpreted by others. You should see yourself as important and necessary. Guadalupe speaks the Indian's own language, "The deity . . . takes sides with the weak." Defending the Indians, she emerges as the mother of a struggling people, favoring the poor and the downtrodden: mirroring the *Magnificat*.[11]

Guadalupe also serves as a restoration or a return of faith in the Indians, "a larger dimension touching on broader social relations among different groups in society--the interpretation . . . to consider the conflictive reality experience in colonial Spanish America" (Gebara & Bingemer 148–9). "I choose you." "You are dignified," not just an Indian, poor, wretched, and conquered. These feelings were similar of other prophets in the Old Testament (Gebara & Bingemer 152). They also have a message to convey.

As the Scriptures exhort that we heed the poor, Gebara pleads that we pay attention, especially to poor women. She clarifies in this story, having learned a valuable lesson from the wife of an industrial laborer. Gebara was meeting with several laborers to discuss their work conditions. After Gebara attempted to invite one of the wives to their home meetings, the woman finally revealed why she would not attend. "The woman bluntly explained that she did not understand what was discussed during the meetings: 'this is not a language of my world and you Miss [Gebara], speak like a man.' The woman continued to explain that Gebara only spoke about the male reality of the industrial laborers, their claims, their needs for a better salary, and their political struggles." "I never heard you seeking [any information] about our children, about the women industrial laborers' difficult life conditions, about their particular struggles during work hours when having their menstrual cycle or when they have to breastfeed and work at the same time. You never speak about our sexuality and submission to men. You don't speak about our daily reality" (Nogueira-Godsey 31–32).

As we listen to women and the poor, Gebara adds that "every cultural group needs to be free to speak its own world in its own way, and to develop its own religious expressions, using whatever approaches it chooses; it should not be expected to interpret its heritage in the light of the Western Christian tradition or through the use of the kinds of academic tools we tend to impose on it with virtually no reflection" (*Longing* . . . 9).

While in Recife, Gebara, after listening to many women, has advocated for women. Childbearing is usually celebrated in most families; however, it is a tremendous struggle if the family or mother is in poverty. In 1995, Gebara was penalized for supporting abortion in Brazil. She argued that at that time in Brazil, those living in poverty were about 80% and were provided little help from the government to prevent pregnancy. Poor women were often malnourished. In Brazil, many employers will not employ pregnant women. With abortion being against the law, what were women, especially single women, to do? Gebara argued that a poor single mother is condemned to a life in poverty when forced to have children with little or no resources. Besides, illegal abortions in Brazil are unsafe and often leave women frightened and alone, at risk, since abortionists quickly leave women for fear of being caught. Gebara argued that governmental decisions should not be made without regard to listening to women and that the church was obstructive to this (*The Abortion Debate* . . . 129–35). She added that the "option for the poor," advocated by liberation theology, should add women's decision-making over their own bodies (Nogueira-Godsey 35). During her two-year exile, Gebara earned a second doctorate in Religious Science. She returned to Brazil and continued her criticism of the androcentrism of the Church, especially given the continued abuse of women and impending environmental devastation.

Finally, three is the daily experience of creating the kingdom of God on earth. This is in a combination of the first two, surviving and dialogue. Women in poverty collectively participate in building a family and community by building a home with a livable environment. Their struggle to survive leads to care for clean water, clean air, and healthy soil, which also helps to save our planet from devastation. Women usually advocate for these critical resources. Guadalupe said, "I sent you forth to . . . build my *templo* (which in Spanish and Portuguese also means *church*, which implies that building God's kingdom is the mission). Instead of destroying it, humanity can turn this around because there is hope.

These three gifts: survival, dialogue, and creating, emerging from the experiences of poor women, offer pathways for communal survival in a world on the brink of devastation. Gebara, like many of these poor women, reflects from the experience of Catholicism. Therefore, we might ask what the procession might look like on the way out if we heeded Gebara's words. How would Latina ministry look different if these ideas were applied? How might it be a ministry not only of the Church but also to the world? With Gebara's ideas on poor women's contributions, Latina ministers would be moved to do the typical current actions: caring, offering financial support, and encouraging other women to consider ministry or service. Something extraordinary would occur.

Part Three: *Las Hijas de María*

As an example, I would like to offer my experiences in Central Texas as a young Latina in ministry. I will provide introspection and then apply Gebara's ecofeminism to envision an updated version of this young women's group. In 1978, I was involved in an old Mexican American Catholic organization called *Las Hijas de María*/Daughters of Mary. The pastor revitalized this old sodality of which my own mother had been a member in the fifties. Since then, this church ministry has been inactive for almost two decades. The pastor's idea was to involve young unmarried women in the much-needed fundraising. Our parish, heavily in debt, needed groups to raise money to reduce the crippling interest.

At Sunday mass, the announcement of the start-up of the sodality invited all unmarried women, teenage, and older to join. I was eager to participate as I wanted to serve the church, and I knew that I would gain new friends in a safe environment. I learned that being unmarried meant that you promised to stay a virgin before marriage. At the meet and greet, a group of about thirty young women as young as me, seventeen and over, attended. One single woman was in her forties. She seemed out of place, and we spoke only Spanish to her as we did with our parents. The rest of us spoke only English to each other. She also did not drive like few women and, consequently, someone always had to pick her up and drive her home. Nevertheless, the older unmarried woman, I will refrain from calling her a spinster or old maid, put up with us. I admire that she demonstrated responsibility to the organization as if she had made a vow. I wondered if the rest of us would be as faithful. Looking back, I wish that I had been more grateful to her and had talked to her more.

The whole subject of virginity was one reason we would be in good graces in the organization. For *Las Hijas de María*, the tradition was that on your wedding day, you symbolically relinquished your virginity to Mary by placing your belt near Mary's statue. This gesture was archaic in my mind. It was demoralizing to me that your virginity, not how you helped your family, served the church or community, and not how worked on your education or other accomplishments, was all that mattered. Meanwhile, no one questioned your future husband's virginity. Nope, we are not going there! How is this not androcentric thinking? What about those whose virginity was taken from them? Where did this leave our member who had been raped? There was no good answer for her. Nevertheless, she wore her belt. I felt that, at times, we were being made marketable for marriage to good standing Catholic men. Gebara reinterprets virginity as more than it is rejecting everything that is not from God. The complete understanding of virginity, especially Mary's, allows one's poverty or barrenness to be opened to God's endless possibilities (Gebara & Bingemer 106). This is why she is called the ever-virgin Mary. This is a more profound meaning that includes the role of women as creators or builders of the kingdom instead of the Genesis creation story when God breathes life into the clay (Gebara & Bingemer 105). The first version is proactive, while the second is passive.

At our initiation Mass, we wore white dresses and white veils; we were given a necklace with the oval medallion of the Immaculate Conception and a crochet belt, both the Virgin's color: baby blue. The whole manner of dress symbolized our intentions of purity (virginity), obedience, and an imitation of Mary. In reality, we were more naïve and afraid than anything else and did not know what we were walking into.

We were taught to love JOY, Jesus, others, and yourself last. As a child, I was always obedient. But as an older teenager, I questioned the tasks given to us by Sister, our spiritual director. She did not concern herself with our spiritual growth other than it would come through obedience. Sister was thoroughly focused on making as much money for the church as possible. It surprises me that even though she took a vow of poverty, she was caught up in making money. Perhaps it gave her prestige and power or simply the recognition of the pastor. When

I questioned Sister why I always had to be perpetually selling raffle tickets, she simply reminded me to obey. When I refused, she gave me the silent treatment. She instructed the girls through her body language to ostracize me. It took a while before I back was in her good graces. Gebara talks about the quest for freedom to be herself; my search for freedom meant that I had to love myself first and not last. I had to do this first before I could love others and Jesus. This came at a cost.

The pastor called the adult women's society, our *madrinas/godmothers*, our mentors. I do not think the pastor asked them, but no one objected. This is how it was then, and some would say that no one questions the priest even today. A few women took this seriously since they were also our mothers. They showed us about fundraising and other ways to serve the church, such as attending rosaries, going to funerals, cleaning the church, and participating in *el santo entierro*/the Holy Burial.[12] Our *madrinas* would later come to our defense when there was gossip about us. Like our *madrinas*, we processed monthly for Sunday mass with our brand-new banner that carried the image of the Immaculate Conception.

Believing that fundraising was the best way to serve the church, we immediately began running the *Lotería* for both of our two *jamaicas*/fund-raising festivals. We were expected to ask for donated prizes for the *Lotería*, but we often bought the prizes ourselves. Everyone enjoyed *Lotería*—but not as much as Bingo, which had money prizes. The Men's group ran the *Jamaica Bingo*, and nobody touched their Bingo unless you came to play. *Lotería* brought in some money, was a game of our culture, and was great fun. We were young and did not mind standing for hours. We passed out the cards, picked up the money, and yelled out the characters of the *Lotería*: "*tu Tío*/your uncle, '*el Borracho*/the drunk, "*la Luna*/the moon, *comiendo su tuna*/eating your cactus fruit," and "*la Sirena*/the Siren," of course, had a drawn-in bra. I realized that if I put my mind to it, I could endure for long hours and come back early the next day to begin the games again. I was there from beginning to end.

As we became better at fundraising, we began a summer-long campaign to raise money for our queen candidate, the prettiest one. The church group that raised the most money won. The campaign would end with a coronation ceremony of the queen candidate by our pastor. Second place would be crowned Princess; third would be Duchess, and so on. All the queen candidates, their maids of honor, and escorts were dressed in conservative, "prom-like" style. The royalty had crowns, scepters, and robes. *Las Hijas de María* would compete with other church groups. This was an effort to make the campaign more fun and motivate church groups and families to work hard so their daughters would not be humiliated if they came in last and made little money. While some families had good fun and were fine that they did not come in first, other families and church groups had hurt feelings. Once in a while, a church group would accuse another group of cheating. "She was selling raffle tickets when she wasn't supposed to," or "the family of the queen candidate, well; they are good friends of the pastor's."

We held smaller bingos in people's yards nightly; this was good community building. We had Sunday dinners, sold raffle tickets, and had bus trips to San Antonio, Laredo, and Corpus Christi. We had an advantage in that the pastor let us use the bus. That rinky-dinky school bus was likely the same one used more than ten years before for the Catholic School. Only two men drove that miracle-on-wheels for free, and one of them was my Dad.

When I look back, I have a fondness for the support and involvement of family and the friendships that I made, a few of which continue today more than forty years later. I was having safe fun with mostly decent girls. As a young woman, I also found that this experience opened opportunities to confront my inadequacies and fears. I learned to question the purpose of everything. It opened questions about my emotional and social development; I asked: How is this helpful to my self-development? Do I need the acceptance of others? Of what am I afraid? For my spiritual development, I asked: How was this so-called ministry a connection to Jesus and Mary? How is this helpful in growing my love for the church? The typical statement, "it's for the church," did not cut it for me anymore.

After two years, *Las Hijas de María* disbanded and has not reemerged in 44 years. Some things worked, but many things did not work. What would *Las Hijas de María* be like today if the work of Gebara were applied? I believe that something extraordinary would occur. I want to share a few mutual understandings that I think would develop in the struggle to view the mission of *Las Hijas de María* holistically. The sodality would be an inclusive process that helps us see the beauty of femininity and the gifts it offers. Our group would have women and men, Catholic and non-Catholic of all ages, cultures, and genders. We would be daughters and sons or just children of *Tonantzín, Shiva, Gaia*,[13] and so on.

Latina ministers such as *Las Hijas de María* would find that they receive as much as they are giving. We become part of the sacred body that Gebara talks about, and we would use our gifts to save each other and our environment. We might fundraise, depending on the need, but we would also minister and serve each other. Through Gebara's insights, we become one in which everyone listens to everyone's own experiences, education, and so on. Everyone would tell their story. Everyone participates and contributes. Everyone is valued, and self-esteem and self-efficacy are something that would be taught and encouraged, especially in cultures that historically have been oppressed.

We would learn how to connect, which we long to do as Latinas. We would also integrate everything we do to care for creation and the environment. We would have integrated what we learned in school in the seventies about pollution and the effects of the rainforest being cut down because this would have been relevant to our culture and our world. We would demonstrate how connected we all are with nature and therefore have the authority to care for our environment since we need it, and it requires us to respect it.

Finally, with the right leaders and opened hearts, we would learn about Catholic Social Teaching and learn to practice social justice for all. We would remember the vulnerable such as ourselves and our families and find that the struggle to turn this around is what saves, restores, and gives hope to our world. Indeed, there is a lot to be done in this process that probably would take years, but we were young and full of hope! What is important is the journey.

During the time, I was involved in *Las Hijas de María*, there were many conflicts to remain uniform, but through Gebara's insights on the struggle, we would be open to diversity, to connect to each other and to the divine. We would learn to unburden ourselves from having to believe and do the same things. There is a reason why each of us is unique. In my rebellion through constant questioning, I found what continues to be my salvation.

To "build the Church" and the kingdom of God in a world of ecological crisis, Gebara argues that we need to move away from seeing things only from an androcentric (male) and an anthrocentric (human) view of the world to a more holistic view that includes the voice of women especially those in poverty and all genders, cultures, and nature. When there is a connection to each other and nature, there is a connection to the divine. The Divinity is not a separate entity; it is a relationship. Among Latinas, we hold this as precious. In the process and the struggle, we save each other and ourselves. We are restored and resurrected in our daily experiences and gifts.

Latinas such as *Las Hijas de María* have much to offer, like those in the procession on the Feast of Our Lady of Guadalupe. Having similar daily experiences with the poor women of Brazil who inform Gebara's thoughts, they too brought gifts. For the gift of survival: *Las Hijas de María* demonstrated hard work toward their parish's financial survival, driven by all of us needing to work to help our families and ourselves. Dialogue: for *Las Hijas de María*, there was a desire and need to grow in self-esteem and self-efficacy to defend ourselves and express our path to freedom. Finally, with education and support, a future *Las Hijas de María*, through their talents, would have the kind of creativity necessary to organize a procession and save the world.

If more women rise to their equal place in caring for our community and our earth with the freedom to use their daily experiences and gifts, then there is hope for the salvation of creation. Is this not finally a procession of love? Let's hold in our hearts the words of Guadalupe: "I will listen to my children . . . Let not your heart be disturbed . . . Do not fear sickness nor any other anguish . . . Am I not here, who am your Mother? Are you not under my protection? Am I not your health? Are you not happily within my fold? What else do you wish? Do not grieve nor be disturbed by anything."

Notes

1 Vicki Sheenstra echoes the centuries-long oral history of this quote in "Prayers, Quips & Quotes: Our Lady of Guadalupe, Feast Day December 12," on the website *The Mystery of Faith, Discovering Catholic Spirituality: Faith, Prayer, Saints*.
2 All references to the Church or Catholic refer to the Roman Catholic denomination, which still claims the highest number of members among all of the targeted groups from the title of this book.
3 Susan Buckingham, in *International Encyclopedia of the Social & Behavioral Sciences* (2nd. Ed.), 2015, defines "Ecofeminism, like the social movements it has emerged from, is both political activism and intellectual critique. Bringing together feminism and environmentalism, ecofeminism argues that the domination of women and the degradation of the environment are consequences of patriarchy and capitalism. Any strategy to address one must take into account its impact on the other so that women's equality should not be achieved at the expense of worsening the environment, and neither should environmental improvements be gained at the expense of women. Indeed, ecofeminism proposes that only by reversing current values, thereby privileging care and cooperation over more aggressive and dominating behaviors, can both society and environment benefit."
4 *Nican Mopohua* is the Nahuatl title of the multiply translated document recounting the oral history of the Our Lady of Guadalupe encounter with the indigenous man, Juan Diego, near what is now Mexico City in the mid-16th century.
5 Norma Cantú, on the Texas State Historical Society website, details "*Los matachines* [as] a traditional religious dance and the dancers, musicians, and elders who participate in it. Its roots go back to a type of widespread medieval sword dance called a *morisca*. Originally, the dances acted out the battle between Christianity and paganism. The Spanish brought the

ritual with them to the New World, where over time it incorporated Mexican, Indian, and American religious and social symbols. Most modern versions rely heavily on representations of the Virgin Mary and the Holy Cross,"

6 *Miriam Webster* defines a sodality as "a confraternity or association, especially a Roman Catholic religious guild or brotherhood."

7 Fellow scholar, Dr. John Francis Burke, a political scientist whose work appears in this volume and others of the Hispanic Worlds book series published by Sussex.

8 Those words of Our Lady of Guadalupe have been extracted from the *Nican Mopohua*, a 16th century historical account of the apparitions and miraculous event written in Nahuatl by Antonio Valeriano. These words of the Blessed Virgin Mary were spoken to Juan Diego over the course of several days.

9 *Wikipedia* lists "Rosiska Darcy de Oliveira is a Brazilian journalist and feminist writer . . . born in Rio de Janeiro in 1944, she graduated in Law from the Pontifical Catholic University of Rio de Janeiro. In the 1960s, she began her professional career as a journalist . . . In 1970, her journalistic career was interrupted by exile. Accused by the military dictatorship of denouncing the systematic practice of torture against political opponents, she was forced to take refuge in Geneva, Switzerland . . . With the reestablishment of democracy in 1980, she returned to Brazil and continued her writing activity on the issues of education and the feminine . . . In defense of the female cause, she strove to promote the arrival of women in the places of knowledge and power as a requirement for the improvement of democracy. In 1991 she founded and chaired the Coalition of Brazilian Women."

10 *Academia.edu* lists Bila Sorj as a professor of sociology at the Federal University of Río de Janeiro, who publishes widely on gender and social issues.

11 *Magnificat* is a Church-associated, multilingual, website intended as a spiritual guide.

12 Latino tradition of a procession of burial of Jesus on Good Friday.

13 Goddesses from various cultural traditions.

Bibliography

Buckingham, Susan. "Introduction to Ecofeminism. *International Encyclopedia of the Social & Behavioral Sciences*, 2nd Ed., 2015. Print.

Catechism of the Catholic Church, 2nd Ed. Washington D.C.: Librería Editrice Vaticana, 1997. Print.

Espinosa, Patricia. "COP 26 Opening Remarks by UNFCCC Executive Secretary." United Nations Framework Climate Change Conference. Bonn, Germany (UNFCCC). Web.

Gebara, Ivone. "The Abortion Debate in Brazil: A Report from an

Ecofeminist Philosopher Under Siege." *Journal of Feminist Studies in Religion* 11, no. 2 (1995100): pp. 129–135. Print.

——. "Daily Life Challenges as the Criterion for Biblical and Feminist Theological Hermeneutics." In *Faith and Feminism*. Eds. B. Diane Lipsett, and Phyllis Trible, pp. 203–16. Louisville, KY: Westminster John Knox Press, 2014. Print.

——. *Longing for Running Water: Ecofeminism and Liberation.* Minneapolis: Fortress Press, 1999. Print.

——. *Out of the Depths: Women's Experience of Evil and Salvation.* Minneapolis: Fortress Press, 2002. Print.

——. "What Scriptures are Sacred Authority? Ambiguities of the Bible in the Lives of Latin American Women," In *Women's Sacred Scriptures* Eds. Kwok Pui-Lan and Elisabeth Schussler Fiorenza, pp. 7, 9. Maryknoll, NY: Orbis Books, 1998. Print.

Gebara, Ivone & María Clara Bingemer. *Mary, Mother of the Poor.* Sao Paulo: Orbis Books, 1989. Print.

Nican Mopohua. Accessed May 23, 2022. Web. https://springfieldop.org/wp-content/uploads/nican_mopohua_english.pdf

Nogueira-Godsey, Elaine. "The Ecofeminism of Ivone Gebara" (PhD diss., University of Cape Town, 2013), accessed May 23, 2022. Web. https://open.uct.ac.za/bitstream/item/9489/thesis_hum_2014_nogueiragodsey_e.pdf?sequence=1.

Ress, Mary Judith, *Ecofeminism in Latin America: Women from the Margins.* Maryknoll, New York: Orbis Books, 2006. Print.

Sheenstra, Vicki. "Prayers, Quips & Quotes: Our Lady of Guadalupe, Feast Day December 12," in *The Mystery of Faith, Discovering Catholic Spirituality: Faith, Prayer, Saints.* Web.

Valeriano, Don Antonio, ed. "The Story of Our Lady of Guadalupe in Nahuatl." Trans. Fr. Johann Roten, S.M., *Stream of Light, Queen of Tepeyacac.* Trans. Elise Dac. Illust. Fernando Leal. Mexico, c1952. Web.

CHAPTER

11

The Pursuit of the Beloved Community in the 21st Century

John Francis Burke

Over the past decade, a growing polarization between the left and right wings of the political spectrum has characterized the politics of the United States, Europe, and other countries around the globe. Whereas in the second half of the 20th century center-left and center right parties negotiated budgets and public policies, be it the Democrats v. the Republicans in the US, the Labour v. Conservative parties in the UK, and the Social Democrats v. the Christian Democrats in Germany, today parties and groups on the far left and the far right have increasingly gained support and have adapted a position of no compromise with the other side. Especially in countries such as Hungary and Poland, right-wing populist governments seemed poised to overturn the principles of liberal democracy to put their policies into action. The presidency of Donald Trump also illustrates that the United States is not immune to such temptations.

In the past, the notion of civil religion has been a mediating factor in such disputes. As articulated by Robert Bellah, civil religion is the "'founding myth' of a political community" (Bellah in Gorski 16). Entailed in civil religion is a set of principles and practices informed both by faith-based and philosophical traditions that set the acceptable parameters of a democratic civil community. Bellah's founding myth, which "interprets its historical experience in the light of transcendent reality" (Bellah in Gorski 16), is fully compatible with "religious freedom, individual rights, and cultural diversity" (Gorski 16). In concrete terms, civil religion promotes feelings and rituals that provide a sense of stability to a community's institutions and a shared sense of identity for its members – such as the ceremony of the unknown soldier on Memorial Day or the speeches, songs, and events surrounding the 4th of July.

US civil religion has largely been, as Philip Gorski contends, a combination of the Judeo-Christian prophetic tradition with a civil republicanism derived from Western philosophy. However, this legacy is increasingly being challenged by a secular humanism on the left and religious nationalism on the right. Religious nationalism, largely informed by apocalyptic thinking and a conquest narrative, seeks to combine religion and politics under a fundamentalist political creed. Secular humanism, on the other hand, seeks to separate the realms of religion and politics as far apart as possible and to rely on rationality, in and of itself, as the sole guide for political life (Gorski 16–19).

Seemingly, one has to choose between an almost anti-religious social justice movement on the left and a rigid clerical hierarchical rendering of religion on the right. What hope is there then for what Massimo Faggioli has termed, "a theology grounded in an optimistic evaluation of creation, a stand that emphasizes incarnation and sacramentality?" (Faggioli 161).

I will explore in this essay sources from the past century that can be drawn upon to revitalize a civil religion that draws upon both spiritual insights, philosophical reflection, and political experience to promote a "unity-in-diversity" that neither culminates in an ideological secularism or a sectarian nationalism. In addition to balancing unity and diversity, I will explore the sources in terms of their capacity for integrating prophetic critique with practical action and to what degree they project a crucial engagement, and not just resistance to dominant political norms.

I confess from the outset that I am examining civil religion from the standpoint of the perspective of personalist philosophy. Personalism accents the human person as the locus though which humans come to a full understanding of their possibilities and can resist their objectification by both natural and technological processes. In philosophical and spiritual terms, personalism navigates the dynamic intersection of transcendence and immanence. In political terms, personalism stresses both personal liberty and responsibility to the common good. In this regard, it is critical of both libertarianism whose preoccupation with individual liberty blinds it to community responsibilities and statism or collectivism which imposes an impersonal common good on human beings. Personalism stresses rational reflection, but also is open to the mystery of faith perspectives, unlike secular humanism. Conversely, unlike religious nationalism, as much as personalism draws upon faith-based insights, it does not allow them to become a rigid theocracy.

My ensuing presentation is comprised of the following sections. In the first section, I explore lessons we can draw from the personalist project of the personalist ideas of Emmanuel Mounier, who sought to navigate stark political divides in 1930s and 1940s France. He also had an intellectual impact on the Christian Democratic movement in Latin America. Second, I explore the fascinating work of the theologian, Luke Bretherton, who contends that it is possible to foster on consociational democracy in which secular and faith-based perspectives can come together to work on common political goals. Third, I examine respectively the work of both Martin Luther King, Jr. and Virgil Elizondo, whose respective use of the Black Social Gospel heritage and US Latinx spirituality to project a "beloved community" in which the marginalized become integral contributors to the moral and political fabric of community life (King, "Facing the Challenges" 140). Fourth, I critically examine African American and Latinx thinkers who contend that the beloved community is too accommodationist to past US American political norms. Specifically, I contend these "separatist" critics end up being mired in resistance to dominant norms rather that grasping that intersectionality should lead us to engagement, not separation from others. Fifth, I examine the contributions, positive and negative, of Nicole Flores' relational ethics, as well as Jacqueline Hidalgo's work on the spiritual dimension of the Chicano movement for fostering a beloved community animated by an open-ended unity-in-diversity. My ensuing conclusion will project how a personalist beloved community, recognizing the many accents of intersectionality, offers a vital alternative to the prevailing entrenched perspectives of the culture wars.

Emmanuel Mounier—The Prophetic and Political Poles of Action

1930s France was a locale bubbling with ideological divides, from Marxists on the left to fascists on the right, with an array of ideological perspectives in-between. In the French Catholic world, a renaissance of sorts was ensuing. Led by Jacques Maritain, Nicholas Berdyaev, and Gabriel Marcel, a personalist communitarian vision emerges that articulates a Catholicism much more open-ended than traditional authoritarian articulations of religion and politics – Charles Maurras' *Action Francaise* being a prototype of the latter. Currently the support of right-wing Catholic groups for Marie Le Pen is a political descendent of Maurras' perspective. On the other hand, French personalist communitarianism also challenges left-wing secularism to retain and incorporate a sense of the transcendent in their effort to effect social change.

The figure who not only represents this personalist communitarianism, but seeks to put in into action, is Emmanuel Mounier, who at the age of 27, founds the journal, *Esprit*, in 1932. Mounier leads a group of young French activists to articulate, through their journalism, an alternative to the atheistic materialism of the Marxists and the rigid, if not repressive, traditionalism of the fascists–in their words, to "remake the renaissance" (Mounier, "Refaire," 5). Throughout his life, Mounier is committed to dialogue with both the political left and right. During the Vichy regime, he coordinated an educational youth program hoping that the collapse of bourgeois order would create the opportunity to chart a new course for France and Europe in a personalist way. Ultimately though, he is imprisoned by the Vichy regime for supposedly working with the communists to overthrow the regime. Subsequently in the 1940s, Mounier's work becomes much more pluralistic in temperament. He turns to existentialism as a basis for people to envision the capacity to dream and realize new lives. Mounier died at the age of 45 in 1950, but his articulation of personalist communitarianism not only had an impact on political debates of 1930s & 40s France, but also on the U.S. Catholic Worker movement of the past century as well as Christian Democratic outlooks in Latin America. In many respects, his thought and work anticipate many of the themes of liberation theology, especially the preferential option for the poor, and the possibility, if not the urgency, for the articulation of Christian Left perspectives.

Mounier's contributions for contending with today's political divides are twofold: his distinction between the prophetic and political poles of action and his commitment to *engagement* as opposed to pure resistance. Going back to the *Old Testament*, prophets are absolutely essential for providing a critique of prevailing trends. Prophets call contemporary political partisans to assess critically contemporary events, from external, if not transcendental norms. On the other hand, the shortcoming of prophets, is that if their critique does not lead to a practical and achievable course of action, their normative stances become ethereal. These ideals become too detached from the nitty-gritty interchanges of politics (Mounier, *Personalism* 88–94).

The political poles of action, conversely, are the actual initiatives and deliberations that bring about public policy. It is nice to have ideals, but one has to know how to put them into practice. To give a contemporary example, global warming and climate change are very challenges, but the politics of initiating public policies across the globe to address these issues is a very sticky wicket. The shortcoming of politicians, however, is all too often, they lose sight of the norms for which these policies are initiated or simply become corrupted by the give and take of practical politics. One such example would be when legislation if passed or opposed by an elected representative merely for the sake of ensuring one's reelection. Mounier argues for "integral action" between these two poles of prophecy and politics (Mounier, *Personalism* 88–94).

Engagement for Mounier is the activist integration of these two poles of action. In his personalist communitarianism, it is insufficient simply to critique the dominant norms and structures of society or purely to resist them. Instead, we are called to roll up our sleeves and work with others to transform the political, socio-economic structures that impede the gifts and contributions of diverse persons and groups.

At the same time, Mounier's own engagement of French politics in the 1930s and 40s leaned more to the prophetic rather than the political pole. He never formed a political party, nor did he run for office. He relied on the journal *Esprit*, his scholarly works, his interaction with ideologues of all stripes, and the *Esprit* discussion circles and communities as a means of engaging politics.

In this regard, the connection between his personalist communitarianism and the US Catholic Worker tradition reveals a great deal. Catholic Worker houses in the United States, politically speaking, are a counterculture to politics as usual. Catholic workers tend to the poor and marginalized, which increasingly are migrants from Latin America and other places. In this regard, they manifest Christian works of mercy. This spirituality is informed very much by Catholic liturgy and piety and Catholic workers choose to embrace both material poverty and poverty of spirit. Their Christian anarchist model is an alternative to the capitalist, consumer-oriented politics that animates contemporary liberal democracies.

As much as the Catholic Worker movement provides an important counterpoint to what Mounier termed "the established disorder" (Mounier, "Manifesto" 46), this Christian anarchist model is not about to transform or supplant current liberal democracy, which was much more the aim of Mounier. But this outcome unfortunately also characterizes Mounier's vision. He envisioned society as a collection of personalist groups encompassed by a Christian understanding of reality—basically a 20th century "'an-archaic'" democratic recasting of a corporate guild society (Mounier, "Manifesto" 248).

As much as Mounier sought to counter the relativist and materialist character of French and European politics in the first half of the 20th century, his corporatist framework does not lend itself to cultivating a widespread moral community in the much more pluralistic politics of the 21st century. Worse yet, the communitarianism than animates his politics can too easily be twisted, contrary to his own intent, to fascism—for example, Peronism in Argentina and other analogues in 20th century Latin America and elsewhere. Instead, our task, I submit, is to revitalize, not reject, liberal democratic institutions, in the face of both assaults from an increasingly secular left and a religious nationalist right.

Luke Bretherton's Articulation of Democracy Through the Framework of *Secularity*

A contemporary US theologian whose ideas hold more promise in terms of articulating how secular and faith-based perspectives in tandem can revitalize liberal democracy is Luke Bretherton. Instead of secularism, he argues that we need to focus instead on secularity. He defines secularization as "a regime of liberal statecraft" (Bretherton, "Christ" 229). By contrast, secularity, as he sees it, is "a political good (Bretherton, "Christ" 229). Secularism, in his eyes, seeks to exclude religious traditions in its pursuit of politics and public policy. On the other hand, with secularity, multiple traditions seek, be they religious or secular, seek to foster a common life "amid difference, disagreement, and asymmetries of power" (Bretherton, "Christ" 229).

Rather than focusing on uniformity or homogeneity, a tendency somewhat evident in Mounier's personalism, secularity entails a commitment to plurality. On one level, Bretherton is building upon Hannah Arendt's insight that the human condition is one of plurality (Arendt 7–8). He is also seeking to foster a rich civil society that serves as a basis for personal expression and fulfillment and serves as a counterpoint to bureaucratic administrative states and the impersonal "hands" of economic markets. In this regard, Arendt emphasizes people discover who they are in the company of other people in the public realm. Bretherton, though, envisions this interaction as ensuing between people of different faith and philosophical traditions. Essentially, he argues, we share this world together; therefore, how through our respective philosophical and spiritual traditions can we cultivate a common good that does not culminate or deteriorate into "us v. them" or "my way or the highway" political arguments.

Bretherton's engagement of secularity has four key aspects. First, He emphasizes the outlook of the citizen over that of the consumer. Whereas the latter seeks material well-being and reduces other people and things to a cost-benefit analysis, the citizen cares about the public realm and grasps that one may have to sacrifice or compromise for the common good. Second, civil society, for Bretherton, is characterized by political judgement, not just serving the market or what is technologically efficient. Both the market and technocracy reduce human beings either to their economic transactions or their bureaucratic identities such as social security numbers or driver's licenses. Third, he maintains we need to learn from and live together with other people not like ourselves. Even before racial, ethnic, and religious diversity has come to comprise our political communities, diverse personalities have distinguished each of us from others. Not only do we need to navigate such divides in practical terms, we will likely grow through encountering the presumed stranger. Finally, Bretheron's articulation of secularity seeks to foster human and economic flourishing, not through a dog-eat-dog competition between people, but in the dynamics of people, despite their value differences, trying to cultivate a life in common (Bretherton, "Christ" 445–65).

The concrete case study Bretherton shares is how in London, diverse and secular groups came together to articulate a set of political goals, especially stressing the pursuit of a living wage. The organization that they formed, London Citizens, is connected to the Industrial Areas Foundation (IAF) originally founded by Saul Alinski. Alinski promoted and pursued working with people in church congregations to articulate the political needs they have for their surrounding neighborhoods and municipalities. In addition to Christian congregations, synagogues, mosques, or potentially any organized religious community, are fertile locales for mobilization. Nor are secular groups excluded as long as they are willing to work in common with their faith-based brethren on issues of common concern. IAF organizers have had great success actually in mobilizing Latinx congregations, in Texas and elsewhere, on how to effect political changes in school boards, city councils, and county commissions. In many of these faith-based communities, women, who otherwise might be just effective prayer group leaders, take this aptitude and through the training they received from IAF organizers to becoming political organizers. The capacity of Latinas to work through female networks—*madres, abuelas, tias,* and *hermanas*—has proven to be a very successful vehicle of political mobilization in the US Southwest. The current group, Angry *Tias and Abuelas*, in south Texas regarding immigration issues is a prime example.

The London coalition of groups, Bretherton shares, is not only focused on exterior political goals such as a living wage, but on creating a process in which representatives from distinct secular and faith-based commitments come to trust each other and work toward a common political goal. In mutually determining the rules by which they engage each other, they create a safe space in which then they can articulate their common goals and how best to pursue them, without any fear of being evangelized in a sectarian sense. Similarly, I have found in the work I have done on intercultural issues in faith-based communities, that if one establishes a set of boundaries to the discussion that were predictable, then it was unlikely that the ensuing discourse between diverse groups would degenerate into self-interested group politics.

Bretherton characterized this dynamic democracy by which diverse traditions come to foster a common life as a consociational democracy (Bretherton, "Resurrecting" 219). Basically, there are different groups in society that share a common concern. In the process of addressing how they mutually can work together to address this issue; these groups mutually develop a trust that not only leads to addressing the issue at hand but cultivates a commitment for caring for the political community. Unlike corporatist frameworks in which each sector of society has an organic role in the body politic coordinated by the state, consociational democracy thrives on a pluralism of philosophical and faith-based perspectives. Conversely, in contrast to self-interested group politics, these diverse heritages can come together to cultivate the political community that sustains each of them without such interaction culminating in uniformity.

Bretherton does support populism, but not of the variety that we have seen of late coming from the far right both in the US and in Europe. This latter type of populism, he argues, seeks to circumvent the give and take intrinsic to democratic political interaction. Instead, some demagogue seeks to eliminate checks and balances to speak for an undifferentiated PEOPLE. The populism Bretherton supports, and in this regard, he draws on the work of Arendt, Margaret Canovan, Bernard Crick, Ernesto Laclau, and Sheldon Wolin, is one steeped in the above plurality. Democratic populism acknowledges that we have to navigate conflict in the political worlds but do so in a way that is "a richer sense of what is the good of the whole body politic" (Bretherton, "Christ" 435). By contrast, with "antipolitical populism," one responsibility is solely to oneself and immediate surroundings, and not to the political institutions and processes "that make up the commonwealth on which all depend" (Bretherton, "Christ" 436).

It must be noted that IAF organizations, such as featured in Bretherton's case study, have not had much success in the United States at expanding their political mobilization beyond local politics to the regional or national politics. Nevertheless, the civil religion that Bretherton articulates brings both secular and faith-based groups together in a way that fosters relational politics built around the dynamic between values and politics. Bretherton's democratic populist seeks to enable the common good as a good in itself and yet has an appreciation for pluralism missing in Mounier's framework. Toward this end, a consociational rendering of democracy moves in-between suffocating uniformity and nihilistic chaos.

Martin Luther King Jr's "Beloved Community" and Virgil Elizondo's "Mestizo Spirituality"

On what sources can we draw upon within the US tradition, in addition to the IAF heritage, to pursue the ethos of either the personalistic communitarianism articulated by Mounier or the consociational democracy articulated by Bretherton? In this section, I will review the visions and actions of Martin Luther King, Jr. and Virgil Elizondo. This examination will not only give further insight into not only how to build bridges in our political life between diverse moral and spiritual perspectives, but it will also do so from the experience of longstanding marginalized communities—that of African Americans and US Latinx.

Martin Luther King, Jr.'s personalist perspective, both in word and deed, straddles the prophetic and political poles of action in his mobilization against racial segregation and discrimination. In particular, King effectively utilizes the Western philosophical and religious heritage as well as the founding ideals of the United States to advance the ends of the civil rights movement. Much in the vein of Bretherton's perspective, King does not seek to overthrow liberal democracy but to seek substantial necessary *inclusions* to realize its promises.

King does not reject the U.S. American political project but rather argues for inclusion on a basis in which African Americans or for that matter any marginalized group, do not have to leave their cultural heritages behind as the price of admission. Elements of King's writings and protests at times reminds one of Mounier and Bretherton. For King, our personality is what connects us to the divine. Therefore, our capacity for freedom, the fact that we are equal to each other, and that we have rights, all derive from God's choice to create the world. As opposed to an atomism that puts irreparable gaps between people, humans in a personalist way are fundamentally called to community life. (Gorski 155–56; Brooks). In King's own words: "We caught in an inescapable network of mutuality, tied in a single garment of destiny" (King, "Letter" 597).

At the same time, rather that rejecting longstanding U.S. political ideals, King extensively draws upon faith-based and philosophical arguments from these heritages to advance democratic inclusion. For example, in the "Letter from a Birmingham City Jail," he cites Socrates, Augustine, and Aquinas to justify civil disobedience in the face of unjust laws. In the "I Have a Dream Speech," he praises "the magnificent words of the U.S. Constitution and the Declaration of Independence" and passionately employs the lyrics of the hymn, "My Country 'Tis of Thee" to "let freedom ring" (King, "I Have" 602–4).

Unlike religious nationalists who uncritically embrace these norms, King makes it clear that the promises of the U.S. Founding documents were a "promissory note" that the country had not yet fulfilled in regard to people of color (King, "I Have," 602). Hence, he concludes that we need to overcome repressive practices and structures so as to bring about a country in which "all of God's children, black men and white men, Jews and Gentiles, Protestants and Catholics, will be able to join hands and sing in the words of the old Negro spiritual, "Free at last, Free at last, Great God a-mighty, We are free at last'" (King, "I Have," 604).

However, King's legacy is not just prophetic, for he engages in concrete political confrontations with exclusionary political, social, and economic structures and this especially distinguishes him from Mounier. King had a learning curve in this regard. In the early stages of his civil rights activism, he thought he could persuade the oppressor to abandon their unjust ways and therefore move toward realizing a more just community. King and his fellow organizers come to realize in time they had to stage nonviolent protests where it would be met by extremely violent actions by Southern local law enforcement actions. Such violence would in turn bring nationwide media coverage regarding the subjugation of oppressed African Americans. In contrast to just pure prophetic critique, the nonviolent resistance practiced by the civil right organizers sought to widen the conflict beyond local Southern communities to the nation as a whole. This expansion would generate political pressure that would affect major political and economic changes. Indeed, the very successful campaigns led by King and the Southern Christian Leadership Conference in Birmingham (1963), and Selma (1965) ultimately lead to the Civil Rights Act of 1964 and the Voting Rights Act of 1965 (Garrow, 212–36).

King's political realism is indebted to the theology of Reinhold Niebuhr. Niebuhr, as a young preacher, vehemently criticized Henry Ford's corporate practices and lent support to union organizers of auto workers seeking justice. Niebuhr cautions, though, that due to the capacity for love of self in our human wills, power politics is an integral part of human life. Consequently, protest movements have to develop concrete strategies to counter the norms and conduct of the prevailing order—a lesson upon which King draws. He also derives from Niebuhr, reservations about the "children of light" who naively think that the move toward human emancipation will automatically unfold in history and conversely the "children of darkness" who reduce everything to power politics and therefore reject appeals to conscience (Niebuhr). The former, Niebuhr contends, are blind to the degree pridefulness can infect their pursuit of good intentions, whereas the latter are only too willing to impose their will-to-power on others.

King's overall vision, tempered by Niebuhr's realism, is that of "the beloved community:" But the end is reconciliation; the end is redemption; the end is the creation of the beloved community. It is this type of spirit and this type of love that can transform opposers into friends. It is this type of understanding goodwill that will transform the deep gloom of the old age into the exuberant gladness of the new age. It is this love which will bring about miracles in the hearts of men (King, "Facing" 140). As Bryan Massingale notes, the beloved community is a vision of human interaction that calls each of us to welcome the others as full participants in the political, social, and economic decision-making networks (Massingale 2010, 141).

The beloved community, has at least four components, as articulated by Kenneth Smith and Ira Zepp. First, personal and community development ensues through interrelationships. Consequently, King advocates for integration as opposed to just desegregation so as to cultivate community and solidarity between racial groups: "America must be a nation in which its multiracial people are partners in power" (King, "Where" 54). Second, we must strive for a society which seeks to eliminate racism and domination over poor people. Specifically, King states: "it is not the race [white] per se that we fight, but the policies and ideology that leaders of that race have formulated to perpetuate oppression" (King, "The Trumpet" 9).

Third, racial equality will never be achieved as long as economic inequality of income and wealth is based on race. Toward this end, King, long before Andrew Yang, proposes a guaranteed minimum income for people (King, "Where" 87). Fourth and finally, King shares that though the beloved community is yet be realized, he emphasizes that God works with us in our political struggles toward its realization: "With this faith we will be able to work together, to pray together, to struggle together, to go to jail together, to stand up for freedom together, knowing that one day we will be free" (King, "I Have" 604).

In summary, like Mounier, King in his political theology and civil rights activism prophetically challenges the established political order. But rather than simply rejecting the dominant political norms of "the established disorder," his activism is closer to Bretherton's articulation of a consociational democracy in that he seeks ways through nonviolent resistance to recast the norms of US liberal democracy so as to realize their full promise. Moreover, both in the voter rights campaign in Selma for voting rights and the subsequent "Poor People's Campaign," he organized an interracial and interreligious coalition that confronted structural injustice and proposed programs that would seek to realize political and economic justice.

King's exquisite rhetorical use of Western, American, and Christian ideals is an animated lived language of civil religion that seeks to eliminate exclusionary practices on the basis of race, ethnicity, or class in US democracy. As much as this civil religion resembles civil discourse between secular and religious people put forth by Bretherton, King is able to stage successful protests that culminate in major pieces of federal legislation that change forever the landscape of US political, social, and economic life. His integration of the prophetic and political poles of action moves beyond just the local level.

At first glance, King's beloved community may seem rather idyllic, not unlike the rather harmonious communitarianism put forth by Mounier, yet it is steeped, via Augustine and Niebuhr, in a sense of proximate justice. A political movement inspired by a just cause, needs also to have prudent objectives and tactics to realize their just ends. Again, as Niebuhr stresses, conflict is an integral part of human affairs due to the human preoccupation with self-love. Therefore, the steadfast pursuit of a proximate, not absolute, justice is what we can realistically hope to achieve—in Christian terms, the space in-between "the already" and the "not yet."

In the U.S. Southwest, Virgil Elizondo articulates the beloved community through the Latinx experience of *mestizaje*—being caught in-between cultures. *Mestizaje* has had a controversial history. Originally, it referred to the mixture of the Spanish conquistadors and their indigenous subjects in the conquest of what is now Latin America. Unfortunately, during the Latin American colonial period, it was articulated as a "whitening" or uplifting of indigenous and African persons to European standards. On the other hand, more recently, during the Chicano and other US Latinx movements, activists recast the concept so as to identify more with their indigenous heritage as a form of resistance to white domination, captured especially by Corky González's "I Am Joaquín."

Elizondo's rendering of cultural mixing, especially, in his autobiography, *The Future is Mestizo*, moves in-between solely identifying with either the oppressor or the oppressed. In his reflections, on the subjugation of Mexican Americans in the U.S. Southwest, he does acknowledge pervasive Anglo domination: "Anglo-American society has no doubts that it was the Master Race! Indians, Mexican half-breeds, and blacks were inferior and therefore to be keep down for the good of humanity" (Elizondo, 21). Especially in the first half of this text, he also shares numerous examples of how Mexican Americans have been historically subjugated in the United States and have consequently internalized a "disabling" sense of shame about their background (Elizondo 128).

At the same time, similar to Martin Luther King, Jr., Elizondo invokes U.S. ideals as something yet to be realized:

> If we had defeated the genetically pure "Master Race" in Germany and Japan, now we had to defeat the "Master Race" concept within our own USA so that authentic Americanism—freedom and justice for all and the right to the pursuit of happiness— could be truly be enjoyed by all the citizens of the land and not just the WASPish whites. (Elizondo 34)

Toward this end, again like King, Elizondo suggests that God intends for us to live in mutual interrelatedness: "Segregation . . . is a sin against the Creator who made all of us descendants of Adam and Eve" (Elizondo 55).

Not unlike W.E.B. DuBois' articulation of the "double-consciousness" that African Americans face in being both African and American (DuBois 456), Elizondo articulates Mexican American identity as being both Mexican and American. And unlike those who dwell on the indigenous heritage as a form of resistance to the dominant European culture, Elizondo envisions a lateral *mestizaje* in which the European-American, Mexican American, and other U.S. cultural communities engage and transform each as equal without culminating in uniformity defined by any one of these communities. Indeed, he contends that white and Latinx cultures are increasing transforming each other: "both are forming a new human space wherein all feel more at home" (Elizondo, 56).

Ultimately though, Elizondo's political theology is a critique of philosophical and spiritual celebrations of purity: "In his existence, Jesus was the antithesis of all human quests for "'purity,' which in effect lead to segregation, degradation, exploitation, and death" (Elizondo 80). In great detail, he cites Our Lady of Guadalupe and Jesus as moral exemplars of mixing (Elizondo 57–86), as well as political and spiritual liberation (Elizondo,57–86). Beyond just empirical mixing though, Elizondo articulates an ethos of embracing racial, religious, and cultural mixture as edifying: "What needs to change radically is the social appreciation of *mestizaje* from that of being a pariah to that of being a gift" (Elizondo 130). In so doing, he suggests, we enable the realization of "a united family of the planet earth" (Elizondo 111).

Elizondo, in comparison to King, does not have the same extensive record in print of staging civil rights protests or putting forward public policy programs—the political pole of action. At the same time, he was a very institutional person. He was one of the founders of the Mexican American Cultural Center (MACC) in San Antonio. For several decades, MACC provided a space through which clergy and laity could come together in liturgical celebrations and pastoral and political theology on how to foster inclusive faith-based and political communities. During his time as rector of San Fernando Cathedral in San Antonio, Texas, comprised primarily of Mexican Americans and US Latinx, this parish manifested vibrant popular religiosity, liturgical experimentation, and spirit-filled inclusion. Essentially, as the "dean" of US Latinx theologians in the 1980s and 90s, he mentored and created opportunities for scholars and pastoral ministers involved in intercultural ministry and in the grassroots pursuit of politics and theology envisioned in the Vatican II document, *Gaudium et Spes*.

Elizondo also had political savvy. In *The Future is Mestizo*, he shares that back in the mid-1960s, he was very excited by Lyndon Johnson's Great Society programs. Taking advantage of these new programs, as a priest in a country parish, he intended to establish a job training program for the youth. Yet the parents of these same youth asked him not to do so, because in all likelihood, members of their community would disappear through retaliation by the white landowners who controlled the dominant power structure. Ultimately, he opted not to push for the jobs program, not as matter of surrender, but of anticipating that moment when "the ultimate liberation of the people" could realistically be realized (Elizondo 31).

Without a doubt, Elizondo's initiatives do not lead to major political and social transformations in comparison to King. Nevertheless, Elizondo, in his scholarship and ministry, does integrate the prophetic and political poles of action. In terms of the prophetic pole, his recasts *mestizaje* as a *lateral* mixing of cultures as opposed to the dominant culture "uplifting" the subjugated culture or conversely the subjugated "resisting" the dominant culture. In terms of the political pole, he expands the institutions and forums through which participants can learn both the pastoral and civic skills that are essential for participating in the civic discourse between diverse groups articulated by Bretherton.

The Beloved Community as A Subtle Assimilation?

Critics within the African American and Latinx theological communities have taken to task sanguine articulations of U.S. intercultural relations within theology that do not take sufficiently into account the power dynamics of white privilege. These critics contend that such calls for integration, such as King's beloved community or Elizondo's rendering of *mestizaje* are actually a subtle form of assimilation.

For example, James Cone in *Black Theology and Black Power* and later *A Black Theology of Liberation*, is highly critical of the integration ethos of the African America Civil Rights Movement. First, he suggests that "all whites were responsible for white oppression" (Dorrien 449). Second, he contends black theology was principally for and responsible to the black community. Third, the acid test for Cone of black theology is whether it connects to the life experiences of subjugated blacks and then, in turn, it leads to black liberation. Finally, as Gary Dorrien notes perceptively, this liberation accountability test has "gained wide currency as the defining principle of Latin American, feminist, and other liberationist theologians" (Dorrien 455).

In turn, Nestor Medina's critique of Elizondo work in *Mestizaje: Remapping Race, Culture, and Faith in Latina/o Catholicism of Elizondo is two-fold*. First, he contends that Elizondo does not recognize how historically in Latin America the discourse on *mestizaje* has privileged the European or white over the African or indigenous components of the mixing. Elizondo, according to Medina, overlooks the political power dynamics of intermixture. Second, Medina argues Elizondo universal rendering of *mestizaje* as hybridity or inclusivity detaches *mestizaje* from its notorious Latin American history (Medina, *Mestizaje* 33–35). The net consequence of such sanguine articulations of mestizaje has been to erase the identities and in some instances the very lives, of African, Asian, indigenous, and Latinx peoples (Hidalgo, "Adelante" 203–4).

Given MLK Jr's untimely death in 1968, his assessment of such separatist arguments is limited. But we can also take some cues from King's thoughts about the Black Power Movement of the late 1960s to project his thoughts on the matter. It should be noted that some of the writings I am drawing from could very well have been written by some of his key advisors in the civil rights movement under his name. First, King opposes separatism on the grounds that it was unrealistic and no "salvation" would issue forth from "isolation" (King, "Where" 48). Second, given that African Americans are both African and American, he added that they needed to work with other Americans to realize "a nation in which its multiracial people are partners in power" (King, "Where" 54). In this regard, he is echoing W.E.B. Du Bois's double consciousness. Third, King, although he understands the justification for the urban riots of the mid-to-late 1960s, ultimately insists violence of this variety is an act of futility and does not lead to the "concrete improvements" brought about by organized non-violent mobilizations (King, "Where 58). Fourth, King fears that protestors motivated by malice, hate, and violence would not only end up mimicking the conduct of "our oppressors," but that this hatred would "corrode" the personalities and souls of the protestors (King, "Where" 64). Here he draws upon Niebuhr's accent on the impact of human pridefulness.

In turn, Elizondo in an epilogue to the revised edition of *The Future is Mestizaje*, acknowledges, that at times he insufficiently discussed the negative side of *mestizaje* in Latin American history: "I did not dwell sufficiently with the negative and soul-destructive aspects of the medieval *mestizaje* of Spain, the *mestizaje* of Latin America and of our own *mestizaje* process within the United States" (Elizondo 119). At the same time, this recognition does not alter Elizondo's conviction that the prevailing political system has to be transformed in order for the previous relationship between conqueror and conquered to realize a genuinely inclusive democracy. One has to move beyond the domination—resistance binary to lateral mutual engagement between equals.

The drawback of adopting solely a resistance stance to hegemonic cultural domination, as do the early Cone and Medina, is to overlook the interconnectedness of human beings across heritages. As much as some thinkers revel in deconstructing universals or claim that theologies such as King's or Elizondo's are too inscribed by the dominant culture, these same critics end up thinkers unfortunately *reifying* and petrifying *particular* heritages as an alternative. This petrification, ironically, is a consequence of remaining mired in the prophetic pole of action.

Moreover, the history of conflict embedded within the respective legacies of slavery and *mestizaje* is precisely why these heritages need to be in the discourse regarding how to have a liberal democracy that genuinely enables diverse peoples, cultures, and faiths to create a just society in concert. Medina acknowledges as much: "the debates of *mestizaje* offer great insight for understanding the power relations and dynamics at play when cultural groups encounter each other under asymmetrical conditions" (Medina, *Mestizaje* 142).

Undoubtedly, critiques by African American and U.S. Latinx separatists are vital for ensuring that the vision and practices of the beloved community not lapse into a cozy Kumbaya fellowship. Still, the almost allergic reaction of some faith-based advocates of resistance to notions of fostering unity or community is perilous. Fostering dialogue between distinct racial, ethic, and religious groups is qualitatively different than imposing uniformity. The latter is indeed a dominating politics of assimilation. Civic dialogue, as Bretherton documents in his London case study, can be cultivated through intersubjective personal relationships and intercultural encounters however flawed by present inequalities. Such dialogue does not necessarily eradicate particular heritages, nor does it culminate in homogeneous community.

In addition, liberation movements can too easily degenerate into another oppressive power structures if they do not grasp, as Niebuhr suggests, how easily our best of intentions can be contorted by our willfulness into becoming just another form of domination. Without a commitment to what we share in common as human beings, well-intended attempts to transform unjust power structures can easily degenerate into an agonal us v. them politics—Samuel Huntington's "clash of civilizations."

No, when prevailing political socio-economic structures privilege some groups over others, political action indeed needs to be taken so that democratic discourse and interaction comes closer and closer to being one between equals. None of King's or Elizondo's critics, have achieved the legislative and/or institutional accomplishments that they did. At some point, prophetic critique has to lead to achievable political action, lest it become just another fool's paradise. Even a critic as well-known as Gloria Anzaldúa, acknowledges, that "it is not enough to stand on opposite" riverbanks; one has to cross the cultural divide on to way "to a new consciousness" (Anzaldúa 100).

In the end, the difficulty with assimilation schemes is that they erase the space through which mutuality ensues. The difficulty with separatist schemes is they petrify identities and strive to barricade participants from doing the hard work of transforming structures of domination so as foster a space where mutuality can ensue. Both Bretherton's case study of London Citizens and King's multiracial mobilizations illustrate how multiple secular and faith-based communities alike can come together can bring about substantial legal and political change.

The Intersectional Dimension

The truth is many scholars, within the African American, US Latinx, and other racial/ethnic cultural circles realm of people of color are moving in-between the opposition between assimilation and separatism. Bretherton, for example, cites how contemporary Black scholars such as Tommie Shelby and Cornel West, and the later James Cone, put forth a vision of the future that "does not require territorial separation, a homogenous, or even a shared [separatist] consciousness" (Bretherton, "Christ" 103). West, in particular, stresses that pursuing a more inclusive democracy entails African Americans forming alliances with Latinx, Asians, American Indians, and European Americans (West in Bretherton, "Christ" 104). Toward this end, Angela Davis suggests, notably, that the basis of the mobilization against oppressive politics needs to be grounded in politics, rather than "the politics on identity" (Davis in Bretherton, "Christ"104).

Womanist and *feminista/mujerista* authors also suggest that issues of class, gender, and sexuality are interwoven into race politics and therefore an intersectional approach to achieving justice needs to be pursued. Such a sensibility also entails putting a critical eye to one's own community. For example, Jacqueline Hidalgo in *Revelation in Aztlán* emphasizes, how in the early stages of the Chicano movement, feminist and queer perspectives were subjected to marginalization and domination (Hidalgo, "Revelation"172–73). In feminist contexts, both Audre Lorde and Ada María Isasi-Díaz respectively challenge the way European American feminists all too often set and dominate the terms of feminist discourse (Isasi-Díaz18–19, Lorde 393–95). To borrow a phrase from Lorde, what has one gained if "the tools of a racist patriarchy are used to examine the fruits of that same patriarchy" (Lorde 393). Liberation movements criticizing terms of engagement which privilege one group of people over another have to also examine whether within their movement, there are actually other patterns of domination that need to be recognized and changed.

In terms of fostering a beloved community, these intersectionality scholars are each accenting that fostering relationships of mutuality has multiple vectors. These relationships of mutuality are indeed affected, and at times, disabled, by power relationships of race, ethnicity, gender, sexual orientation, and spirituality among other categories.

A very promising political theology in this regard is Nicole Flores' *The Aesthetics of Solidarity*. Building on the aesthetic orientation of Alejandro Garcia-Rivera's theology, Flores contends that Our Lady of Guadalupe articulates a solidarity that fosters the equality, mutuality, and participation essential for "fostering a just democracy" (Flores 27). As Flores shares, Guadalupe's interaction with Juan Diego enables him to realize his own dignity, both through the aesthetics of the encounter and through her enabling of putting truth to power. However, such liberation, Flores contends, is not just for the past, but as a sensibility for enabling the marginalized to resist contemporary "colonization, slavery, and segregation" (Flores 37).

The heart of her work is a critique of a liberal aesthetics that she contends cannot foster the pursuit of solidarity in a pluralistic democracy. In particular, she critiques the work of John Rawls and Martha Nussbaum. She finds that Rawls' exclusion of spiritual values and discourse from deliberation on the principles of justice to be very problematic. Flores contends that Rawls' reduction of the political role of religion to religious violence ignores the "potential role of religious traditions in undermining violence" (Flores, 65). In Nussbaum's case, Flores is drawn to the integral role of emotions to fostering public life. Unfortunately, Nussbaum's "'civic poetry'" Flores finds too limiting because it precludes non-Western "art, literature, and music that . . . can be legitimately engaged in the formation of political emotions" (Nussbaum in Flores, 96–97). In particular, Flores accents that Nussbaum too easily excludes the critical role of rage manifested in the Black Lives Matter Movement. Ultimately, she concludes that both Nussbaum and Rawls limit political discourse to traditions that are too narrow and largely, Eurocentric.

Flores's articulation of how aesthetic spiritual encounters can forge community across social purposes is very cogent. Her criticism of liberal ethical and political discourses that exclude faith-based and non-European perspectives is spot on. In this regard, she is a kindred spirit to Mounier, Bretherton, Martin Luther King Jr., and Elizondo. Finally, she also provides several examples of specific groups that have effectively drawn upon aesthetics to further social justice—the political pole of action (Flores 131–36).

On the other hand, at times, her argument too easily subscribes into Medina's argument that the discourse over *mestizaje* erases "the genuine racial, cultural, and religious differences inherent in Latine identity" (Flores 118). Again, as accented above, if one becomes too preoccupied with countering erasure perpetrated by a dominant group against a marginalized community, the very space through which the intersection of differences that can create a rich, dynamic political community is never entered. Helpful, in this regard is Bretherton's contention that unlike "hybridity, nomadism, and fugitivity" which lacks a sense of a common space, both in terms of a specific place and over generations, "*mestizaje/mulatez* and *neplanta* recognize the possibilities of a common life or *convivencia* while contending that one voice or culture cannot determine it, and any form of shared life must attend to the brutal histories that inevitably form its backdrop"

(Bretherton, "Christ" 318). Flores comes closer to this outlook when she suggests, once one puts more stress on differences rather than unification, it becomes possible to pursue "a vision for the common good" based not on "oneness," but on "wholeness" (Flores 118).

In addition, Flores's criticism of Nussbaum for insufficiently grasping how vital emotions are to moral and political discourse, such as rage, are integral to strategies of pursuing justice is quite valid (Flores, 90). At the same time, as shown by the protests organized by King and the Southern Christian Leadership Conference, if such legitimate rage leads to violent riots by protestors, it loses the support of many Americans and thus any hope of bringing about legislation addressing the oppressions that incite such rage (Garrow 212–36). The focal point of the protest should be exposing the underlying violence structural. Without a concrete protest strategy, cognizant of what will and will not gain nationwide public support, righteous rage in-and-of-itself will often prove politically counter-productive.

Hidalgo's work on scriptures, utopias, and the Chicano movement, in turn, further develops the notion of cultural intersections that neither eliminate differences nor petrify them. She articulates the notion of Aztlán as "pliable, fluid, dynamic, and contested" (Hidalgo, "Revelation" 202). Whereas Flores relies on García-Rivera, Hidalgo draws from the work of Fernando Segovia. Specifically, Flores stresses Segovia's contention that we resist the temptation as scholars to perpetrate a comprehensive perspective. Instead, she insists "the experiences of living caught between worlds . . . forces many of us to recognize the constructedness of those multiple worlds, the possibilities and flaws of such constructions, and the necessity of perceiving the particularity of one's own" (Hidalgo, "Revolution" 271). Given the multiple power relationships highlighted by intersectionality, both Hidalgo and Flores ultimately illustrate that political spaces forever need to be reconstructed continually by the intersection of particular narratives, many of which were previously excluded.

Engagement, Not Just Resistance

At the outset of this essay, I outlined three key considerations for revitalizing a civil religion, especially in the context of the United States, which could be a constructive alternative to a secular humanism that does not permit faith-based arguments and religious nationalisms that are too ready to impose faith-based norms on others. First, unity needs to be balanced with diversity. Second, the prophetic and political poles of action need to be in integral relationship. And finally, any critiques of the prevailing political order, need to be committed to concrete strategies of engagement, and not just resistance.

After finding Mounier's personalist communitarianism too corporatist to be a model for such a civil religion, I have shown how Bretherton's depiction of secularity and Martin Luther King Jr's articulation of the beloved community lead to an inclusive civil religion. Secular and faith-based sources are mutual contributors to this community. Diverse groups are integral to bringing about a unity which is continually reconsidered. These prophetic norms in turn lead to political action that actually reshape political, socio-economic networks so as to become more inclusive and democratic. Subsequent insights post-King by figures such as Cornel West, Jacqueline Hidalgo, and Nicole Flores pinpoint that the vision of the beloved community needs to be recast by intersectional power considerations. Still, out of all the scholars I have reviewed, Bretherton and King are the ones that illustrate *specific* concrete strategies on how to engage in political transformations.

Undoubtedly, the beloved community needs to be updated from its origins in the 1960s protest era. Indeed, Eddie Glaude has called for a "Third American Founding" that in true democratic fashion sets aside pernicious notions like a "shining city of a hill" or "the redeemer nation" that all too often have served as normative justifications for slavery, genocide (of American Indians), genetic experiments on people of color, and policies that either have fostered forced assimilation—the Indian Christian schools or exclusion—the Chinese Exclusion Act (Glaude 202–3). In this regard, Donald Trump's backward-looking "make America great again" has a lot of deleterious historical antecedents.

Whereas John Courtney Murray could confidently claim six decades ago that there were truths in common between the Jewish, Catholic, and Protestant traditions that provided a civic forum by which diverse creeds and philosophies could argue over politics and public policy, today political discourse ensues in a much more dissonant, postmodern universe. A unity-in-diversity perspective faces polemical resistance from both the political left and right. The almost allergic reaction of those on the left to notions of fostering unity or community is perilous. By the same token, the too-ready embrace of uniformity by those on the right is suffocating.

Frankly, in personalist terms, pursuing unity is different from imposing uniformity. The latter is indeed a dominating politics of assimilation. In turn, a personalist recognition of diversity in distinct from rigid separatist articulations of cultural identity. Unity-in-diversity, rather, is cultivated through pluralistic, intersubjective personal relationships and intercultural encounters, however flawed and incomplete due to prevailing inequalities and dominations.

Pursuing a beloved community in an age of deep moral cleavages may very well prove utopian. However, King never gave up on working toward the promises of U.S. democracy in his critique of prevailing injustices. The ideals of the beloved community, calls each of us to envision and pursue, a political community characterized by egalitarian relationships between diverse faiths, races, and ethnicities. Toward this end, we need to engage and transform prevailing unjust political socio-economic structures and relationships to enable diverse persons and groups to enrich our shared community life with their respective gifts—an ethos that Emmanuel Mounier projected almost a century ago and which increasingly is articulated in this country with a Mesoamerican verve.

Bibliography

Angry *Tías and Abuelas*. 2022. Available online: https://www.angrytiasandabuelas.com/

Anzaldúa, Gloria. *Borderlands: La Frontera: The New Mestiza*. Fourth Edition. San Francisco, CA: Aunt Lute Books, 2012.

Arendt, Hannah. *The Human Condition*. Chicago: University of Chicago Press, 1958.

Bretherton, Luke. *Christ and the Moral Life: Political Theology and the Case for Democracy*. Grand Rapids, MI: Ww. B. Eerdmans, 2019.

Bretherton, Luke. *Resurrecting Democracy: Faith, Citizenship, and the Politics of a Common Life*. New York, Cambridge University Press, 2015.

Brooks, David. "Personalism: The Philosophy We Need." *The New York Times*. 2018. Available online: https://www.nytimes.com/2018/06/14/opinion/personalism-philosophy-collectivism-fragmentation.html .

Cone, James. *Black Theology and Black Power*. Maryknoll, NY: Orbis Press, 2019.

——. *A Black Theology of Liberation*. Maryknoll, NY: Orbis Press, 2020.

Dorrien, Gary. *Breaking White Supremacy: Martin Luther King, Jr. and the Black Social Gospel*. New Haven, CT: Yale University Press, 2018.

DuBois, W.E.B. "The Souls of Black Folk." in *American Political Thought: Readings and Materials*. Editor Keith E. Whittington. NY: Oxford University Press, 2017, 456–61.

Elizondo, Virgilio. *The Future is Mestizo: Life Where Cultures Meet*. Revised Edition. Boulder, CO: University of Colorado Press, 2000.

Faggioli, Massimo. *Joe Biden and Catholicism in the United States*. Translated by Barry Hudock. New London, CT, 2021.

Flores Nicole. *The Aesthetics of Solidarity: Our Lady of Guadalupe and American Democracy*. Washington, D.C.: Georgetown University Press, 2021.
Garrow, David. *Protest at Selma*. New Haven, CT: Yale University Press, 1978.
Gaudium et Spes. 1965. Available online: https://www.vatican.va/archive/hist_councils/ii_vatican_council/documents/vat-ii_const_19651207_gaudium-et-spes_en.html .
Glaude, Jr., Eddie S. *Begin Again: James Baldwin's American and Its Urgent Lesson for Our Own*. New York: Crown, 2020.
González, Rodolfo Corky. "I Am Joaquín," Available online: https://www.latinamericanstudies.org/latinos/joaquin.htm
Gorski, Philip. *American Covenant: A History of Civil Religion from the Puritans to the Present*. Princeton, NJ: Princeton University Press, 2017.
Hidalgo, Jacqueline M. "*Adelante* in Difference: Latinxs in the Age of Trump." In *Faith and Resistance in the Age of Trump*. Editor Miguel A. De La Torre. Maryknoll, NY: Orbis Press, 200–7.
———. *Revelation in Aztlán: Scriptures, Utopias, and the Chicano Movement*. Palgrave Macmillan, 2016.
Huntington, Samuel P. *The Clash of Civilizations*. New York: Touchstone, 1996.
Isasi-Díaz, Ada María. *Mujerista Theology*. Maryknoll, NY, 1996.
King Jr., Martin Luther. *The Trumpet of Conscience*. New York: Harper and Row, 1967.
———. *Where Do We Go from Here: Chaos or Community?* New York: Harper and Row, 1967.
———. "Facing the Challenges of a New Age." In *A Testament of Hope: The Essential Writings of Martin Luther King, Jr*. Edited by James Melvin Washington. New York: Harper & Row, 1986, 135–51.
———. "I Have a Dream Speech." In *American Political Thought: Readings and Materials*. Edited by Keith E. Whittington. New York: Oxford University Press, 2017, 602–4.
———. "Letter from a Birmingham City Jail." In *American Political Thought: Readings and Materials*. Edited by Keith E. Whittington. New York: Oxford University Press, 2017, 597–601.
London Citizens. 2022. Available online: https://www.citizensuk.org/chapters/london/
Lorde, Audre. "The Master's Tools." in *Twentieth Century Political Theory: A Reader*. Second Edition. Edited by Stephen Eric Bronner. NY: Routledge, 2006, 393–95.
Massingale, Bryan. *Racial Justice and the Catholic Church*. Maryknoll, NY: Orbis Press, 2010.
Medina, Néstor. *Christianity, Empire, and the Spirit: Reconfiguring Faith and Culture*. Boston: Brill, 2018.
———. *Mestizaje: (Re)mapping Race, Culture, and Faith in Latina/o Catholicism*. Maryknoll, NY: Orbis Press, 2009.

Mounier, Emmanuel. *Personalism*. Translated by Philip Mairet. Notre Dame, IN: University of Notre Dame Press, 1952.
———. *A Personalist Manifesto*. Translated by Monks of St. John's Abbey. New York: Longman, Green, and Company, 1938.
———. "*Refaire La Renaissance*." Esprit. Vol. 1, No. 1 (*Octobre* 1932): 5–51.
Murray, SJ, John Courtney. *We Hold These Truths: Catholic Propositions on the America Proposition*. New York: Sheed & Ward, 1960.
Niebuhr, Reinhold. *The Children of Light and the Children of Darkness*. Chicago: University of Chicago Press, 2011.
Smith, Kenneth L. and Ira G. Zepp, Jr. 2020. "Martin Luther King's Vision of the Beloved Community." Religion Online. 2020. Available online: https://www.religion-online.org/article/martin-luther-kings-vision-of-the-beloved-community/
Zepp, Jr., Ira G. *The Social Vision of Martin Luther King, Jr.* New York: Carlson Publishing, Inc., 1989.
Zwick, Mark and Louise Zwick. *The Catholic Worker Movement: Intellectual & Spiritual Origins*. New York: Paulist Press, 2005.

PART III

Rites, Rituals and Indigenous Religions for Control of Physical Space, Real & Fictional

Introduction to Rites, Rituals & Indigenous Religions for Control of Physical Space, Real & Fictional

Environment & Nature. Myth & Geography. Sacred & Secular. Indigenous & Conqueror-Imposed

Part III of this eighth volume in the series has come full-circle, emphasizing efforts for control-of-physical-space from some of humans' earliest periods (which may continue contemporarily in different configurations and/or purposes), whether the art represents documentation, the simple beauty of décor—or perhaps as historically "one of the most popular of the sympathetic magic theories," the "magical" aspect of controlling or influencing reality, whether animals, the hunt for food in the cave art featured on the front cover of the first volume, *Body*, or other religious contexts. This reproduction of one of the multiple negative human hand stencils from the Paleolithic period, located specifically in *Cueva El Castillo*, one of about a dozen caves near Puente Viesgo in the north central Spanish province of Cantabria . . . arguably some of the earliest European visual representations of the body (of animals as well as humans). Thus, this hand is one of the first "selfies," among other cave art body representations in both hemispheres of the Hispanic world over the ages.[1]

What the motives or purposes or combinations of same behind these prehistoric representations may be debatable but each possibility includes some degree of control, whether over space itself, preserving documentation or projected outcomes in physical, psychological and/or religious settings.

Clearly, Jeanne Gillespie, whose academic specialty is everything which was real-life Aztec religion, ceremonies, gods, etc., emphasizes indigenous control efforts in all of her chapters over the eight-book series, as her titles reveal. For example, in *Body*, her three chapter titles make the intended power of the rites, rituals and religious overlay clear: *The Body and Indigenous Control of Environment. The Fluids of Life: Blood, Water, Power and Bugs à la Tlaxcalteca*; *The Body Cured by Cleansing: Washing Away the Evidence: Midwives and Ritual Cleansing in Mesoamerica and Colonial New Spain*; and *The Body Cured by Plants: Where have all the (Chocolate and Popcorn) Flowers Gone? Recovering Healing Botanicals in Nahuatl Poetry*. Her chapter in the eighth volume continues that focus, *Sacred Geography and Gendered Ritual Violence as Social Control in Anahuac*.

The next two chapters in this part also deal with attempted control of physical space via indigenous efforts, those spaces which still are, and have been, important to the indigenous populations and their religious beliefs. However, these chapters are based on the interpretation of those spaces in literary works—and the applicability of indigenous legends and myths in those modern works, while focusing on previously not-as-common geographic areas, emphasizing physical place, for this book series, i.e., the South American Andes. Haiqing Sun's *A Literary Mystery to Solution: The Andean Rituals in Lituma* addresses the Peruvian Andes and how the indigenous legends from there figure in the efforts by a detective, a novel by Nobel Prize winner, Mario Vargas Llosa (interestingly, admittedly a "new" focus for the writer himself, in spite of his nationality, as he confesses—but not totally without explanation, as he was raised elsewhere due to his father's government positions). Elizabeth White Coscio's *Mythic Consciousness and Sacred Space in the Works of the Bolivian Poet, Óscar Cerruto* concentrates on indigenous myth in the Bolivian Andes as portrayed in Cerruto's poems.

Both contributors have participated in past volumes, though Sun's chapters have focused on various other countries and genres: films from Mexico and China: *Family, Food & Fighting: A Comparative Study of the Mexican Film, 'Como agua para chocolate,' directed by Alfonso Arau, and the Chinese Film, 'Eat Drink Man Woman,' directed by Ang Lee* first published in *Family, Friends & Foes* and reprinted in *Sustenance; China and 'Chinago:' Globalization of the Kung Fu Genre and the Interpretation of Hero and History* in *Crossroads*. A related, at least in terms of Southern Cone and detective fiction, chapter she has written focuses on Argentina but her interest in mystery genre: *Vision & Confession: The Murder Mysteries by Jorge Luis Borges* from *Death & Dying*.

A mystery behind a mystery is part of Vargas Llosa's combination of criminal case and Andean ritual in Sun's chapter for *Rites, Rituals & Religions*. As *is* usual in the author's works, socio-political reality plays a major role, in this case, underlying the crime—but in the unique sense of both modern Perú and its pre-Conquest history. The detective is a "stranger in a strange land" but in terms of *regional* Perú. Both the superstitions of the local indigenous and the goals and actions of *Sendero Luminoso*/Shining Path[2] twist and turn as the mysteries unfold.

In Coscio's chapter, the last in this book, she describes the concept of both physical space and how mythic consciousness mixes/supplants it in Cerruto's works. She defines the sacred space of the Andes "as a step beyond realism and naturalism, the environment is psychological rather than telluric, but the Andes are the ever-present hallowed space. That space can be called sacred because it is a secret place in each person. Each of us has a kind of gloomy fence (*un cerco de penumbras*) that surrounds a place where we subconsciously keep what is our mythical past." At the same time, the religion brought by the conquerors, Roman Catholicism, plays a role. In some stories, the reader identifies the physical space "immediately with the Bolivian landscape, while in others, there is only a presentation of individual indigenous elements local to the region."

In contrast, Coscio's other chapters in earlier volumes have focused on all manner of diverse topics from all sorts of genres, depending on the volume's theme, as evidenced by the titles: *The Evolution of Hispanic Artistic Violent Imagery Through Postmodernism: Federico García Lorca, Carlos Fuentes, Roberto Bolaño* from *Insult*; *Latinas and Responsibilities. Searching for the Map: An Early Revelation of Latina Identity Crisis in Bilingual Theatre—'Coser y Cantar/Sewing and Singing' by Dolores Prida* from *S/HE*; and *Architecture and the Constant Hispanic Postmodern Project* from *Crossroads*. Those prior chapters mostly in the contexts of Roman Catholicism include *Euthanasia and Bioethics Within the Catholic Intellectual Tradition: The Film 'Mar adentro/The Sea Inside'* from *Death*; *Food Culture in (Catholic) Higher-Education Courses: Political Allegory in 'Lazarillo de Tormes'* from *Sustenance*; and now, indigenous beliefs, for this eighth volume, *Mythic Consciousness and Sacred Space in the Works of the Bolivian Poet, Óscar Cerruto*.

Notes

1 From *Acknowledgements* in *The Body*.
2 "The Shining Path (Spanish: *Sendero Luminoso*), officially
the Communist Party of Perú . . .is a communist guerrilla
group in Peru following Marxism–Leninism–Maoism and Gonzalo
Thought . . .
When it first launched the internal conflict in Peru in 1980, the Shining Path's goal was to overthrow the government through guerrilla warfare and replace it with a New Democracy. [An aside] The Peruvian guerrillas were unique in that they had a high proportion of women; roughly 50 percent of the combatants and 40 percent of the commanders were women."
Wikipedia.

CHAPTER
12
Sacred Geography and Gendered Ritual Violence as Social Control in Anahuac

JEANNE L. GILLESPIE

This chapter will examine violence against gendered bodies commemorated in pre-Hispanic colossal sculptures in the Valley of Mexico, Anahuac. The themes and contexts of these sculptures underscore a subtext of mutilation and brutality against female actors in military combat and establish the underpinnings of imperial the Mexica (Aztec) campaigns for hegemonic power. An examination of pre-Hispanic and colonial texts and artifacts corroborates that Mexica narratives employ examples of violence against female bodies to assert Mexica hegemony. This analysis examines the iconography and geography of the pre-Hispanic monumental sculptures of four important female divinities in conjunction with the placement of several of these sculptures in the ceremonial precinct of the *Templo Mayor* of Tenochtitlan. By considering the sculptural record in conjunction with colonial pictorial and oral narratives we can establish that the violent treatment of the female body by male warriors was an organizing principle of Mexica power at the time of the arrival of the Europeans as well as a pattern of behavior on the part of Mexica elite to subjugate and intimidate conquered polities.

The four figures studied here include Chalchihuitlicue (Jade Her Skirt), the embodiment of contained water and the patron of the Fourth Mexica Sun; Tlaltecuhtli (Earth Ruler), the saurian monster ripped apart by Quetzalcoatl and Tezcatlipoca to form the earth; Coatlicue (Serpent Skirt), the mother of the Mexica tutelary divinity Huitzilopochtli; and Coyolxauhqui (She of the Jingle Bells), the sister of Huitzilopochtli and the 400 Southerners. When the representations of these four divinities are considered alongside the narratives of the festivals of Ochpanitzli and Huey Tozoztli, the *Primeros memoriales* compiled by missionary ethnographer Bernardino de Sahagún, a well-structured complex of gendered violence emerges.

Chalchihuitlicue and the Concept of *Altepetl*

To understand the use of monumental sculpture by the Mexica, we must first understand their concept of *altepetl*. Bernardino de Sahagún's encyclopedia, the *Codex Florentino*, explains how an *altepetl*, a civic unit that we could describe as a "city," is organized around, and dependent upon, access to water as well as their connection to the mountains that marked their geography:

> The people from there, from New Spain, the ancient ones, said [that the rivers] came from there, that they came from Tlalocan, and that they are the property of the goddess called Chalchihuitlicue, and that they come from her. They also say that the mountain is no more than a skin, only the exterior is made of earth, of stone, but it is like a vessel, like a house full of water. And if someone tried to destroy the mountain, it would cover the world with water. For that reason, they gave the name of the *altepetl* [water mountain] to the places where people lived. They said that that water mountain, that river from there came flowing from the interior of the mountain; Chalchihuitlicue let it escape from her hands. (*Codex florentino* XI: f. 223v)

From this description, we see that geological features serve as metaphors for socio-political structures and the divinities who control those elements also figure into the imagery. Chalchihuitlicue's body contains precious, life-giving water. In Mesoamerica, water is blood and blood is water, so this water flows from her like amniotic fluid or menstrual blood. Her body also collects rainwater and draining water to nourish the plants and to give life. Representations of Chalchihuitlicue in pre-Hispanic and colonial documents reiterate the function as the patron of contained waters and as receptacle for sacrificial fluids. Images show Chalchihuitlicue seated on the *teoicpalli*, the "divine throne," and depict the divinity with water rushing out of her body carrying several other humans who swim in the flow. The image of Chalchihuitlicue from the *Tonalámatl Aubin* (Figure 1) depicts the divinity giving birth to the divinity, Tlazoteotl, with water rushing out carrying several other humans who swim in the flow as well as a string of beads similar to those worn by the divinity. In this document that tells the calendrical functions related to the twenty-day months, Chalchihuitlicue is seated on the *teoicpalli*, the "divine throne."

Figure 1 Chalchihuitlicue from the *Tonalámatl Aubin* Image 8, Library of Congress.

As stated in Sahagún's encyclopedic compilations on the Mexica world, the *Codex florentino,* the source of all waters, Tlalocan, was, literally, the body of Chalchihuitlicue. Water was (and is) the most precious commodity in Mesoamerica and conflicts ensued over water rights and access. In addition, water events like rain, hail, flood, and drought could ruin crops and lead to disease and mass starvation, a crisis for any polity. Storms, droughts, and hail were the milieu of Chalchihuitlicue's brother/consort, Tlaloc, who also inhabited Tlalocan. Tlaloc's images and representations are prominent at Teotihuacan from as early as 250 CE (Foncerrada de Molina). While Tlaloc's iconography has been studied extensively, very little research has been devoted to his consort/sister, but like her male counterpart, the indigenous record depicts Chalchihuitlicue in many forms, from monumental sculpture to painted codices.

Perhaps the most spectacular representation of Chalchihuitlicue was placed at the base of the extinct volcano known as Tlaloctepetl or Monte Tlaloc. This 167-ton monolith carved into the shape of a reclining figure rested for 1500 years near the *altepetl* of Coatlinchan (Figure 2). In 1964, the sculpture was transported to the capital to grace the entrance to the National Museum of Anthropology and History. While this sculpture has been called "Tlaloc" while in residence in the capital, many residents of Coatlinchan maintain that she is actually Chalchihuitlicue (Figure 3).

Coatlinchan citizens also call her the Tecomate [Gourd] Stone because of the twelve holes in her breastplate that served as vessels when the monolith was reclining (Cruz Barcenas). In this image, we can perceive her as a massive stone effigy that collects rainwater. At Teotihuacan, a 20-ton, 3.2-meter-tall [10.5 feet-tall] stone statue of Chalchihuitlicue dating to between 300 and 400 CE was discovered at the top of the Pyramid of the Moon (Figure 4). A comparison between the two sculptures supports this identification of the monolith as Chalchihuitlicue. They share the trapezoidal head gear, similar stances, similar hand positions, and skirts typical of *Teotihuacano* style.

Figure 2 Chalchihuitlicue at the base of Monte Tlaloc near Coatlinchan

Sacred Geography | 183

Figure 3 The monolith at the INAH (photo by the author)

Figure 4 Teotihuacano sculpture of Chalchihuitlicue
In the section of the *Primeros memoriales*, entitled "How the gods were arrayed," Sahagún recorded a description of Chalchihuitlicue's "array" in both the oral and pictorial traditions. This text collected and edited by informants in Tepepulco, a city in the eastern Valley of Mexico, commemorated written and pictorial information about the culture, geography, and cosmography of the region.

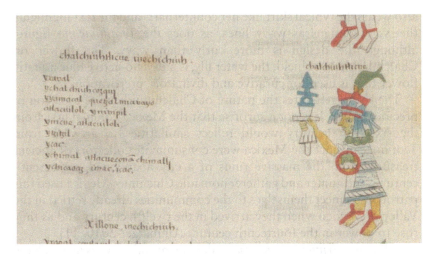

Figure 5: Chalchihuitlicue (*Primeros memoriales* f 263v Biblioteca Digital Mexicana)

The image of *Chalchihuitlicue* (Figure 5) was accompanied by this description:

The Array of Chalchihuitlicue

Her [yellow ochre] face paint
Her green stone necklace.
Her paper crown has a quetzal feather crest.
Her shift has the water design [of horizontal, blue, wavy lines].
Her skirt has the water design.
Her little bells.
Her sandals.
Her shield is the water lily shield.
In her [other] hand is her rattle staff
(*Primeros memoriales* 263v)

The precious jade stones known by the name *chalchihuitl* that make up her necklace appear in many representations of this patron of contained water, highlighting the preciousness of both water and blood. These echo the holes carved into the breastplate of the Cuatlinchan statue, and the sculpture from Teotihuacan also boasts a necklace of beads that may have been painted blue or blue green. Chalchihuitlicue's headdress with its circular ornaments is perhaps her most identifiable feature, echoing the headgear of the Teotihuacan statue and the Coatlinchan monolith. The *Primeros memoriales* image also wears the typical skirt like her counterparts and the text highlights the water designs as wavy lines, as does the *Teotihuacano* figure, although the design is more curly than wavy. The flower on Chalchihuitlicue's shield, the water lily, is a psycho-active blue aquatic flower that is used for curative and divinatory preparations.

The shield reiterates the nature of Chalchihuitlicue as a patron of precious water. It is not a surprise that the Mexica colonial text from the sixteenth century would reflect similarities to artwork from Teotihuacan since the Mexica were consummate collectors of ancient treasures from the massive ruins of a city abandoned it the tenth century. The hunter and gatherer nomadic Chichimec Mexica used this patron to connect themselves to the communities already settled in the Valley of Mexico when they arrived in the twelfth century and as they rose to power in the fourteenth century (Umberger 2010, 11).

Sahagún's *Primeros memoriales* documents other ways in which the Mexica incorporated the geography of the settled, agrarian Toltecs as part of their right to rule Anahuac. In the same section of "How the gods were arrayed," Sahagún recorded the arrays of 36 different divinities. The final image, the only one that is not of a single divinity, presents "The Array of the *Tepictonton*" (267r). *Tepictonton,* literally "little molded ones," were diminutive images of personified geographical features molded from amaranth seed and honey (Figure 6). These figures were crafted for celebrations honoring Tlaloc, Chalchihuitlicue, Quetzalcoatl and other important divinities for festivals marking important seasons in the rain cycle, and they were decorated with the same arrays as each of the divinities. According to Sahagún's informants:

> [a]nyone who fashioned a figure because he made a vow, fashioned images of the mountains. He fashioned as many images as he wanted. Thus, Popocatepetl was first. It was made in the likeness and arrayed in the adornments of Tlaloc. It was covered with amaranth seed dough. It had its paper crown, its paper locks on the nape of its neck, the quetzal feather plumes, its paper vestments, in its hands its reed staff . . . The array of Iztac Tepetl [Iztaccihuatl] was the same. The vestments of both were painted with rubber [black] . . . The Third was Matlacuye, and her paper crown was painted blue . . . The fourth was Chalchihuitlicue, her vestments and paper crown the same. The vestments of both were painted blue. (*Primeros memoriales* f. 267)

Sacred Geography | 187

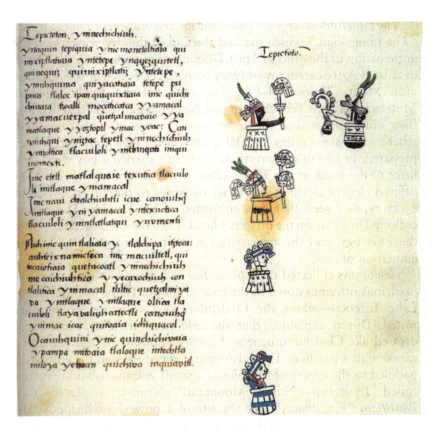

Figure 6 The *tepictonton* Sahagún, *Primeros memoriales* f. 267

The first three *tepictonton* represent three of the surrounding volcanos, visible from nearly every part of the Valley of Mexico as well as the Puebla-Tehuacan Valley. Popocatepetl "Smoking Mountain" and Iztaccihuatl "White Woman" are adorned with the array of Tlaloc, while Matlacuye "She of the Blue-Green Skirt," who represents a dormant volcano in nearby Tlaxcala, wears blue garments. She and the fourth figure, Chalchihuitlicue, are adorned with a similar headdress painted blue. Chalchihuitlicue wears a blue striped skirt similar to the one worn by the Teotihuacano sculpture and has a rounded base rather than a flat one like the others in line with her. Chalchihuitlicue is represented further down than the first three, and all four face the fifth image, dressed in black adornments and paint in the array of Quetzalcoatl. This effigy, like that of Chalchihuitlicue, sits on a rounded base. The rounded bases will be discussed further in the article.

The *tepictonton* were prepared for the celebration of *Huey tozoztli* "The Long Vigil," which marked the end of the dry season and the anticipation of the rains in April. Dominican missionary Diego Durán details an Aztec ceremony of *Huey tozoztli* celebrated at this location atop Monte Tlaloc (84–85). The rulers of the Triple Alliance, Motecuzoma II of Tenochtitlan and Nezahualpili from Texcoco and their allies gathered at the ceremonial precinct atop the mountain where a life-sized effigy of Tlaloc and many *tepictonton* had been prepared. In Durán's description, celebrants carried a boy child on a litter to the front to the Tlaloc effigy where he was sacrificed. They offered elegant clothing and other treasures to the effigy as well as every type of seed that was cultivated in the Empire. These were collected in a vase on the divinity's head. Then they anointed the effigy, the offerings, and the *tepictonton* with the sacrificial blood in an emulation of rain.

Celebrants collected the *tepictonton* and carried another round of luxurious offerings down to the base of Monte Tlaloc to the shore of Lake Texcoco—where the Chalchihuitlicue sculpture would have rested. Durán explained that the celebrants took a female child dressed like Chalchihuitlicue and the *tepictonton* and put her into a canoe with a pavilion. They also mounted canoes, and the entourage paddled to the center of the lake to a small volcanic island that they called *Tepetzingo* "Little Mountain." Nearby, a place called *Pantitlan*, "Flag Place," was the site of a powerful whirlpool. The child was sacrificed. Her blood was stirred into the whirlpool and the rest of the sacrificial and ceremonial materials were offered into this whirlpool. Sahagún recorded an image of Pantitlan (Figure 7) in the *Florentine codex*, and reiterated the narrative of the offerings as part of the veneration of the *tepictonton* in one of the chapters dedicated to Chalchihuitlicue:

> And all their adornments—their clothing, their paper shoulder-sashes, their stout reed staves, their lightening sticks, their cloud bundles, and their green stone bowls, the little wooden bowls, the clay cups, all these they left at Tepetzinco: they threw them into the water, offshore, at a place called Pantititlan. (1:49)

Members of the Triple Alliance sought out a ceremonial precinct constructed in pre-Aztec times and dedicated to the autochthonous rain divinity atop a mountain named for him. They performed ceremonies there and then carried out additional ceremonies at the lakeshore and at Pantitilan in the center of Lake Texcoco. The first part of the ceremony is performed in the realm of Tlaloc and included the sacrifice of a boy child. The second, Lake Texcoco, was the realm of Chalchihuitlicue with the sacrifice of a girl child.

Figure 7 Pantitlan from the *Codex florentino* Sahagún Book 1:42

An analysis of the geography of the ceremony of the *tepictonton* illustrates that the participants traveled the topography of *altepetl*. The ceremony is a vigil for the arrival of the life-giving rains, and it begins atop the mountain (*tepetl*) with effigies of the surrounding mountains dressed as divinities personifying three of those mountains. However, the two figures with rounded bottoms, Chalchihuitlicue and Quetzalcoatl are not personified mountains. I suggest that the Quetzalcoatl image is the embodiment of Venus as the Morning Star rising from the east before the volcanoes, and Chalchihuitlicue, the container of the waters of Lake Texcoco at the base of the volcanoes.

Figure 8 The Sun Stone from Tenochtitlan. Photo Creative Commons by Anagoria.

From Sahagún and Durán we know that Chalchihuitlicue is also linked to Pantitlan and Tepetzinco, the whirlpool and small mountain in the center ... navel ... of Lake Texcoco. Finally, we also know that the ceremonial precinct atop Monte Tlaloc predates the rise to power of the Mexica-Tenochca. The archaeological zone dates to the period in which Teotihuacan dominated the valley, 250 CE–750. This is not the only time that Mexica-Tenochca ceremonial practice appropriated Teotihuacano structures or accoutrements. In fact, the Aztecs exhibited a significant appreciation for antiques and relics from Teotihuacan, and they sought to validate their own existence and right to rule the Valley of Mexico by appropriating many of the images and artifacts they gathered at Teotihuacan. As part of the Mexica-Tenochca justification for their right to rule the Valley of Anahuac, the Aztecs added their "Sun" *Nahui Ollin* (Four Movement) as the "Fifth Sun." They detailed the birth of this sun in the *Leyenda de los Soles* (Legend of the Suns). After the examination of the role of Chalchihuitlicue in the concept of *altepetl*, it may not be a big surprise that the narrative of the Fifth Sun, born at Teotihuacan, confirms that this sun replaced the Fourth Sun *Nahui Atl* (Four Water) presided over by Chalchihuitlicue.

Chalchihuitlicue, the Sun Stone, and the Teocalli of Sacred Warfare

The most famous carved stone monument commemorating the birth of the Fifth Sun, the Sun Stone (Figure 8), depicts each of the Five Suns graphically. It was discovered in excavations from 1790. The center of the stone depicts the glyph for the fifth sun—the era of Mexica dominance—*Nahui Ollin*, Five Movement, with each of the previous suns in cartouches flanking the face of Tlaltecuhtil, the saurian Earth Monster whose (female) body Quetzalcoatl and Tezcatlipoca violently ripped in two to create the land and the sky. The cartouche on the lower right depicts Chalchihuitlicue, the divinity of the Fourth Son, *Nahui atl* Four Water (Figure 9, overleaf).

For most of the rest of Mesoamerica, there were four suns, but in Aztec cosmology, there were five. According to the *Historia de los mexicanos por sus pinturas*, the first sun was called *Nahui ocelotl* (4 Jaguar) and was presided over by Tezcatlipoca. In a disagreement, Quetzalcoatl knocked his rival, Tezcatlipoca, out of the sky and people that inhabited that world were devoured by jaguars. The next sun was ruled by Quetzalcoatl, *Nahui ehecatl*, (4 Wind). When the inhabitants did not pay attention to the divinities, Tezcatlipoca turned them into monkeys and Quetzalcoatl sent a hurricane to blow them away.

Tlaloc commanded the next sun, *Nahui quiahuitl* (4 Rain), but when Tezcatlipoca seduced his wife, Xochiquetzal, Tlaloc sent a rain of fire to destroy that era. The fourth sun was that of Tlaloc's next consort, Chalchihuitlicue, *Nahui atl* (4 Water). When Tezcatlipoca told her she was selfish, and the people did not love her, she cried blood for 52 years and flooded the earth. From this destruction emerged the

Figure 9 Detail of *Nahui Ollin* (left) and detail of Chalchiuitlicue from Sun Stone (right). Photo Creative Commons by Anagoria.

Aztec Sun, *Nahui ollin*, 4 Movement, over which the Mexica tutelary divinity Huitzilopochtli reigned.

While the Sun Stone was discovered in the central plaza, the Zócalo, of Mexico City, it was out of context, so its actual location before the destruction of the *Templo Mayor* is not certain. Nevertheless, another important monument from the same era, the *Teocalli* (Divine House) of Sacred Warfare (Figure 10), offers some perspective as to how the stone might have been used to affirm the right to rulership. In "El trono de Moctezuma (1984)" now available also as "Montezuma's Throne (2010)" Emily Umberger analyzed the *teocalli* in intricate detail. Umberger's insights help us understand how this stone connects power to Chalchihuitlicue and how this connection may refer directly to the Chalchihuitlicue sculpture we have already examined.

This sculpture was discovered in 1936 in the same area of the Zócalo where Motecuzoma Ilhuicamina's palace stood. Umberger identified the sculpture as "Motecuzoma's Throne" and demonstrated that it is of a scale upon which a person could be seated (See Umberger 2010, 32). It shows a carving of the Aztec sun which would appear at the back of a seated ruler as well as an image of the female earth divinity, Tlaltecuhtli (Earth Lord), whom Quetzalcoatl and Tezcatlipoca ripped in half to create the earth and sky. The *tlatoani* (ruler) would sit upon the body of the earth divinity with the sun at his back. The pyramidal structure also represents the *altepetl* as human-created mountain.

Figure 10: El Teocalli of Sacred Warfare (Wikipedia Creative Commons https://ast.m.wikipedia.org/wiki/Ficheru:Teocalli_de_la_Guerra_Sagrada_-_1.jpg)

For our purposes, however, I would like to consider the reverse of the sculpture which offers more insight into the connection between Chalchihuitlicue, Pantitlan, Tepetzinco, and the establishment of Aztec hegemony. The reverse side of the Teocalli of Sacred Warfare (Figure 11) depicts the founding of Tenochtitlan. The eagle screaming "*atl tlachinolli*" (mist and smoke) the Mexica-Tenochca war cry perches atop the prickly pear cactus (*nochtli*). This image recreates the portent established by the Mexica warrior divinity Huitzilopochtli indicating the place the wandering Chichimecs should establish themselves for success in the Valley of Mexico. The cactus image also reinforces the name of the Mexica capital, Tenochtitlan as a glyph. The *nochtli* cactus rises out of a "stone" (*tetl*) in the middle of Lake Texcoco, spelling out *tenochtli*. There is no indication of suffix -*tlan* that signifies "place of" but the positioning of the image surrounded by wavy lines like those indicated as water on the divinity's skirt in the *Primeros memoriales* concretely locates the image in the place where the Mexica did establish their city, on an island in Lake Texcoco, and that is no ordinary rock. The *nochtli* emerges from the abdomen of the reclining body of Chalchihuitlicue adorned with the fruits of the cactus, called *tunas* in Mexico, that also signify human hearts in Mesoamerican imagery. These bright red, juicy fruits are also embellished with the *chalchihuitli* beads, again linking them not only to human hearts, but indicating that they are bleeding and precious in Aztec conventions.

Chalchihuitlicue wears other elements from her array present in the other representation, including the circular *chalchihuitli* beads. These beads adorn her skirt, embellished by the same wavy lines on the skirt indicating water. Although the monument is effaced on the lower left, a little bit of Chalchihuitlicue's trapezoidal headdress and one of her circular ear-ornaments can be identified. To the right, her feet sport sandals similar to those from the previous depictions. Distinct from the other representations, the cactus seems to explode out of a gaping maw in her abdomen.

If we consider the role of Chalchihuitlicue in the ceremony from Monte Tlaloc as the recipient of the offerings preparing for the rainy season, then we must also revisit the destination of those offerings at Pantitlan, the whirlpool in Lake Texcoco near Tepetzinco (Figure 11), that literally portrays the body of Chalchihuitlicue as a rock or a little mountain, in the middle of Lake Texcoco, which, not coincidentally, is very near the place that the Aztecs chose to build Tenochtitlan. It should not be surprising, then that Sahagún explains that the Aztec arsenal and the launch point of their military boats was located near Tepetzinco (*Florentine Codex* Book 2: 42).

Sacred Geography | 195

Figure 11 Sculpture of Tenochtitlan rising out of Chalchihuitlicue (Umberger used with permission)

The massive Chalchihuitlicue sculptures at the base of Monte Tlaloc near Coatlinchan and Teotihuacan indicate a reverence for the divinity as patron of waters and perhaps as the personification of the Lake Texcoco. For the Mexica, she embodies the concept of *altepetl* graphically and geographically. The Sun Stone records that the Aztec Sun, *Nahui Ollin* emerged after the destruction of the previous historical eras of Mesoamerica, including *Nahui Atl*, the sun in which Chalchihuitlicue presided. On the Teocalli sculpture, the hieroglyph of the *altepetl*, Tenochtitlan, rises from this female body. The Mexica constructed their capital city atop the female body of the divine patron who presided over the previous cosmological era. The Teocalli sculpture confirms it, reiterating the literal meaning of *altepetl* from the passage about Chalchihuitlicue in Sahagún: she is a mountain and the waters flow from her body.

Works Cited

Aubin Tonalamatl. [Place of Publication Not Identified: Publisher Not Identified, to 1599, 1400] Pdf. Retrieved from the Library of Congress. Web. <www.loc.gov/item/2021668125/>.

Batres, Leopoldo; Mexico. *Tlaloc:? exploración arqueológica del Oriente del Valle de México*. Secretaría de Instrucción Pública y Bellas Artes, Mexico, 1903. Print. Wikisource. https://es.wikisource.org/wiki/Tlaloc%3F June 2, 2022. Web.

Cruz Barcenas, Arturo. "Tláloc sigue enterrado aquí; se llevaron a Chalchiuhtlicue." *La Jornada*. sábado 5 de abril de 2014, p. 8. Web. http://www.jornada.unam.mx/2014/04/05/espectaculos/a08n1esp

Garza, Mercedes de la. "Análisis comparativo de la *Historia de los mexicanos por sus pinturas* y *La leyenda de los cinco soles*. Estudios de la Cultura Nahuatl 16. 1983. n 123134. Print.

Sahagún, Fray Bernardino de. *Florentine Codex. General History of the Things of New Spain*. Eds. Arthur J. O. Anderson and Charles E. Dibble. 12 vols., Santa Fe (New Mexico): The School of American Research and the University of Utah. 1950–1969. Print.

———. *Primeros memoriales* f. 267 (DG037169) Web. http://bdmx.mx/detalle_documento/?id_cod=34&codigo=DG037169&carp=06

———. *Primeros Memoriales*. Paleography of Nahuatl Text and English Trans. Thelma Sullivan. completed and revised, with additions, by H. B. Nicholson, Arthur J. O. Anderson, Charles E. Dibble, Eloise Quiñones Keber and Wayne Ruwet. Norman, Oklahoma, University of Oklahoma Press, in cooperation with the Patrimonio Nacional and the Real Academia de la Historia, Madrid, 1997. Print.

Umberger, Emily, "El trono de Moctezuma" published in Estudios de Cultura Náhuatl 17 (1984), pp. 63–87. Print.

———. "Montezuma's Throne" arara 8, 2010. Web https://www1.essex.ac.uk/arthistory/research/pdfs/arara_issue_8/umberger.pdf

CHAPTER
13
The Mystery to a Solution
The Rituals in *Lituma en los Andes* by Vargas Llosa

HAIQING SUN

> *Ahí estaba:*
> *inmenso, misterioso, verdegrís,*
> *pobrísimo, riquísimo, antiguo, hermético/*
> There it was:
> immense, mysterious, metallic greenish-blue,
> so poor, so rich, ancient, sealed.
> Mario Vargas Llosa

Vargas Llosa's criminal mystery novel, *Lituma en Los Andes* (1993) provides a unique perspective— a genre-structured narrative for the reader to examine the writing of the Peruvian social-political conditions in the 20th century. This novel, written years after his defeat in the 1990 presidential election by Alberto Fujimori in Peru, which also won the Planeta Prize for Vargas Llosa, marked a new start for the writer who had chosen to exile himself from Peru and acquire Spanish citizenship. In contrast to his previous novels, the story is set in the Andes, a region that, although being internationally renowned for scientific studies and tourist interests, had seldom been represented in Vargas Llosa's fictional works before the 1990's. The writer himself states in 1985: "Los Andes no aparecen en mis libros, o aparecen apenas de paso, creo que por una razón, porque mi experiencia del mundo andino es una experiencia muy pobre, muy escasa/The Andes do not appear in my books, or they appear only in passing, I think for a reason, because my experience of the Andean world is a very poor, very meager experience" (Coloquio 31). This study will analyze how the author approaches the truth of a strange homeland through an access to a criminal case and the Andean ritual—a mystery behind the crime mystery. *Lituma en los Andes* can be read as a sequel to *Quién mató a Palomino Molero/Who Murdered Palomino Molero*, the author's 1987 novel, which continues the adventure of police sergeant Lituma who faces the challenge of a mystery in both his community and his personal life.

The Andes, as depicted in this novel, represent a world full of mysteries and conflicts in the eyes of the protagonist Lituma, who has been transferred from his warm costal hometown to a post in the Andean Naccos area, to protect a road construction. The text contains two parts and an epilogue. The first part is divided into five chapters. The story begins with three missing-person cases in the area of Lituma's jurisdiction. The missing people are Pedro Tinoco, a mute and intellectually disabled boy who used to be a servant for the police station; Casimiro Huarcaya, an albino; and Demetrio Chanca, a highway foreman. The narrative in each chapter contains three sections, each following a different clue. The first section is about Lituma's investigation of the disappearance, which presents the encounter between Lituma and the Andean world; the second section narrates incidents happening in the Andes, among the "Andeans," including the Shining Path (*Sendero luminoso* or *Senderistas*) guerrilla's attacks and past encounters between this military rebellious force and the three missing people. The third is a love story between Tomás Carreño, Lituma's assistant, and Mercedes, a young prostitute from Lituma's hometown Piura. Before coming to the Andes, Tomás is a fugitive, who has killed a drug dealer in order to save Mercedes. The third story also provides a narrative connection between the Andes and the outside world that involves the police's past. The investigation of the crime serves as a major clue that moves through the different stories.

During the investigation, Lituma frequents Don Dimnisio's and Doña Adriana's bar at the Naccos camp, as he suspects that the barkeepers may know some secret of the disappearance. There he hears different rumors about the three vanished people, that they might run away to join the *Senderistas*, or might be killed by the guerrillas, or be taken away be the *pishtacos* (vampires), the Andean monsters in which many local people believe (65). While Lituma feels lonely and helpless in the "strange" land, as well as troubled by the lack of clue to the cases, the second section of the first five chapters, which focuses on the *Senderistas*' activities, reveals more information about the social and political situations in the Andes, which can be considered a background for the missing cases. Under their stiff Marxist doctrines, the guerrillas maintain strong hostility to all government officials, property owners, and foreigners. Since the disappearances happen around the same time that the guerrillas attack some other innocent people, Lituma suspects them to be the guilty party. Moreover, all three missing people have had previous encounters with the guerrillas. Pedro had witnessed their killing of the *vicuña* herd in a natural reserve. Casimiro had been sentenced to death due to his affair with an Indian girl who later became a guerrilla. Demetrio Chanca, formerly Llantac, the lieutenant governor of Andamarca, had escaped from the *Senderistas* when they attacked his village, and has lived in Naccos under his new name since then. By the end of the first part, it seems that the guerrillas are the center of conflict in the Andes, a threat for everyone including the two policemen, and the major suspense of the mystery hangs over the relationship between the three missing people and the guerrillas.

However, in Part II, which consists of four chapters, the narrative focus changes from the *Sendero Luminoso* to don Dionisio and Doña Adriana, the barkeepers. In this part, Lituma survives an avalanche and learns from a Danish engineer Stirmsson about the still-performed indigenous ritual that sacrifices human beings to the Andean spirits or monsters. This discovery makes him link the missing people with the superstitions that reign the local community. In parallel with Lituma's continuing investigation of the mystery, Doña Adriana talks about her fighting with the Andean monsters and life in the Andes in the past. Her narration develops gradually from fantastic tales of human beings who once challenged the Andean monsters to more realistic observations of the depression in the Andean region, which is connected to the cases of the missing people; these stories help Lituma to figure out this couple's role in the mystery. By the end of the novel's second part, the mystery is apparently solved as a tragedy caused by the superstitions of the indigenous people who try to avoid the recession of the local economy through human sacrifices to the Andean spirits. But, in the epilogue, while Tomás recuperates his once lost love with Mercedes, and the two policemen receive orders to abandon their post in Naccos, Lituma makes a last investigation at the local bar and finds out that the *Senderistas,* in fact, are an indirect cause of the murders of the three victims. Thus, although the different parties of the Andean society—the police, the workers of road construction, the indigenous people, and the guerrillas—seem ideologically diverse or in contrast, they prove to be interrelated and together form the world of mystery in which Lituma feels lost.

Throughout the investigation, Lituma is repeatedly struck by nostalgia for Piura, his coastal hometown, which makes him feel more alienated from the harsh environment of Naccos. Even the solution of the missing-murder cases does not help him to feel adapted to, or accepted in, the Andean region, but confirms his status as a stranger.

The rebellion of *Sendero Luminoso* and the Andean myth are central themes of the Andes, a literary image of Peru. Vargas Llosa himself also connects explicitly the rebellion and the superstitions, although without mentioning the crime investigation in the novel and comments: "The phenomenon of the shining Path is present [in the text] because its members, the Senderistas, appear there . . . there is something more that if not dialogical and not at all political, which is a mythology . . . that is why I have also re-created this in the case of Dionysus, the world of the Pishtacos, and the world of Andean mythology" (Rebaza-Soraluz, 21).

However, in the study of the narrative, one should ask how these two phenomena, rooted in different socio-cultural soils of the Peruvian life, are set together to provide the reader an experience of mystery solution; and also, what is the common ground for their representations? Penuel suggests that the Andes are depicted as a world of different types of violence, and, indeed, the theme of violence functions as a key connection for the stories in the novel (453–454). Berg views the stories as an ambitious "narrative multiplicity" with simultaneously juxtaposing and contrasting representations of the Peruvian life that have "calculated and often very dramatic effects" (25). The two critics prefer to examine these phenomena as independent issues, somehow ruling out the criminal mystery as a constructive factor basic to either the representation of different types of violence or the conforming of different stories. Meanwhile, as the above summary of the novel's narrative structure indicates, the core of the narrative is to bring a solution to the crime, on which the development of all other themes depends. That is to say, the text is following a "ritual" of mystery-display-resolution per narrative's sake. The detective Lituma's work serves as a vehicle that moves forward the representations of different problems in Peruvian life. The narratives about the *Senderistas* and the Andean myths follow the rhythm of Lituma's criminal investigation, unfolding in response to his questions and becoming more mysterious as his uncertainties about the crime itself grow.

The *Senderistas* are under immediate suspicion when the three missing persons cases are reported to the police: "A éstos (the missing people) no creo que los hayan matado . . . se los habrán llevado, más bien, a su milicia. A lo mejor hasta los tres eran terrucos. ¿A caso Sendero desaparece a la gente? La mata, nomás, y deja sus carteles pare que se sepa/I don't think these (the missing people) have been killed . . . they will have taken them, rather, to their militia. Maybe even the three of them were *terrucos*.[1] Perhaps Sendero disappears[2] people? He kills her, no more, and leaves his posters so that it is known " (15). The three cases also initiate the suspense of the two policemen's fate in the Andes: "'Ya los tenemos encima a los terrucos,' pensó Lituma ... 'Cualquier noche vendrán'/'We already have them on top of the terrucos,' thought Lituma ... 'Any night they will come'" (12). The community's fear of the *Senderistas* is maintained through an episode which describes the guerrillas' attack on some innocent tourists. In the following chapters, while Lituma and his subordinate try to find out the possible relationship between the missing cases and the guerrillas, the narrative about the past encounters between the three vanished people and the guerrillas reveals more details of the guerrillas' doctrines and activities. This rebellious force is extremist and irrational, and it has been committing atrocities against the Nature and communities. One may regard these revelations as a sign of the social conflicts in Peru. On the other hand, such information also provides the reader a chance to consider the guerrillas' role in the mystery, since their activities concern all the parties related to the crimes: the victims all have confronted them before their disappearance; both the detective and local people feel their threat; and they keep executing innocent people in the area during the time of Lituma's investigation. The narrative of the *Senderistas'* atrocities forms a clue that parallels Lituma's suspicion of the guerrillas in the missing case and gives the reader access to the mystery. That is to say, such information makes the mystery open and puts the reader in a position not inferior to the detective character's in terms of examining the available clues. Therefore, the *Senderistas'* involvement in the missing case should be regarded not only as a social problem or setting for the criminal case, but also as an important element in the mystery-solving ritual of the narrator.

While the police wonder about the possible connection between the guerrillas and the missing people, the past encounters between these two parties help to clear the *Senderistas* of further suspicion, as they, in fact, have spared the lives of two of the victims and lost the trace to the third one (56–57 and 227). Another question thus rises: who else can harm the victims? In the meantime, police sergeant Lituma, as a representative of the state-ruling machine in the Andes, feels himself constantly under the threat of the *"Terrucos'* fatal attack" (*Senderistas*), placing him in the boots of a potential victim before a heroic detective.

With the investigation proceeding, Lituma's attention is drawn from the *Terrucos* to another dimension of the Andean life—myth and superstition. The key figures in this transformation are Don Dionisio the barkeeper, and his fortune-telling wife. This couple, who are the only people that talk openly about the victims, hold a different "theory" about the crime. They comment on the third vanished person that "[a Demetrio Chanca] lo iban a sacrificar para aplacar a los malignos que tantos daños causan en la zona. Y que lo habían escogido a él porque era impuro . . . porque se había cambiado de nombre/[Demetrio Chanca] was going to be sacrificed to placate the evil ones that cause so much damage in the area. And that they had chosen him because he was impure . . . because he had changed his name" (41). For another victim, Don Dionisio suggests: "A Casimiro Huarcaya tal vez lo desaparecieron por dárselas de pishtaco . . . Era una bola que corría él mismo . . . yo lo oí mil veces gritando como un erraco: 'soy pishtaco y qué. Terminaré rebanándoles el sebo y chupándoles la sangre a todos'/Maybe they disappeared Casimiro Huarcay for representing himself to them as a *pishtaco* . . . It was a ball that he ran himself . . . I heard him a thousand times shouting like a boar: 'I'm *pishtaco* and what. I'll end up slicing the tallow and sucking everyone's blood'" (65). Before actually paying attention to the superstition of the local people, Lituma has wondered that the barkeepers might be the guerrillas' conspirators. As Lituma's attention turns to the local superstitions in the second part of the text, the protagonists in the middle section of the following chapters also shift from the *Sendero Luminoso* to the barkeepers, especially to Doña Adriana, whose narration in Part II of the text offers another perspective from which to view the Andes.

Adriana describes a mythological world, which Lituma's later findings on the indigenous religions and rituals confirm. In the beginning, the policeman does not take the Indian rituals seriously, as he questions: "¿De veras los indios creen eso? . . . ¿Crees que Doña Adriana . . . está cojudeándonos a su gusto con la historia de los diablos de los cerros?/Do the Indians really believe that? . . . Do you think Doña Adriana . . . is messing with us [exploiting] your interest in the history of the devils of the hills (13 and 47). The Danish engineer "Escarlatina" Stirmsson advises him about the Andean "superstition" from the stand of a "civilized" outsider:

> Los huancas eran unas bestias, Escarlatina . . . Tú mismo nos contaste las barbaridades que hacían para tener contentos a sus apus. Eso de sacrificar niños, hombres, mujeres, al río que iban a desviar, al camino que iban a abrir, al templo o fortaleza que levantaban, no es muy civilizado que digamos . . . se encogió de hombros el profesor Stirmson . . . Claro que eran unas bestias. ¿Algún pueblo de la antigüedad pasaría el examen? ¿Cuál no fue cruel e intolerante, juzgado desde la perspectiva de ahora? . . . no tienen explicación racional/The *Huancas*[3] were beasts, Little Red . . . You yourself told us the barbar-

The Mystery to a Solution | 203

ities they did to keep their *apus*[4] happy. That of sacrificing children, men, women, to the river that they were going to divert, to the road that they were going to open, to the temple or fortress that they raised, is not very civilized that we say . . . Professor Stirmson shrugged Stirmson . . . Of course, they were beasts. Would any ancient people pass the exam? Which one was not cruel and intolerant, judged from the perspective of now? . . . [it would] have no rational explanation. (177–78)

Doña Adriana's story provides Lituma a more vivid description of the Andean spirits and local people's worship to them with different rituals. The so-called bruja (witch) tells of her life as if it were an Andean legend. She has helped her first husband to go inside a labyrinth cave and killed a *pishtaco* who takes young girls from their village as offerings. Her second husband, Dionisio, used to lead an entertainers' group. He is a local celebrity who has the power to bring people to carnivals wherever he visits. He settles down in Naccos with his wife when the economy in this region experiences recession.

Critics have not paid as much attention to Stirmsson's comment of the primitive land as to Doña Adriana's mythical tales. Based mainly on the matching of the names of Dionisio and Adriana to the original Greek myth of Dionysus and Ariadne and the tales of the killing of the minotaur, Arnold Penuel suggests: "Of particular interest in *Lituma* are the perspectives issuing from the novel's principal intertexts. The novel displays an impressive interweaving of Greek mythology, Christian iconography, and Peruvian indigenous beliefs and superstitions [as represented by the rituals], both ancient and modern" (441–42). Mary Berg suggests that myth "is a central narrative force in Vargas Llosa's novel; references to the Greek Dionysus and Ariadne are conspicuous throughout the book" (30). She concludes:

> Christian communion in which flesh and blood are consumed . . . Andean belief in cannibalistic *pishtacos* and expiatory rites involving human sacrifice, Greek accounts of human beings sacrificed to the Minotaur . . . all of these are fused by Vargas Llosa into one powerful meditation on the irrational in human civilization and specifically on the force of the irrational in the Andean areas of Peru. (33)

Both Berg and Penuel have provided comparative analysis between the plots of the Dionisio-Adriana story and the Greek Dionysus myth. Within the context of criminal mystery, however, the author's borrowing a myth prototype cannot be read as serving the sole purpose of myth recreation.

Although further examination of the role of myth in Vargas Llosa's novel is necessary, an immediate question is how to detect the textual position of the Andean myth behind the rituals. Myth is a basic literary form with extensions into different socio-cultural dimensions through human history. The "myth" in *Lituma en los Andes,* however, is not the type of mythological representation recounted from what is held in the indigenous traditions that could translate a certain primitive, symbolic significance to the modern world. It is first of all a story within the story, according to one of the main characters, a *bruja,* who claims herself to have some supernatural powers, and tries to persuade the detectives into another direction for their mystery-solving task. It is notable how the context of the criminal investigation and that of the indigenous rituals are interconnected through the narration of the violence in the Andean land and the anxiety for survival among the local people. For the police, the Andean myth, as represented by the blood-shedding rituals, is, first of all, a challenge to their *modus operandi* in the detective work. As David Bidney points out, "Myth is said to have its mode of necessity and its own mode of reality ... Myth is not something freely invented but a necessary mode of feeling and belief which . . . seizes upon human consciousness" (Vickery 5). Therefore, in the case of *Lituma en los Andes,* one has to consider the identity of the myth-teller.

Doña Adriana is, first of all, a suspect instead of a "storyteller" or a "mythological figure" in the novel. Before the account of her *pishtaco*-killing legend in the second part of the text, she has tried to relate the missing-people to the Andean monsters (44–45). Her mythical stories, centered on the Andean gods instead of the victims, start only after the policeman's attention shift from the *Senderistas* to the Andean superstitions and rituals during the investigation of the crime. She is under the pressure to talk, to answer a policeman's questions in order to clear his doubts. The story that involves the Andean rituals is apparently the major subject of her talk, which draws the reader's attention to a matter different from the detective's concern, but this does not mean that the "myth" should be read separately from the narrative of the crime mystery.

To Doña Adriana's storytelling, a first question one may raise, for instance, is what relationship is being suggested between past (the indigenous rituals) and present events (the crime) in the Andes, since, different from a common ancient ritual with supernatural factors and symbolic meanings, her story makes explicit a serious concern about the social and economic conditions in the current Andean region. In her story about how a *pishtaco,* who demands human sacrifice, threatens her village, and how she and her first husband manage to kill it, she comments: "Así ocurrió cuando Naccos [the local economy] vivía de la mina Santa Rita y así está ocurriendo ahora, que vive de esta Carretera... Las desgracias no vendrán de los terrucos... ni de los pishtacos... éstos vienen siempre en los tiempos difíciles/So it was when Naccos [the local economy] lived from the [profits of] Santa Rita mine and so it is happening now, that he lives on this highway... Misfortunes will not come from the *terrucos*... nor of the *pishtacos* ... these always come in difficult time " (184). Then, she reveals how the social conditions have affected her own life: "Seguíamos viajando ... Hasta que los caminos empezaron a volverse peligrosos con tanta matanza y los pueblos a vaciarse y a encerrarse en una desconfianza feroz hacia los foráneos/We kept traveling... Until the roads began to become dangerous with so much slaughter and the villages to empty themselves and lock themselves in a fierce distrust of foreigners" (248).

The final part of her story, however, describes a more tangible concern of the Dionisio couple—the current road construction in Naccos:

> Se habló años de años, antes de que se decidieran a construirla [la carretera]. Lástima que cuando empezaron los trabajos y aparecieron ustedes [la policía] con sus picos, palas y barrenos, fuera tarde. La muerte le había ganado la pelea a la vida. Estaba escrito que la carretera nunca se terminaría... También las oigo, en el corazón que late dentro del árbol y en el de la Piedra... La muerte de Naccos está decidida. La acordaron los espíritus y ocurrirá/There was talk for years of years, before they decided to build it [the road]. Too bad when the work started and you [the police] showed up with your picks, shovels and holes, it was late. Death had won the fight against life. It was written that the road would never be finished... I also hear them, in the heart that beats inside the tree and in that of the Stone... Naccos' death is decided. It was agreed by the spirits, and it will happen. (270)

With this concern for her village's fate, Doña Adriana's narration transforms from a pure storytelling to a justification of the human-sacrifice ritual as a means of inviting a supernatural power to save the region, with even an insinuation on how the victims of the sacrifice are chosen:

> yo he visto lo que fue Naccos antes de que se llamara Naccos y antes de que la decadencia le ganara la pelea a las ganas de vivir. Aquí hubo mucha vida porque hubo también mucha Muerte... Antaño la gente se atrevía a enfrentar los grandes daños con expiaciones. Así se

mantenía el equilibrio. La vida y la muerte como una balanza de dos costales del mismo peso . . . ¿Qué hacían para que la muerte no le ganara a la vida? . . . el varón que el pueblo elegía en cabildo como cargo para las fiestas del próximo año, temblaba. Sabía que sería principal y autoridad sólo hasta entonces; despúes, al sacrificio. No se corría, no trataba de escaparse . . . conforme y orgulloso de hacerle un bien a su pueblo/I have seen what Naccos was before it was called Naccos and before decadence won the fight against the will to live. Here there was much life because there was also much Death . . . In the past, people dared to face great damage with atonements. This was how the balance was maintained. Life and death as a scale of two sacks of the same weight . . . What did they do so that death would not win over life? . . . the man that the people chose in cabildo5 as a position for the festivities of the next year, trembled. He knew that he would be principal and authority only until then; then, to sacrifice. He didn't run, he didn't try to escape . . . satisfied and proud to do good to his people. (271–72)

A differentiation, if not a gap, is notable between the beginning of her narration—a mythical story from long ago—and its ending, which comments on current social-economical situations. Nevertheless, two basic ideas remain unchanged throughout her narration: that of the superstition and rituals for the Andean spirits (or monsters), and of herself as a heroine who tries to save the village. In this sense, her story is more of a self-justification than a description of the Andean ritual. Doña Adriana reasons: "Repito lo de tantas veces: a grandes males, grandes remedios" (270). Also noteworthy in the narrative is that Doña Adriana's explanation of human sacrifice in the Andean ritual parallels Lituma's accusation of her and her husband as guilty in the missing-murder cases (268). Such "mythtelling" and justification of a ritual (human sacrifice) serves the purpose of a character before serving the construction of the text. Doña Adriana's story, aside from its persuasive defense against Lituma's suspicion, bears a logical explanation for the superstition: it is due to the local people's desperation when facing the unstable, foam-like prosperity. Economic depression is the social background for both Adriana's story and the *Senderista* movement. It is as well a cause of the missing-murder cases, as the narrative later discloses that the vanished people have been sacrificed in a secretly performed ritual to "appease" the mountainous spirits and to "bless" the road construction, a project on which the Naccos' economy depends.

Although the social depression is related to different aspects of the mystery—the criminal cases, the *Senderista* activities and the secret rituals—it is explicitly present only in Adriana's story. Therefore, her explanation of the performance of the ritual can be considered a truth-telling that affords the reader access to the solution of the crimes, which strongly implies the criminals' motives. As William Righter notes, "to represent something is to become the mark of a truth, either occult or abstract" (8). In other words, the more supernatural or irrational her story may seem, the closer it reaches (implicitly) to the solution of the criminal mystery.

The different themes of the Andean life—from the *Senderistas* to the mountainous ghosts, are not independent of each other in the textual scope. They share with the criminal mystery a common social ground of depression, and they are both represented within the detective's tracing of a crime. Both issues are revealed first as possible causes of the crime, and in the end, as social factors that strongly motivate the guilty party. Thus, the reader can examine the *Senderista* movement and the Andean superstitions not apart from, but within the presentation of the mystery. On the other hand, the different aspects of Andean life that appear within the crime novel does not mean that they function only as part of the narrative of the mystery or that they are insignificant outside the context of the detective's work. With the exposure of the different kinds of crisis, the policeman's investigation expands to a more complicated experience through which the Andean world is observed as a mystery that any solution to it may seems insignificant—at least it is so in the eyes of Lituma the protagonist.

It is not unusual for a detective story to present a criminal case in the context of some pressing social issues, but *Lituma en los Andes* does this so as to develop a sense of mystery not only around, but also well beyond, what is typically the primary tension of a crime story—that between the detective and the criminal. Rather, it "mysterizes," as it were, the Andean world and puts under examination not only a concrete crime but also an expanded mystery of the region. In this novel's end, it is not the criminal case but the Andean world that remain mysterious for the detective.

For the people of Naccos, especially those who perform the human-sacrifice rites, the fear of the economic crisis has made them succumb to barbarism. The multiple conflicts at different social levels reveal a loss of power for the "powerful"—the ruling machine of the country. Although they are the official representative of the surveillance and disciplinary force in Naccos, Lituma and his assistant are isolated from the community, estranged from the Andean natural environment, and threatened by the Marxist *Senderistas*. They try to perform their duty as detectives, only to find themselves impotent to restore the social order or impose justice.

When Lituma regards the *Senderista* guerrillas as primary suspect in the missing-murder cases, he also believes himself to be their potential victim: "¿Por qué [los senderistas] no los habían ajusticiado a él y Tomasito? Por sádicos tal vez. Querían romperles los nervios/Why hadn't [the hikers] executed him and Tomasito? For being sadists, perhaps. They wanted to unnerve them" (35). Lituma's view of the Andes is that of defeat: "No tengo más remedio, entiéndome . . . Esas tormentas andinas, con rayos y truenos, no lo hacían feliz; nunca se había acostumbrado a ellas. Siempre le parecía que iban a aumentar, aumentar, hasta el cataclismo/ I have no choice, understanding me . . . Those Andean storms, with lightning and thunder, did not make him happy; he had never become accustomed to them. It always seemed to him that they were going to increase, increase, even the cataclysm" (135).

If one reads the text as a detective story, the turning point of the narrative seems to be the Danish engineer's disclosure of the human-sacrificing rituals. However, in the epilogue, Lituma eventually finds out that he and his police partner have been spared *Senderistas'* attack because the local people—those who are involved in the rituals, have "labeled" the two policemen to be decent and harmless. In other words, Lituma realizes in the end that he himself is also among the sacrifice-to-be under the huge altar called "the Andes." Albeit reaching a key to the murder cases, Lituma, in the interwoven relations of the sacrificed and the ritual's performers, finds himself incapable of accessing a society doomed to know only failures.

For Lituma, the Andean problems represent a meta-mystery that he could leave alone but not solve. The Andean people appear as a community holding its own view of mystery, one that is rooted in the social and natural conditions, which Lituma detests as superstition and judges as unacceptable to a modern *modus operandi*. As I [Sun] have noted, he can only observe the Andean world from the stand of a stranger or outsider (106). His conclusion of the journey in the Andes is pessimistic while the Andean society remains in his eyes a land of terrorism, barbaric rituals, and unpredictable natural disasters. He says, "Ya no me importa . . . ya bajé la cortina, ya eché llave. Me ha llegado mi nuevo nombramiento. Me iré . . . y me olvidaré de la sierra/I don't care anymore . . . I already lowered the curtain; I already threw away the key. My new appointment has come to me. I'll leave . . . and I will forget about the mountains" (304).

In the last part of the narrative, when an avalanche destroys the last hope of the road construction, it seems that the harsh natural environment severs the final connection between the police and the Andes. However, the novel's examination of the Andean mysteries from a stranger's perspective, one marked by Lituma's nostalgia and confusion that recognizes only chaos in this society, presents the reader with yet another "mystery:" should this novel be read as an entry into the Andean world or as an alienation, a "mysterization" or a "demonization" of this remote site in the author's literary world? Besides presenting a case of loss, Vargas Llosa does not provide more answers to the mysteries of Andes. The *Senderistas*, the *pishtacos*, and Nature itself are depicted similarly as untraceable and life-threatening, meanwhile all of them contribute to the formation and execution of the rituals directly or indirectly.

Moreover, Lituma, the novel's central figure, fails to gain any insights into this primitive land of his country, but must himself depend on a foreigner, a Danish engineer, to uncover the secret of the crime. "Gracias a Escarlatina lo aclaré, antenoche. Le juro que hubiera preferido no averiguarlo. Porque eso que les pasó es lo más estúpido y lo más perverso de todas las cosas estúpidas y perversas que pasan aquí/Thanks to "Little Red," I clarified it, the night before. I swear I would have preferred not to find out. Because what happened to them is the stupidest and most perverse of all the stupid and perverse things that happen here" (261). From the beginning and throughout the narrative, Lituma's feeling of being lost in the mysteries and his shock at the natural and human atrocities leave little space for further understanding of the mountainous region. The rituals performed behind the textual scenes, whose details are not explicitly revealed, gesture a critical portrayal of the Andean world contrary to what the author believes to be progressive: safe community, sound economy, and openness to the outer world.

In *The Location of Culture*, Homi Bhabha describes the post-colonial elites' cultural function as mediators between Western influence and their homeland. Following Homi Bhabha's post-colonial theory of "liminality," Ed Christian points out that in the case of the detective in a post-colonial land, there is the condition of "being within a space made by the meeting of two borders, a space which serves as a threshold between the two . . . Often, the detective is this space, this area of overlap, this space of meeting" (13).

For Lituma in particular, his investigation in the Andes probes into a meeting of the modern and the ancient—the highway project labeled and re-defined by local superstitions, an overlap of the rational and the irrational—the police's *modus operandi* challenged by the killings under primitive doctrines, and the confrontation between the desire for progress and the disillusion caused by human and natural disasters. Notably, the Andean rituals—their formation and consequences, stand for a "threshold" at each of these encounters, where the main characters from different social spheres have their fates interwoven.

Vargas Llosa claims that his motivation for writing about these Andean problems is to show "how certain myths are perennial, are always there because evidently the types of questions that brought them about have not been resolved (they are questions that reappear under certain circumstances); and also how the idea of modernity and progress is such a precarious idea; and how beneath all these lies an atavistic force belonging to a certain tradition that is not easily uprooted" (Rebaza 21). Therefore, the mythical stories and the rituals in the novel have as their background what the author perceives as social vulnerability and the loss of order, which contributes to an allegorical representation of the lack of confidence in this society, where a crime is solved only to reveal a bigger mystery for humanity.

Notes

1 According to the *Urban Dictionary*, *terruco* is a derogatory term in Peru related to communist of socialist.
2 Post-the *Guerra Sucia*/Dirty War in Argentina and the atrocities in Chile especially in the 1980s, the term, "to be disappeared" is a common usage for "murdered."
3 Inhabitants of the Huancayo area in Peru.
4 *Wikipedia* notes that *apu* refers both to an actual bird and to a constellation, which may have held sacred value for the *huancas*.
5 *Cabildo* refers to the later Spanish term for a ruling council.

Works Cited

Berg, Mary G. "Narrative Miltiplicity in Vargas Llosa's Lituma en los Andes." La Chispa '95. Ed. Claire Paolini. New Orleans: Luisiana Conference of Hispanic Language and Literature, 1995. 25–38.
Bidney, David. "Myth, Symbolism, and Truth." Ed. Vickery. 3–13.
Christian, Ed. The Postcolonial Detective. New York: Palgrave, 2001.
De Castro, Juan. *Critical Insights: Mario Vargas Llosa*. New York: Salem Press, 2014.
Kluckhohn, Clyde. "Myth and Rituals: A General Theory." Ed. Vickery. 33–44.
Penuel, Arnold M. "Intertextuality and the Theme of Violence in Vargas Llosa's Lituma en los Andes." Revista de Estudios Hispánicos. 3 (1995): 441–60.
Rebaza-Soraluz, Luis. "Demons and Lies: Motivation and Form in Mario Vargas Llosa." *The Review of Contemporary Fiction*. 1(1997): 15–24.
Righter, William. Myth and Literature. Boston: Routledge and Paul, 1975.
Sun, Haiqing. "Reflection on the Absurd: A Comparative Reading of *Death in the Andes* and *The Time of the Hero*." Ed. Juan de Castro. Salem Press. 2014. 175–87.

Vargas Llosa, Mario. *Lituma en los Andes*. Madrid: Planeta, 1993.
———. "Coloquio/Respuestas." *Semana de Autor: Mario Vargas Llosa*. Madrid: Instituto de Cooperación Iberoamericana: Ediciones Cultura Hispánica, 1985. 218–19.
Vickery, John, ed. *Myth and Literature: Contemporary Theory and Practice*. Lincoln: U of Nebraska P, 1973.

CHAPTER
14
Mythic Consciousness and Sacred Space in the Works of the Bolivian Poet, Óscar Cerruto

ELIZABETH WHITE COSCIO

There are authors who display a mythic consciousness very much a part of the literary movement, magic realism, whose production has been sometimes ignored since they began to write before the decade[1] known as the "Boom."[2] The very interesting history of the actual development of the literary denomination, magic realism, is an important part of this story. As the term most commonly used to define a uniquely Latin American style, other denominations included "*surrealístico* and *fantástico*," the "*real maravilloso*" proposed by Alejo Carpentier[3] and the "*real imaginario*" suggested by Mario Vargas Llosa[4] in his study of *Cien años de soledad/A Hundred Years of Solitude* (1982 Nobel Prize-winning novel by the Colombian writer, Gabriel García Márquez).

Mythic realism defines the special vision exhibited in *Cerco de penumbras/Fence of Dark Spaces,* an anthology of parables by the Bolivian poet, Óscar Cerruto. This work represents a prelude to that new realism that defined the years of technical and linguistic experimentation that were the sixties. As a step beyond realism and naturalism, the environment is psychological rather than telluric, but the Andes are the ever-present hallowed space. That space can be called sacred because it is a secret place in each person. Each of us has a kind of gloomy fence (*un cerco de penumbras*) that surrounds a place where we subconsciously keep what is our mythical past. Cerruto closes the reader within that fence, not artificially, but in an intuitive way that testifies to the validity of a mythic cosmovision. This mythical meaning permeates each story. Being a poet, Cerruto conjures a portentous atmosphere with only a few words beginning each story. The incidents do not seem forced at all, rather they seem to be born instinctively from a predisposed mythic mentality, receptive to the poet's technique of introducing each story with the unexpected. This study of the sacred space includes only a selection of the poet's allegorical stories including in the anthology, "*Cerco de penumbras.*" The focus is certain themes and ancient myths that still populate the sacred Andean space in these parables imbued with indigenous fatalism alongside classical imagery.

Óscar Cerruto was a poet of great stature in his time. He was also a narrator, biographer, and diplomat, but in *Cerco de penumbras* (1958), it is his experience as a journalist that is revealed in these parable stories. This anthology represented that step beyond realism and naturalism when the environment becomes psychological rather than telluric but, again, the eternal Andes are always present. Cerruto's worldview was an inherent faith in the phenomenon of special meaning in everyday occurrences. By acknowledging a mythical conscious in the stories of *Cerco de penumbras*, mythical, non-chronological time is recognized, that mix of past, present, and future that resides both in memory and an area of semi-shaded sub-consciousness. In this area, this sacred space, within our own being, reside the ghosts of remote and future times that torment us asking for an explanation of the human condition.

By means of indigenous cyclical time, a break in chronological time or an overlay of realities in a flexible time/space, we manage to enter into the very spirit of man. The subtle signs of our immersion in another environment come at the beginning of each story. The atmospheric changes produced by the cold, the rain and the wind from the *altiplano* (Andean plateau) facilitate this metamorphosis. The stories use a set of protagonists with individual names, still in contact with the forces of nature revealing Andean peculiarities dating from an Incan past. This base provides a strong contrast to other characters in the stories: anonymous *bourgeois* men who renounce their heritage in the hostile environment of the city. Physical/social isolation, lack of communication, loneliness and even the relationship man/woman come from an unconscious indigenous fatalism. The importance of death as a main theme cannot be denied. The omens are clear and man feels his lack of importance in this world.

This generalization is made through a purely Andean environment. The very name of this anthology, *Cerco de penumbras*, is probably based on a Callahuaya[5] custom. When the diviner foretells with coca leaves, he sees the future or the answer to the question in the falling leaves. Enrique Oblitas Poblete warns in *Cultura Callahuaya*: "Cuando forman círculo o cerco quiere decir que la suerte ha quedado cercada y no podrá el consultador salir de su actual situación/If the leaves form a circle or fence, it means that fate has been surrounded and the consultant will not be able to get out of his current situation" (178).

This deterministic prophecy is almost always told in a parable. Perhaps because of the use of this genre developed from an oral tradition, deceptively simple and condensed, this anthology in its entirety has not been considered of much importance in the general canon of Hispanic literature. The classic definition of a parable includes little characterization, a condensed plot, and a startling inversion with an underlying moral or spiritual intent. Cerruto's stories deserve the parables label in the broadest sense of the word.

If some do not have a didactic purpose at first glance, it is because of the monstrosity of the twentieth-century world that they reflect. These stories are parables of an alienated world with self-absorbed men, who metaphorically show hopelessness in a world that rejects its own myths and beliefs. By way of complex and exquisite analogies, there is no longer a need for mere similes. It is an indirect communication in the manner of Kierkegaard[6] where truth is the subjective. It follows that truth cannot be communicated in the same way that factual information is communicated (PIC).

There is a double reflection: the narrator presents imaginative alternatives and the reader decides how to untie the dialectical knot by his own subjective consciousness. There is self-questioning at different levels: personal, Bolivian, and universal. It is an act of discovery because the reaction brings all the mythic consciousness to a conscious level. In that way, besides introducing new possibilities by way of metaphors, there is an intention to alter the reader's very own consciousness.

Óscar Cerruto offers a good example of a parable with a didactic purpose with "*El círculo*/The Circle," which is the simple story of a relationship: Vicente leaving and returning to Elvira. But, read critically, this could be the return of the infidel to religion. However, the end provides an unusually ironic twist: "God is dead." There are several symbols that reinforce this religious path. First of all, Miss Elvira's last name, *Evangelio*/Gospel, means the good news of the world's redemption through Jesus Christ. Returning to his mistress inadvertently, the man proceeds to apologize like a child and ends in a useless "*mea culpa*" (15). This prayer of confession in the Roman Catholic Church is used by Catholics to confess sins. In Latin, it means literally "through my fault" and represents an apology, as well as remorse when asking for God's forgiveness.

The cyclical time provides a leitmotiv with the repetition of the word "*tiempo*/time," enclosing the reader in that circle. This enclosure affects the physical space, resulting in transition to that mythic consciousness. Another line from the same story brings in nature by way of the wind: "*Un viento desasosegado arrastraba su cauda de rancor por las calles*/a restless wind dragged its bitterness through the streets" (12), which represents a metaphor that again has to do with the Roman Catholic Church: the *cauda* refers to the tail of the consistorial layer (consistory from the Latin *consistorium*, the assembly of cardinals presided over by the Pope, place where the canonization of the saints is verified according to Larousse.[7] The narrator comments on the problem of man and free will planted in religious beliefs. The soul in conflict is revealed in Vicente's split personality, one that hastens his return and another that delays it. He follows the first, revealing the eternal existentialist struggle when describing his freedom as a burden that weighed him down and her absence that ""*no parecía al amor ni era el anhelo de la carnal presencia de Elvira, sino una penosa ansia, la atracción alucinante de una alma*/did not resemble love, nor was it the longing for Elvira's carnal presence, but rather a painful longing, the hallucinatory attraction of a soul" (20).

In "The Circle," already from the second paragraph, there is a feeling of something strange. "*Esto ya no es para mí*/This is no longer for me" says Vincent referring to the "*frío de la tumba: que siente porque viene de otro clima*/the cold as in the tomb: that he feels because he comes from another climate" (10). The double meaning of these words is not clarified until the end. What no longer exists for him is the love he felt in another time and the cold he feels so tomb-like is due to the mythical space recognizing the possibility of other worlds parallel to ours.

The fatalism in these stories does not inhibit their presentation as parables. Perhaps by the very fatalistic nature of the Andean myths, they are pessimistic in that man can never meet the demands of the gods, so he seeks another way to satisfy his needs through his own imagination. Cerruto brings to light these moments man faces in the shadows of his own sub-consciousness by way of a mythical fusion of dreams and concrete realities presented in the format of a parable.

As in "*El círculo*," fatalism is often related by early signs of the character's own mythic consciousness predisposing a return to a sacred space. Instead of a circling of fate, we find a rather elliptical format in "*Iphigenia, el zorzal y la muerte*/Iphigenia, the Thrush/Songbird and Death" where the little man is conditioned to a routine and a deterministic destiny. There is the gratuitous death that occurs within the confines of revolutions. The protagonist is constantly thinking about returning home, symbolic of the Andean man's destiny to reunite with *Pachamama*, Mother Earth.

The title speaks of human sacrificial symbols: the very word 'death' is reinforced by the double meaning of the word "thrush." as bird and scapegoat. The cry of this macabre thrush is a bad omen that repeats in different moments both day and night as a Greek chorus in the darkness of the revolutionary chaos foretelling the man's death. Iphigenia could be symbolic of salvation or liberation since in Greek mythology she was the daughter of Agamemnon and Clytemnestra destined to save Troy. Her father had to sacrifice her for having offended Artemis, but the gods saved her, leaving a deer or a bear (depending on the version) in her place (Oxford). In the story, the mysterious Iphigenia is a blonde woman, a political symbol of the foreign influence in that revolution. The symbolic title once again hits like a stone thrown in a lake allowed to ripple into three concentric circles: the character in chronological time and space in subjective fiction, the Andean mythic fatalistic consciousness, and a universal political parable in the objective reality of the Bolivian Revolution of 1952.

The storyline follows others where we find Man with all his faults, deceptions, and complaints. He lives in social isolation that does not allow him to share the enigmas or misfortunes of life with another, resulting in his solitary stance against political situations revealed in a dream-like landscape with a hostile natural environment. Home is the sacred space in this story, and it is definitely La Paz, where the 1952 revolution began, by the name the major streets and best-known boulevards of the capital. The socio-political theme of a revolution meant to better the country that does not is shown by the protagonist who in order to improve his own future, needs to change his present tranquil lifestyle.

The story begins with gunfire waking the protagonist, who has an interview the next day for a new job as an auditor. Of course, he is worried that the revolution will spoil his plans for a better-paying job. He ventures outside the front door in the night air to smoke and hears the first call of the thrush or did he really? He may imagine or dream what happens next because he runs into a beautiful woman (Iphigenia) who dashes into his apartment looking for protection. What starts as a romantic interlude ends in an argument where she reproaches him for his lack of ambition, insisting the revolution could change everything. He insists they are just too diffent for a relationship to work. He longs for his selfish solitude and describes himself as like "*esas aldeas del altiplano que confinan por sus cuatro costados con la estepa, con el vacío*/those villages of the altiplano that border on all four sides with the steppe, with the emptiness" (Pastor Poppe 119).

As in a weird nightmare, he wants to kill the woman, or maybe stop the revolution with her as a symbol, although the very thought of the act is repugnant to his very nature. The next day, he risks his life to go to the interview and finds La Paz in total chaos with dead animals on the streets, populated by desperate people running by destroyed homes in the pouring rain. At that point he hears the thrush's call again. While his thoughts alternate between random pleasantries and sheer panic, he thinks he sees Iphigenia in camouflage and then he takes a bullet in the head and dies while the thrush calls from afar.

Beyond his search for identity, he has never really loved the big city and longs for the small-town life. In the quote above, he speaks of his rural past in the *altiplano* and the quiet tranquility of his own apartment. As he witnesses the street violence, he thinks of a return to his childhood home or his present apartment as a sacred safe space. Even as a middle-class urbanite, he retains that mythic consciousness:

*Debo llegar a mi casa, se dijo. Debo llegar. Por suerte estoy muy cerca. Si logro llegar a mi casa, tomaré una buena taza de té. Gracias a Dios, tengo un té inglés excelente; té de la India, claro. ¿Conoceré un día la India? Qué curioso debe ser tomar el té en las propias plantaciones. O en una casa de té, servido por camareros con turbante, tal vez por mujeres semidesnudas de ojos exóticos". Ya al finalizar su trayectoria a través de la ciudad, se detiene en la casa de su amigo Covarrubias y comenta, 'Podría entrar; estaba nervioso, peor aún, estaba temblando. Un miedo irracional se había apoderado de él'/*I must get home, he told himself. I must arrive. Luckily, I'm very close. If I can make it home, I'll have a nice cup of tea. Thank God I have excellent English tea, Indian tea, of course. Will I one day see India? How curious it must be to drink tea in the plantations themselves. Or in a tea house, served by turbaned waiters, perhaps by half-naked women with exotic eyes." At the end of his journey through the city, he stops at the house of his friend Covarrubias and comments, "I could enter;" he was nervous, worse still, he was shaking. An irrational fear had seized him. (*Pastor Poppe 125*)

In "Iphigenia, the Thrush and Death" the second line makes us think, where are we? He was awakened by the first shot, but was it really the first? All of the stories involve this early transition to another space and time. In "*Retorno con Laura*/Return to Laura," in the fifth paragraph, there is the behavior of the dog disturbed, agitated. In "*Los buitres*/The Vultures" also the second sentence leaves us expectant, saying he didn't know why he was there. "*La calle abierta como un ancho sueño hacia cualquier azar*/the open street as a wide dream towards any chance encounter), a quote from Jorge Luis Borges that introduces the story "*Un poco de viento/* A little wind" represents the path to destiny." Also, there is a quote from William Shakespeare at the beginning of "*Alimento profético*/Prophetic Sustenance" that introduces us to the other world: "The key that opens my nocturnal dwelling to the furies". The first sentence of "*La junta de sangres*/The Blood Junta" gives the reader a restless anticipation: "*nunca se sabe la muerte que nos está destinada*/you never know the death that is destined for us." To show the entrance to a special time/space in "*Morada de ébano*/Ebony Abode," the first sentence warns us that "*Fue aquel para la familia un día de agitación*/It was a day of turmoil for the family.

The use of italics points to stream-of-consciousness in various stories including "*El rostro sin lumbre*/The Face without Light:" "*Aquella noche Ana presintió, supo que Andrés no iba a Volver*/That night Ana sensed, *she knew* that Andrés was not going to return (161).

The story that perhaps best exemplifies the author's plan to move the reader in an almost imperceptible way into a dream or imagined world is "The Vultures." There is nothing superfluous about this grotesque journey that appears to take place in Buenos Aires but then it moves to a lunar plain, an *altiplano* in diffused light (74). Although it is an unreal, other world, or dream landscape, it is implicitly described as the flat highlands of the Andes.

The fable is simple. It's a man's journey on a tram. The first sentence advises the presence of another, retrospective narration, with a phrase in italics: "*If they get on, I will take it*" (60). Thus, throughout the story, again the method is a stream-of-consciousness commenting subjectively on the mythical space. "*They're going to kill me any day*" (64), he thinks when he almost collides with a truck. "*It's ridiculous,*" he says when he feels something tie him to his seat. "*This can't go very far . . . They have to get off soon*" (66) he observes about the women who have fascinated him during the tram ride. "*Maybe I'm dead?*" (67) is his last comment before the arrival of a flock of vultures who suddenly appear in the tram devouring people and forcing him to "throw himself into the void" (74) to escape.

Little by little the change moves from a completely normal situation to a nightmare full of transformations of objective reality. Although the reader does not feel any abrupt change in the first reading, when reading it critically, a well-defined structure is established. In the first 'real' part, there is a stream of strange sensations: "there was something irregular inside, in people or in the atmosphere . . . what we call omens" (60). But it's "crossing . . . the stream thick as wine" (66) that launches us into mythical space. Óscar Rivera Rodas draws a parallel between the realities of the two parts but does not comment on the demarcation of the river as a transition to the second part (53–63). There is "the declining light of the evening . . . the shadows . . . Night fell . . . A perverse personified wind appears . . . " wandering "in the corners of the streets, dragging desolation and dead leaves [which] brings confusion to the protagonist. He didn't know where or why he was there or where he was going. The inside of the tram dripped with a yellow clarity" (67). This repeats the emphasis on atmospheric change. The wind gets more furious, then there are lightning and thunder that will bring the storm. Suddenly it's cold, the character on the tram feels icy, "a dangerous humidity like a fever penetrated him to the bones" (68). Comparing humidity to fever causes chills at the thought that a weather change could affect both the body and a physical illness.

On the same page, there are three synonyms: "*tormenta, temporal, y tempestad*/storm, rainy and/or windy weather, and tempest. Lightning chases the vehicle. The tram rolls for at least three days, marking the rise and fall of the sun. Already on the third day, when the storm passes and the sun rises again, it is pale and looks on a strange city he had never seen" (68). This insistence on atmospheric changes completes the total transfer of space/time from one plane to another. "The clear rain, red, blue, bright" (79) of the day in "Un poco de viento/A Little Bit of Wind" changes to a "dry rain at night" (87). The oxymoron serves the purpose of transporting the reader from one environment to another, where it intensifies the absurdity to its apocalyptic end.

The coldness, loneliness, oppression and conflict of other realities are compared to the environment of the highlands. The landscape represented corresponds to that area, but it serves as an image for other more frightening places, such as that psychological desert that each of us carries inside. If we call it a mythical space, it must be clarified that this term can also include the destruction of the same myths that define the Andean man turned city dweller. Rivera Rodas refers to Cerruto's heroes as a true reflection of *altiplano* reality. "*Este hombre se encuentra en un círculo del que no puede salir y vive en él en un estado de inconciencia. Sus héroes duermen una pesadilla y viven en un ambiente que les parece coherente, donde lo absurdo e imprevisto es lógico para ellos*/This man finds himself in a circle from which he cannot get out and lives in it in a state of unconsciousness. His heroes sleep in a nightmare and live in an environment that seems coherent to them, where the absurd and unforeseen is logical for them" (*La Razón*, 17 September 2001).

"*La calle estaba oscura y fría. Un aire viejo, difícil de respirar y como endurecido en su quietud, lo golpeó en la cara . . . en la noche estancada*/The street was dark and cold . . . an old air, difficult to breathe and as if hardened in its stillness, hit him in the face . . . in the stagnant night" (9). This is how Cerruto defines the rarefied night air of "The Circle." Rivera Rodas notes the progression present in the stories by defining abstract space without limits, no matter how present the Andes are, it could also be any dark and cold street anywhere (43–44).

By giving a sense of stagnation to the air and night, it also suspends chronological time. In the same way that the storm can serve as a transition to a mythical space, the cold of a stagnant night of old air places us within that space at the beginning of the story. Vicente comes out in the rain after the cold and darkness of his encounter with Elvira. On the other hand, when he returns the second time, it is sunny, symbolizing the exit from one environment to another. Also, as in other tales, the mythical encounter takes place during a storm. There is thunder, rain and restless wind (17). The importance of the wind is based on an Aymara myth that respects the Huayra-Tata as "a god that originates and produces winds and hurricanes" and "his relationship with the earth is close, being she is *Pachamama* (Mother Earth)" and also the "female side of the wind" (Paredes 32).

The wind is also of paramount importance in the story of "Adelaide and the Fury," which describes in just five pages the death of Fermín Rosales because of the fury of the wind and Adelaide's whims. Chasing her through the streets of the town, Fermín finds himself taken over by the typhoon forces that eventually leave him in an open ossuary. Just like in "The Circle," the air slaps him in the face, only no longer the old, stale air, rather *"repentinas iracundias del vendaval*/sudden wrath of the gale." Instead of the preterite tense that fixed that stale air in "The Circle," the imperfect tense provides more of a sensation of the wind blowing in gusts: "*se llevaba sus palabras . . . Arreciaba, oscuro, lo golpeaba en medio del pecho, le llenaba la cara*/took away his words . . . It raged, dark, hit him in the middle of the chest, filled his face (266).

The *altiplano* environment is a special one, and in these stories the details are important, but other critics have noted the universality of man's mythic space. Yvette Ostria describes the space as the world itself, places where Man lives. She also brings up the importance of that wide street charged with symbols that could be anywhere, an indefinable space without limits (59). It is in the transformation of the physical Andean highlands to a psychological space. Those who are not part of the belief or destruction of the Andean myths, will see the space in this way. She is correct in recognizing that space but gives little credence to the fragments of Bolivian soul that are a part of that metamorphosis.

Cerruto employs the environment both directly and indirectly: in some stories, the reader identifies immediately with the Bolivian landscape, while in others, there is only a presentation of individual indigenous elements local to the region. As in Romanticism,[8] the characters reflect their surroundings: the cold, the wind, and the rain form a part of their innate pessimism.

An example of the explicit occurs in "*La estrella de agua*/The Water Star," where there is an exact description of a highland drought. In "*El aviso*/The Warning," there is the bone-chilling cold again: *esos aires de la sierra calaban hasta los huesos*" (248). Stories are situated not only by way of climate, but also topography, and by the mention of specific cities, streets, plazas or mountains: "Lo había elegido ella misma en La Paz (hizo un viaje con ese solo propósito, a riesgo de enemistarse con los carpinteros de Corocoro/She had chosen it herself in La Paz (she made a trip for that purpose only, at the risk of antagonizing the carpenters of Corocoro" (*Morada de ébano/Ebony Abode* 145); "El sol de Llallagua/The Sun of Llallagua" (una montaña/a mountain en *La araña/The Spider* 183).

There are also abundant classical metaphors such as the traditional romantic sun as a boat, "el sol-nave desmantelada por las llamas postreras del día/the sun-ship dismantled by the last flames of the day" (*La estrella de agua* 133); "el sol navegaba ya de bolina hacia el horizonte, en busca de puerto . . . Quedaba todavía, sin embargo, un par de horas para arriar las velas/the sun was already sailing bowline towards the horizon, in search of a port . . . There were still, however, a couple of hours to lower the sails" (*Alegría del mar/Joy f the Sea* 235), the night as a temple, "al templo de la noche . . . permanecieron largo tiempo contemplando, con recogida devoción alzarse las catedrales de agua/ to the temple of the night . . . they remained for a long time contemplating, with collected devotion, the water cathedrals rose" (*Estrella de agua* 211); and the bells ringing as teardrops in the same story. Some stories reveal a more *costumbrista*[9] tone when the bells become the "*polleras de muchachas/girls' skirts*" (*Alegría del mar* 218) or the Andean plateau after the long drought becomes "un inmenso tambor resonante/an immense resonant drum" (*Estrella de agua* 139).

Metal, as the substance which gives life to a mining community is apparent in a number of stories: "El sol de LLallagua brillaba con luz hirienta en las techumbres de los ingenieros, se deslizaba en millares de arroyuelos e oro líquido por entre el cuarzo pórfido de los montes y era una llamarada hirvienta en la patena de las represas/The sun of Llallagua shone with a burning light on the roofs of the engineers, it slid in thousands of streams of liquid gold through the porphyry quartz of the mountains and was a boiling flame in the patina of the dams" (*"La araña"* 183). The day is described as gray as steel in another story, *El aviso,* and the miners themselves are "*hombres y mujeres de piel atezada y con los flejos del metal de Pampanaya/ men and women with tanned skin and with the metal flakes from Pampanaya* (Morada de ébano 157).

The countryside becomes another protagonist that suffers and enjoys. The wind can be "perverso, ambulante, arrastrando desolación y hojas muertas/perverse, wandering, dragging desolation and dead leaves" (Los buitres 7); it crosses the *altiplano* "tropezando en los tejados y sacudiendo puertas y ventanas o ululando en los confines de la pampa/tripping on rooftops and shaking doors and windows or howling in the confines of the pampas" (*Morada de ébano* 149); and in the same story the wind "arrastraba su gran capa húmeda y fría por los charcos del camino/he dragged his big wet and cold cape down the puddles of the road" (157). In *"Adelaida y la furia/*Adelaida and the Fury," the wind has huge treacherous hands that push the man along (268). Man struggles obstinately against the wind in an eternal battle between man and environment. The Indigenous people's arid land is personified, as in other Bolivian works, as a villain or executioner (35).

Beyond the explicit examples provided, there are many implied evocations of the high plateaus of the Andes. Who hasn't commented on the desert-like silence of the highlands as Fermín does in "Adelaida y la furia" (264)? Actually, the notion of a cold desert as a specific place and the idea of a solitary silence in a place not only unpopulated by people, but also by most vegetation truly fits the *altiplano*. In that space, Fermín finds himself "entre la furia del calor y la furia de los tifones/between the fury of the heat and the fury of typhoons" (264). The constant assault of the elements is only part of the Andean man's environment. The description of the graveyard with its wide promenade bordered by trees (268) provides the one sure path of all men and a typically Bolivian scene. This can be whichever area of the Bolivian highlands, where the small towns stand out in the vast frigid wasteland as mirages with their adobe huts, a simple plaza, the church, and those few trees leading to the *campo santo/*graveyard. In a few words, the author defines the Andean man's destiny and the constant lack of change in certain regions. Even the dead do not decompose, rather they compose, become stiff and the bare bones cleaned by the weather extremes. If a man were to fall into an open crypt in a tropical region, the sensation would be totally different. The lack of insects, tropical foliage and humid dirtiness creates a rather meticulous sense of dry cleanliness. For that reason, the reader may accept with less repugnance the description of the boneyard where "*sus huesos crujieron,* *con ruido seco, al confundirse con los restos dispersos de los esqueletos definitivamente pulidos por las lluvias y por el tiempo*/his bones creaked, with a dry noise, as they merged with the scattered remains of the skeletons definitely polished by the rains and by time" (269). The quote speaks to the brusque changes of this region: a sun that burns in the day and makes you feel colder in the night, just as in the desert, in spite of a rainy season barely allows for the sparse vegetation that maintains the sheep, llamas, and the indigenous crops. Although the mining cities are completely different today, the cold and contrary environment is ever present.

These tales represent a probe into the deepest level of human experience. Like subtle poetry, they signify riddles without solutions, parables that deceive the reader until he is confronted with the truth itself. Due to the transfiguration of reality in a mythical space/time, we are presented with images so exact, so well-employed, that they give credence to the existence of a strong mythical realism by way of a popular Andean saying that introduces Cerruto's poem, *Altiplano*: "*Porque el altiplano es más ancho, siempre un poco más ancho de lo que es posible imaginarlo*/Because the altiplano is wider, always a little wider than it is possible to imagine it" (http://escritordebrochagorda.blogspot.com/2017/06/altiplano.html).

Notes

1. The timing of this movement and what writers are included has been the subject of rather hotly debated controversy. *Wikipedia* has extensive articles about these aspects. "The Latin American Boom . . . was a literary movement of the 1960s and 1970s when the work of a group of relatively young Latin American novelists became widely circulated in Europe and throughout the world. The Boom is most closely associated with Julio Cortázar of Argentina, Carlos Fuentes of Mexico, Mario Vargas Llosa of Peru, and Gabriel García Márquez of Colombia. Influenced by European and North American Modernism, but also by the Latin American Vanguardia movement, these writers challenged the established conventions of Latin American literature. Their work is experimental and, owing to the political climate of the Latin America of the 1960s, also very political."
2. *Wikipedia* goes into explanatory detail about the literary movement most associated with the period: "Magic realism is a style of literary fiction and art. It paints a realistic view of the world while also adding magical elements, often dealing with the blurring of the lines between fantasy and reality. Magical realism, perhaps the most common term, often refers to literature in particular, with magical or supernatural phenomena presented in an otherwise real-world or mundane setting, commonly found in novels and dramatic performances. Despite including certain

magic elements, it is generally considered to be a different genre from fantasy because magical realism uses a substantial amount of realistic detail and employs magical elements to make a point about reality, while fantasy stories are often separated from reality. Magical realism is often seen as an amalgamation of real and magical elements that produces a more inclusive writing form than either literary realism or fantasy. The term *magic realism* is broadly descriptive rather than critically rigorous, and Matthew Strecher (1999) defines it as "what happens when a highly detailed, realistic setting is invaded by something too strange to believe." The term and its wide definition can often become confused, as many writers are categorized as magical realists. The term was influenced by a German and Italian painting style of the 1920s which were given the same name."

3   Alejo Carpentier y Valmont (December 26, 1904–April 24, 1980) was a Cuban novelist, essayist, and musicologist who greatly influenced Latin American literature during its famous "boom" period. Born in Lausanne, Switzerland, of French and Russian parentage, Carpentier grew up in Havana, Cuba, and despite his European birthplace, he strongly identified as Cuban throughout his life, according to the biography on *Wikipedia.*

4   Jorge Mario Pedro Vargas Llosa (born 28 March 1936) . . . is a Peruvian novelist, journalist, essayist, and a former politician, who also holds Spanish citizenship. Vargas Llosa is one of Latin America's most significant novelists and essayists, and one of the leading writers of his generation. Some critics consider him to have had a larger international impact and worldwide audience than any other writer of the Latin American Boom.[3] In 2010 he won the Nobel Prize in Literature, "for his cartography of structures of power and his trenchant images of the individual's resistance, revolt, and defeat," also from *Wikipedia.*

5   *Encyclopedia. com* says that "The name, *Callahuaya* derives from an Inca province of the same name. Bolivians refer to them as *Qollahuayas*, meaning *place of the medicines*, because the *Callahuaya* are renowned herbalists in Andean countries. They cure with plants, minerals, animal products, and ritual. Peasants refer to them as Qolla kapachayuh or *lords of the medicine bag.* The *Callahuaya* have earned this title on account of their knowledge of over 1,000 plants used for curing."

6   The *Wikipedia* biography lists "Søren Aabye Kierkegaard (5 May 1813 – 11 November 1855) was a Danish theologian, philosopher, poet, social critic, and religious author who is widely considered to be the first existentialist philosopher. He wrote critical texts on organized religion, Christendom, morality, ethics, psychology, and the philosophy of religion, displaying a fondness for metaphor, irony, and parables. Much of his philosophical work deals with the issues of how one lives as a 'single individual,' giving priority to concrete human reality over abstract thinking and highlighting the importance of personal choice and commitment."

7   The publisher's website identifies itself as primarily dedicated to dictionaries.
8   Wikipedia defines Romanticism (also known as the Romantic movement or Romantic era) [as] an artistic, literary, musical, and intellectual movement that originated in Europe towards the end of the 18th century, and in most areas was at its peak in the approximate period from 1800 to 1850. Romanticism was characterized by its emphasis on emotion and individualism, idealization of nature, suspicion of science and industrialization, and glorification of the past with a strong preference for the medieval rather than the classical.
9   *Miriam Webster* defines this literary movement as "a Spanish or Latin-American . . . work . . . marked by usually realistic depiction of local or regional customs and types."

Works Cited

Cerruto, Óscar. *Cerco de penumbras,* La Paz: Ed. Difusión, 1975. Print.
Carpentier, Alejo. Prologue, *El reino de este mundo.* Mexico: Ediapsa, 1949.
"Iphigenia," in *Oxford Classic Dictionary.* Print.
Kierkegaard, Søren. *Practice in Christianity.* Trans. Howard V. Hong and Edna H. Hong. Princeton, NJ: Princeton UP, 1991. Print.
——, and Thomas Oden. "Prologue" in *Parables of Kierkegaard.* Princeton, NJ: Princeton UP, 1978. Print.
Oblitas Poblete, Enrique. *Cultura Callawaya.* La Paz: Ed. Populares Camarlinghi, 1978. Print.
Ostria, Ivette. "La obra en prosa de Óscar Cerruto." Doctoral Thesis: University of Paris, 1966. Print.
Paredes Candia, Antonio. *Diccionario mitológico de Bolivia.* La Paz: Ed. Puerta del Sol, 1972. Print.
Pastor Poppe, Ricardo, ed. "Ifigenia, el zorzal y la muerte" in *Los mejores cuentos bolivianos del Siglo XX.* Segunda Edición. La Paz, Bolivia: Editorial Los amigos del libro. 1989.
Rivera Rodas, Óscar. *El realismo mítico en Óscar Cerruto.* La Paz: Ed. Abaroa, 1973.
——. *"Cerruto ante el espejo de 'Cerco de Penumbras.'" La Razón.* 17 Sept. 2001.
Vargas Llosa, Mario. *Historia de un deicidio.* (Barcelona: Barral, 1971), pp, 528–538.

Conclusion

Wrapping up an eight-book, one a year, series has been bittersweet, encompassing a decade of all of our lives and careers, which has constituted the last decade of my own nearly five-decade formal professional teaching career before retirement in late 2020. This decade was marked (marred and/or enhanced?) for all of us by the unprecedented pandemic during the last three volumes, not to mention expected and unexpected personal changes for so many of us: geographic and professional changes of residence and/or professional association for at least a dozen of us, dramatic medical challenges for at least two of us, and more.

I have included the biographies of not only the editor and contributors to the current eighth volume but an addendum with those of collaborators in earlier volumes in recognition of their contributions to the series, this being the final volume in the series.

The overviews for each volume are reproduced in reverse order by year to highlight the threads that run through the series.

The Editor and Contributors

Debra D. Andrist, PhD, retired Professor of Spanish, formerly founding Chair of Foreign Languages at Sam Houston State University, formerly Chair of Modern & Classical Languages/Cullen Professor of Spanish, University of St. Thomas/Houston and before that, Associate Professor of Spanish, Baylor University, holds the BA, Fort Hays Kansas State University; MA, University of Utah; PhD, SUNY/Buffalo; and a Mellon Post-Doctoral Fellow at Rice University. A sociologist of created societies (literature) in works by and about women, her scholarly works include international conference papers and other presentations, books of criticism and textbooks, translations, critical articles, reviews, interviews and movie study guides, plus current books in progress. She has received internal and external grants plus awards and honors for teaching (SUNY) and service (Baylor and UST). She has personally studied abroad in Mexico and Spain and taught in study abroad in Mexico, Spain, Ireland, and Costa Rica, was an exchange professor in Chile and Canada and a Fulbright-Hays Scholar in Morocco. A member of many professional organizations, an officer in most, she was, e.g., president of SCMLA and of the Houston Area Teachers of Foreign Language and Senior Vocal of AILCHF. Active in service, e.g., she is a docent at Bayou Bend, has been secretary of Houston Hispanic Forum (a Board member for 17+ years), on the Montgomery County Arts Council Grants Committee and others.

Mary Jane DeLaRosa Burke, MEd. A native of Central Texas, Mary Jane earned her bachelor's degree in Bilingual Education from Texas State University San Marcos, holds two master's degrees, in Reading and Language Arts from the University of Houston and in Counseling Education from the University of St. Thomas/Houston, and is currently pursuing a third master's in theology at the Oblate School of Theology in San Antonio. A retired bilingual elementary teacher and middle school counselor, she served thirty years in Austin, Mississippi, Houston, Philadelphia, and San Antonio. Married 35 years to her husband, John, together they have three children and five grandchildren. She has been involved in church ministry since her youth and especially enjoys music ministry in diverse settings. She hopes to become a chaplain after she obtains her next degree.

John Francis Burke, PhD, teaches political theory, religion and politics, US Latinx politics, comparative politics and US American politics at Trinity University in San Antonio, Texas. He is an interdisciplinary scholar who has published articles especially on political theory, intercultural relations, social justice and religion & politics in several journals and periodicals, including *The Review of Politics and Commonweal.* He is the author of *Mestizo Democracy* (College Station, TX: Texas A&M Press, 2002), a text on democracy and multiculturalism in the U.S. Southwest and *Building Bridges Not Walls: Nourishing Diverse Cultures in Faith /Construyamos puentes, no muros: Alimentar a las diversas culturas en la fe* (Collegeville, MN: Liturgical Press, 2016), a text on integrating diverse cultural spiritualties constructively in faith-based communities. He has also appeared as a political commentator on many Texas media outlets, both in English and Spanish. In addition to his scholarly work, he has coordinated social justice institutes and programs at the University of St. Thomas in Houston, TX and Cabrini University in Radnor, PA. He has also served on several committees and conducted workshops in Indiana, Pennsylvania and Texas dealing with social justice and intercultural issues. Finally, he has extensive experience in church liturgy and has earned a "reputation" for cultivating vibrant multilingual choirs.

Elizabeth White Coscio, PhD, presently teaches Spanish language, literature, culture, clinical conversation and other Spanish applied language courses at the University of St. Thomas in Houston, Texas. She has been the Cullen Endowed Chair of Spanish and Chair of the Modern and Classical Languages Department since 2007 and has also led study abroad experiences. Although she has also worked in marketing and sales, an area that provided experience in budgeting, staff development, and influencing clients, she has always taught language courses at all levels. Past experience includes many years of teaching secondary level French, university Spanish courses including practical language application courses (translation, business, media, for the medical professions and English as a Second Language at Rice University, University of Houston, and other institutions. As collaborator on a Spanish middle school text, she wrote and edited games and projects and has produced critical articles on a variety of both peninsular and Latin American topics, as well as books, translations, international presentations, reviews, interviews, and other. She is a past vice president and president of the South Central Modern Language Association, Associate Professor of Spanish, Cullen Endowed Chair of Modern & Classical Languages, Director of the Latin American and Latino Studies Program and Sponsor for Sigma Delta Pi Spanish Honor Society.

Gwendolyn Díaz-Ridgeway, originally from Buenos Aires, Argentina, is professor emerita of English at St. Mary's University in San Antonio, TX., where she taught World Literature and Literary Theory. She earned a BA from Baylor University, the PhD from the University of Texas/Austin and did a post-doc on Latin American magical realism at Rice University. Díaz co-founded the *Las Americas Letters* Series in Literature and the Arts, an annual conference held at St. Mary's. She is frequently invited to speak abroad on the topics of her research. Fluent in Spanish, English, French and Portuguese, Díaz has published seven books in both Spanish and English on topics of Argentine literature. Her latest are *Women and Power in Argentine* Literature (Univ. Texas Press, 2009); *Mujer y poder en la literatura argentina* (Emece, 2009); *Texto, Contexto y Postexto en la obra de Luisa Valenzuela* (Univ. of Pittsburgh, 2010) and a collection of her own short stories, *Buenos Aires Noir* (2010). Díaz also has published articles on Latin American literature, literary theory and U.S. Latino literature, as well as on works by Sandra Cisneros, Cristina Garci and others. Her awards include a Fulbright, a Carnegie Mellon Fellowship, the St. Mary's University Distinguished Professor Award for both undergraduate and graduate teaching and an Honorary Professorship at the *Universidad Católica de Salta* in Argentina.

Jeanne Gillespie, PhD, exhibits a passion for finding fascinating stories and rendering them into accessible narratives for reflection and further investigation. She has taught courses at all levels of Spanish language and cultures. In addition, she teaches in the Women's and Gender Studies program and in Interdisciplinary Studies at Southern Mississippi University at Hattiesburg. Gillespie has published on Spanish colonial literary and cultural studies as well as on innovative pedagogies and interdisciplinary inquiry. Her current research project is the documentation of plant materials and healing practices in indigenous Mexican documents, especially poetic and dramatic texts. In conjunction with that research, she is preparing an article on women's voices in the Iberian colonial record that examines Native American women whose words and accounts have been recorded in Spanish documents. Gillespie holds a Bachelor of Arts in Spanish from Purdue, a Master of Arts in Latin American Studies with concentrations in

Anthropology and Art History from the University of Texas at Austin and a doctorate in Spanish American Literature from the Arizona State University. She is currently Associate Professor of Spanish and Associate Dean at Southern Mississippi. Gillespie is married to musician, John Palensky, and is the mother of three vivacious children. Her home is filled with good food, great music, and much love.

Kimberly A. Habegger, PhD, retired Professor of Spanish and formerly chair of languages at Regis University in Denver, Colorado, taught language, literature, culture and interdisciplinary courses. She graduated from Ohio State University with a doctorate in Romance Languages and Linguistics with an emphasis on historical theater from the Post-war period. Participation in several seminars and institutes such as an NEH Summer Teaching Institute have afforded her the opportunity to connect her research interests with the needs of the curriculum. In past years, her research has produced several presentations and publications that explore the iconography and semiotics of the traditional arts of the American Southwest and of Spain. Of late, she has been investigating the phenomenon of the contemporary iconic wineries of Spain designed by widely renowned architects. Recent professional and personal trips to Spain, the Dominican Republic, Costa Rica, and Peru have informed her awareness of the cultural aesthetics of the Hispanic world.

Enrique Mallén, PhD, is a Professor in the Department of Foreign Languages at Sam Houston State University. He completed his Ph.D. at Cornell University. Dr. Mallen has published numerous articles and book chapters on linguistics, literature and art history. The titles of some of his books are: *Con/figuración Sintáctica*, *The Visual Grammar of Pablo Picasso*, *La Sintaxis de la Carne: Pablo Picasso y Marie-Thérèse Walter*; *Poesía del Lenguaje: De T. S. Eliot a Eduardo Espina* and *A Concordance of Pablo Picasso's Spanish Writings*, *Antología Crítica de la Poesía del Lenguaje* and *A Concordance of Pablo Picasso's French Writings*, *La muerte y la máscara en Pablo Picasso*. Dr. Mallen is a recognized expert on Pablo Picasso. He is director and general editor of the *Online Picasso Project*, an encyclopedic digital archive and catalog of the works and life of the Spanish artist, which he created in 1997.

Stephen J. Miller, PhD, is Professor of Hispanic Studies at Texas A&M University. Among his research fields are Nineteenth Century through Contemporary Narrative with special emphasis on Spanish Peninsular and American narrative. He is the author of the following volumes:

El mundo de Galdós: teoría, tradición y evolución creativa del pensamiento socio-literario galdosiano (1983); *Del realismo/naturalismo al modernismo: Galdós, Zola, Revilla y Clarín (1870–1901)* (1993); *Galdós gráfico (1861–1907): orígenes, técnicas y límites del socio-mimetismo* (2001). He is co-editor and contributor to *Critical Studies on Gonzalo Torrente Ballester* (1988; with Janet Pérez) and *Critical Studies on Armando Palacio Valdés* (1993; with Brian J. Dendle). In 2001, he did the introductions to his facsimile editions of three Galdosian graphic narratives: *Gran teatro de la pescadería*, *Las Canarias*, and *Atlas zoológico*, and to two of Galdós's sketchbooks: *Álbum arquitectónico* and *Álbum marítimo*. For the last decade, he has been doing short book reviews for *Choice* of critical studies, biographies and collected letters of Hemingway, Bellow and Updike. As contributor and co-editor with José Pablo Villalobos, he published Rolando Hinojosa's *'Klail City Death Trip Series': A Retrospective, New Directions* in 2013. He is presently working on an original book-length critical study of Hinojosa's *Klail City Death Trip* Series.

Juanita Sena Pfaff graduated summa cum laude with a B.A. in Spanish and a B.A. in Catholic Studies in 2005 from the Honors Program of the University of St. Thomas in Houston, Texas, as a Presidential Scholarship recipient, nominee for outstanding graduate in Spanish, and on the Dean's Honors List. Her Master's in Spanish with a concentration in Southwest Studies is from the University of New Mexico, where she worked as a teaching assistant in the Heritage Language track. She began as a Spanish medical interpreter and translator at North Country Healthcare in Flagstaff, Arizona, where she also began her career in medical transcription, which she has done from home for a decade while raising and homeschooling seven children, concurrently running a small business with her husband. She is also a relationship coach, which flows naturally from her love for language, culture, and relationships that have shaped her education and careers throughout her life. Her presentations and publications, mostly based on oral history research, focus primarily on her great-grandmother, Isidora "Lola" Flores (October 9, 1910–April 3, 2010), with whom she spent a summer dedicated to documenting her stories, prayers, recipes, songs, and memories. Lola was one of the original thirty-six women who created the 265-foot-long embroidered tapestry at Our Lady of Guadalupe Church in Villanueva, New Mexico, for the bicentennial event in 1976 and was featured in 2021 by *Cornerstones* after being delicately cleaned and preserved. Juanita's presentations include *Southwestern Conference of Latin American Studies (SCOLAS)*, Oral History Research Presentation, 2006; *Recovering Religious Hispanic*

Thought in the U.S., Oral History Research Presentation, 2005; *UST Research Symposium*, Research Presentation for Spanish and Catholic Studies, 2004 and 2005; and *National Association of Hispanic and Latino Studies (NAHLS)*, Research Presentation, 2005. Her publication about her great-grandmother, "La Santidad: Devotions of a New Mexican Woman," was published in *Recovering Hispanic Religious Thought and Practice of the United States*, 2007.

Rose Mary Salum Nemer, MFA, founder and director of the bilingual literary/art magazines, *Literal: Voces Latinoamericanas/Literal: Latin American Voices*, as well as the publishing house, Literal Press, and *Visible*, was born in Mexico of Lebanese descent. She holds the MA from University of St. Thomas/Houston. She is the author of four books of short stories, *El agua que mece el silencio/The Water That Rocks the Silence* (Vaso Roto, 2015); *Delta de las arenas. Cuentos árabes, cuentos judíos/Delta of the Sands: Arabic & Jewish Stories* (International Latino Book Award; Literal Publishing, 2013; Vigía, 2015); *Entre los espacios/Spaces In-Between* (Tierra Firme, 2002) y *Vitrales/Stained Glass* (Edomex, 1994). In 2009, she edited the collection, *Almalafa y Caligrafía, Literatura de origen árabe en América Latina/Moorish Apparel and Calligraphy: Literature of Arabic Origen in Latin America*, for the magazine, *Hostos Review*. Her stories and essays have appeared in the anthologies, *Women Writers in the U.S.* (Hostos Review, 2014); *Cruce de fronteras: Antología de escritores iberoamericanos en Estados Unidos/Crossing Fronteras: An Anthology of Iberian-American Writers in the U.S.* (SubUrbano, 2013); *Poéticas de los (dis)locamientos/Poetics of (Dis)Locations* (Literal Publishing, 2012); *Raíces latinas, narradores y poetas inmigrantes/Latin Roots, Immigrant Narrators and Poets* (Vagón azul, 2012); *América nuestra: antología de narrativa en español en Estados Unidos/Our America: An Anthology of the Narrative in Spanish in the U.S.* (Linkgua, 2011); *Professions* (MLA, 2009); among others. For her literary and editorial work, she has received the Author of the Year 2008 from the Hispanic Book Festival, the Hispanic Excellence Award, the International Latino Book Award, four Lone Star Awards, two CELJ Awards, the Classical Award from the University of St. Thomas, a recognition from the U.S. Congress, the Mujeres Destacadas/Outstanding Women Award, from the journalistic agency, ImpreMedia, three nominations for the Nora Magid Award from Pen America (2013), the Ana María Matute (Torremozas, 2008) y the Maggie Award (2005). She is a Fellow of the Academia Norteamericana de la Lengua/North American Academy of the Language.

The Editor and Contributors | 233

Haiqing Sun, PhD, Texas Southern University, is Professor of Spanish, with research focus on Latin American narrative and comparative study of Latin American and Chinese film and literature. She has published research on Latin American detective fiction, on writers, Jorge Luis Borges, Mario Vargas Llosa, Roa Bastos, Rodolfo Walsh, encyclopedic entries, and Chinese translations of works by Octavio Paz, Gabriela Mistral, and Luis Buñuel. She currently serves as editor for journals, *Caribbean Vistas* and *Yangtze River Academic*, and is Invited Guest Professor of Pingdingshan University. She has also worked as principal investigator in literature and culture projects funded with grants of National Endowment for the Humanities (NEH), and Humanities Texas (HTx).

Contributors to Earlier Volumes in the Series

Eduardo Cerdán, MA (Xalapa, México, 1995), adjunct professor of undergraduate studies in Letras Hispánicas de la Universidad Nacional Autónoma de México, is a writer of narrative and an essayist. He has won prizes in national story competitions, has collaborated on collected writings and on periodical publications like *Revista de la Universidad de México, La Jornada Semanal, Literal: Latin American Voices* y *La Palabra y el Hombre*. He studies sinister stories by writers of mid-century Mexico and is a columnist for *Cuadrivio Semanal*. Some of his stories have been translated to French.

Jorge Chavarro, MD, ABD in Spanish, was born in Colombia in a village with jungle heat and sun. The natives called it Tora, it's now known as Barrancabermeja; however, he lived in Bogota from the age of ten months. He graduated from medical school in the turbulent Seventies, met and married his wife, Marthica. Their first child is now a physician in the U.S. Chavarro's medical degree came after his children, including a specialization in urology in the Eighties. His cherished daughter was a gift born during his urologist degree and is now a Spanish teacher in Texas. He practiced his specialty in Colombia and taught urology at his alma mater, the National University of Colombia. In early 2002, he was a victim of kidnapping by the Colombian Self-Defense, the reason for his immigration to the U.S., which led to starting over professionally in the surgery field in the U.S. His avocation and dream to become a writer and teach literature; in fact, his first poetry collection and first short story collection are to be published in 2021. His interest in literature led him to an MA in Spanish at Sam Houston State University in 2014. He is currently a

PhD candidate at Texas A & M University in College Station whose dissertation projected for 2022 is entitled *History of Death in the Modern Period of Poetry.*

Lauren M. P. Derby holds an MA in English and American Literature with a certificate in Empire studies from the University of Houston. Her articles, book reviews, devotionals, and short stories have appeared in various non-academic publications. She has spoken at several conferences, including the South Central Modern Language Association's 2012 conference on Death and Eros. Two of her articles—"Steel-Plated Petticoats: The Heroism of Woman in *Don Quixote*" and "Rudolfo Anaya's *Bless Me, Última*: A *Mestizaje* Education"—have been published in the University of Houston's journal, *Plaza: Dialogues in Language and Literature.* Her area of focus is postcolonial and Nineteenth-century British literatures. After living abroad in Suriname and China, among others, with her diplomat husband, she lives in Washington D.C. in 2021, awaiting another international assignment.

María Montserrat (Montse) Feu López, PhD, is Associate Professor of Spanish at Sam Houston State University. She is the co-advisor of the Spanish M.A. program and advisor of Latinx student organizations. She serves on the CHSS Diversity and Inclusion Committee. She has taught Spanish, Gender Studies and Humanities courses at Hood College, the University of Houston and UH-Downtown; she was a research assistant in the Recovering the U.S. Hispanic Literary Project. Feu recovers the literary history of the Spanish Civil War exile in the United States, US Hispanic periodicals and migration and exile literature at large. With her students, she has examined and translated such recovered texts. Feu has presented her research at academic conferences and her articles have appeared in peer-reviewed journals and publishers in the United States and in Spain. Her article, "The U.S. Hispanic Flapper: *Pelonas* and *Flapperismo* in Spanish-language Newspapers 19201929," won the Research Society for American Periodicals Prize (2015). She is the author of *Correspondencia personal y política de un anarcosindicalista exiliado: Jesús González Malo (1943–1965)* (Universidad de Cantabria, 2016) and co-editor with Christopher Castañeda of *Writing Revolution: Hispanic Anarchism in the United States* (University of Illinois Press, 2019). Her manuscript, *Fighting Fascist Spain,* examines the antifascist activism and culture of workers and anarchists (University of Illinois Press, 2020). She is board member for the Recovering the U. S. Hispanic Literary Heritage and for the Research Society for American

Periodicals. She is a fellow of the Cohort #2 of the Texas Academic Leadership Academy (TALA). She was awarded the 2019 Western Social Science Association Outstanding Emerging Scholar. She can be reached at mmf017@shsu.edu.

Patricia González Gómes-Cásseres, Ph.D, was Senior Lecturer at Smith College, Northampton Massachusetts since 2006 (now retired). She earned a BA in Spanish and Biology from Mary Baldwin College at Staunton, Virginia and an MA from Middlebury College at Middlebury, Vermont. She came to Smith in 1981 after receiving a doctorate from the University of Texas at Austin. She taught courses in Latin American theater and literature for five years and went back to her home in Colombia in 1986. She returned to the United States and taught at Mount Holyoke College from 1989 to 1998. In 1998, González rejoined the Spanish and Portuguese department at Smith and since then has been teaching Caribbean literature and culture courses, as well as Spanish language courses. Her first publication, *La sartén por el mango: Encuentro de escritoras latinoamericanas* published in 1983 by Huracán in Puerto Rico, became a major work consulted avidly by Latin American feminists and was used in Latin American women studies courses in many universities in the United States during the 1980s and 1990s. Her next publications, *Confluencias en México palabra y género*, published at the *Benemérita Universidad Autónoma de Puebla* (BUAP) in 2007, covered issues related to women in academia in Mexico across different disciplines, including history, anthropology, literature and philosophy. Her current research centers on Cuban ritual theater and Latin American women writers, and she has authored many scholarly articles. She was executive director for two programs abroad, one in Córdoba, Spain (2013–15) and one in Puebla, Mexico (2008–11; and 2013). She served as resident director for the Puebla program from 2005–8. In 2015, she received an NEH grant to translate Lydia Cabrera's book *La lengua sagrada de los Ñañigos*. Thanks to the grant, she traveled to Cuba, Cameroon and Nigeria during the summer of 2016 to research secret societies in the *Calabar* region, similar to those known as the *Abakuá* in Cuba.

Luis Meneses, PhD, was a Postdoctoral Fellow and Assistant Director (Technical Development) of the Electronic Textual Cultures Lab at the University of Victoria (Canada) at the time of his participation in this series. He is a Fulbright scholar, and currently serves on the board of the *Text Encoding Initiative* (TEI) Consortium and on the *IEEE Technical Committee on Digital Libraries*. His research interests include digital humanities, digital libraries, information retrieval and human-computer interaction. His research focusses on the development of tools that facilitate open social scholarship.

Norma Adelfa Garza Mouton, PhD, is a researcher, writer and independent scholar who focuses on the subjectivity of U.S. Latinos/as expressed in autobiographical conversion narratives, autobiographical fiction, and other genres. She has published articles on the works of Teodoro Torres, Rev. Gregorio Valenzuela, Rev. Santiago Tafolla, Sr., and Rev. David Maldonado, Jr., chapters in *In Defense of My People: Alonso S. Perales and the Development of Public Intellectuals* (Arte Público Press, 2012) and in *The Body, Subject and Subjected: The Representation of the Body Itself, Illness, Injury, treatment, and Death in Spanish, Indigenous, and Hispanic American Art and Literature* (Sussex Academic Press, 20160, as well as encyclopedia entries on Latino/a literature and culture. Dr. Mouton has presented at conferences in the U.S., Spain, Croatia, and Mexico.

Jason M. Payton, PhD, was an Assistant Professor of English at Sam Houston State University at the time of the volume in which he participated. His research was broadly focused on representations of crime and criminality in early American literatures. He has published essays and reviews in such journals as Early American Literature, The New England Quarterly, and The Sixteenth Century Journal. He was working on a monograph on the literatures of piracy in early America and the early modern Atlantic world. According to the current University of Georgia website, Payton specializes in the literatures of Early America and the Atlantic world. His research interests include maritime and oceanic studies, economic history, political philosophy, and environmental studies. His current book project, *Rogue Ecologies: Piracy and the Environment in American Letters*, examines the relationship between piracy and its aqueous environs with emphasis on narratives produced by and about the Caribbean buccaneers. His work has been featured in Early American Literature and in the edited collections American Literature and the New Puritan Studies (Cambridge UP, 2017) and From Insult to Injury: Violence in Spanish, Hispanic American and Latino art and Literature (Sussex Academic Press, 2016).

His research has been supported by residential fellowships from The John Carter Brown Library in Providence, RI, and The Huntington Library in San Marino, CA.

Michelle Sharp, PhD, is the co-editor of the first critical edition of Carmen de Burgos scholarship in English, *Multiple Modernities: Carmen de Burgos, Author and Activist* (Routledge 2017). This collection was the fortuitous outcome of a series of panels dedicated to Carmen de Burgos's literacy legacy at the 23014 KFLC: The Languages, Literatures and Cultures Conference. Another featured recent publication is a chapter, "Carmen de Burgos: Teaching Women of the Modern Age" in *Kiosk Literature of Silver Age Spain*, Eds. Susan Laron and Jeffrey Zamostny (Intellect 2017). She defended her PhD dissertation titled "The Narrative of Carmen de Burgos: An Innovative Portrayal of the Family and Gender Roles in Spain," inspired by research at the Biblioteca Nacional in Madrid. Dr. Sharp now evaluates Burgos's domestic manuals and cookbooks for their contributions to Burgos's overreaching feminist mission. She was a visiting assistant professor at Macalester College (Satin Paul, MN). She is the co-editor of the first critical edition of Carmen de Burgos scholarship in English, *Multiple Modernities, Carmen de Burgos, Author and Activist* (Routledge 2017). She was the editorial advisor and contributor for the entry on Carmen de Burgos in the *Twentieth-Century Literary Criticism (TCLC)* (Cengage 2016). The chapter, "Vitamin F: The Rise of First-Wave Feminist-Fueled Home Economics," was inspired by a presentation she gave at the inaugural Early Modern Food Studies Conference at the University of Minnesota/Twin Cities in the fall of 2019. An independent scholar, she works as the administrator for the Notre Dame Club of Minnesota and writes a local newspaper column titled "Meet the Minnesota Makers: Land of 10,000 Treats." You can follow her adventures with the makers and growers of the Land of 10,000 Lakes on social media @MeettheMNMakers.

Overviews of Content of Volumes 1–7

Sustenance For the Body & Soul

The food-secure and/or privileged worldwide no longer eat and drink simply to maintain life itself. They have the advantage and choice to regard "sustenance" not just as fuel for the body/machine but as a source of pleasure and entertainment for the mind/intellect. This enhanced concept of "sustenance" embraces all the senses: visual, auditory, olfactory, gustatory, and tactile, thus including not just food & drink but ceremonies & art forms dealing with them. This book explores the substantive ways food & drink impact human existence.

The work comprises five parts: medicine; ceremonies; literature & cinema; art & artists; space/architecture & advertising/art. Food & drink start with the physical, morph into nutrition, the most basic requirements for organic life, but progress from the beginning of physical process to ceremony and expression. The result and the experience highlight physiological and sensual concepts, and indeed, preference. Food & drink staples are determined by geographic availability and cuisine & beverage are closely associated with culture & ethnicity. Contributor exploration is wide-ranging: Aztec, Mexican & Spanish medicine; African & Roman Catholic rites; cookbook discourse and socio-gender influence; literature, including cultural comparisons of cooking and cooks; preparation & representation of food & drink as artistic endeavors, including by Latin American women, and types of inspirational "fodder," especially in the context of Picasso's art in Spain & France, & Spanish wine museums & labelling.

Death & Dying in Hispanic Worlds

The dispassionate intellectual examination of the concepts of death & dying contrasts dramatically with the emotive grieving process experienced by those who mourn. Death & dying are binary concepts in human cultures. Cultural differences reveal their mutual exclusiveness in philosophical outlook, language, and much more. Other sets of binaries come into play under intellectual consideration and emotive behavior, which further divide and shape perceptions, beliefs, and actions of individuals and groups. The presence or absence of religious beliefs about life and death, and disposition of the body and/or soul, are prime distinctions. Likewise, the age-old binary of reason vs. faith.

To many observers, the topic of death and dying in the Hispanic cultural tradition is usually limited to that of Mexico and its transmogrified "religious" festival day of *Día de los Muertos*. The studies in this book seeks to widen this representation and set forth the implications of the binary aspects of death and dying in numerous cultures throughout the so-called "Hispanic world," including indigenous and European-derived beliefs and practices in religion, society, art, film & literature. Contributions include engagement with the pre-Hispanic world throughout the Americas, Picasso's poetry from Spain, cultural norms in Cuba, and the literary works of Isabel Allende of Chile, Jorge Luis Borges of Argentina and Gabriel García Márquez of Colombia. Underlying the arguments presented is Saussurean structuralist theory, which provides a platform to disentangle cultural context in comparative settings.

Crossroads: Time & Space/Tradition & Modernity

Crossroads! Intersections—physical and/or metaphorical—demand processes of consideration, determination, decision, and commitment. Stasis is no longer an option where convergence is poised before the unknown. Where categories such as gender, culture, ethnicity, socioeconomic status, philosophy and religion clash, the multivariate process can reach such complexity that literary, sociological, and psychological tools can have differing interpretations. Real-life intersections range from the mundane (choosing among food items on a menu according to taste preferences) to survival-determinants (evaluating the efficacy of various medical procedures). But such intersections are at the two ends of a very long continuum that takes in issues of form/function, and traditional vs. "modern." For example, "Home" may be defined both as a physical place and/or a mental construct. In more esoteric contexts, artists chiefly known for visual production, representing their ideas with color and form, not infrequently cross media to "paint" with words. Philosophy, religion, art and literature cross paths via symbols and other visual and linguistic constructs. Writers deal with how and where their own or their characters' multiple identities intersect. The Hispanic world is an extraordinarily vivid place to explore these crossroads.

This collection of essays addresses a multitude of crossroads in numerous Hispanic contexts across the intersections of time & space/tradition & modernity. The contexts are wide-ranging, e.g., the visual, architectural: how Spain's age-old oenological tradition meets modern technology, how the vestiges of long-term dictatorship lurk in the spaces of Spain's democracy; and how space/architecture, and art/poetry cross in Latin America. Painters Pablo Picasso and Frida Kahlo's productions cross the visual to the written; and magical realism products of the twentieth century Latin American artistic movement defy nature, science, time, and space.

Family, Friends & Foes in Hispanic Art & Literature

Jigsaw puzzles' notorious complexity and mega-multiple, amorphously shaped pieces provide an appropriate metaphor for the navigating and maneuvering necessary throughout all aspects of human dynamics. Involvement comprises not only efforts by an individual personally trying to fit together a life of relationships with *Family, Friends & Foes* within complex categories and different levels, but the efforts by groups of individuals within those categories, progressively, by those groups within a larger society and/or societies, and then, across so many so-called boundaries: geographic, ethnic, linguistic, artistic and more. Such is the starting point for this particular collection of essays, which focuses on the human dynamics in cultures characterized, mostly linguistically, as Hispanic worlds, and those cultures both in real life and in terms of cultural productions such as movies, visual art, and literature.

Unlike jigsaw puzzles with their convenient guiding box-cover representation of the finished "product" once the pieces are correctly assembled, human dynamics' "pieces" are more like amoebas, ever changing size and shape, multiplying and dividing, sometimes fitting in with other pieces, sometimes not, sometimes overlapping—in short, frequently unpredictable and always challenging for the would-be "assembler(s)." Thus, the title of this book could easily morph ad infinitum with the three elements of *Family, Friends, Foes* reflecting an enormous and unwieldy range of relationship, emotion, and viewpoint. Mixed messages abound. And as can be seen from the individual chapter titles and content so-called successful relationships may be fleeting or unattainable—or may match the imagined, hoped-for "picture" of a working relationship dynamic.

S/HE: Sex & Gender in Hispanic Art & Literature

Hierarchies and disparities based on sex and gender have characterized nearly all hominid societies over almost the entire world of cultures since time immemorial. Nearly without exception, those disparities have created a hierarchy of male over female. Many languages reflect that. But this book is not specifically about language per se. Rather, the chapters within focus on roles in Hispanic societies, "traditional feminine" domestic and biological ones, as enforced by social mores and customs, versus those roles, whether domestic, biological, professional, etc., not necessarily feminist, chosen by those who actively auto-determine, for whatever reason.

To define those foundational terms in the title and/or within the book, for the purposes of *S/HE: Sex & Gender in Hispanic Worlds*, sex refers to biological differences, i.e., reproductive organs and secondary sexual characteristics, which are perceived as oppositional, yet collaborative, in the propagation of the species. Gender, on the other hand, refers to culturally specific expectations and/or stereotypes in terms of an individual's or group's self (re)presentation and/or behaviors.

Sociologists, writers, and artists of both sexes in both languages have always addressed sex and gender concerns, whether overtly or covertly. This book, focused on the Hispanic worlds, by its focus, pays homage to all who do not fit comfortably within the strict parameters of any of the previous definitions by including broadened definitions and aspects of existence as portrayed in the life, literature and art addressed.

Insult to Injury: Violence in Spanish, Hispanic American & Latino Art & Literature

The stark reality of all life, from the biology of the food chain incorporating all living beings to the social stratification and hierarchies of human cultures, revolves around violence—physical or psychological. That unavoidable, black-and-white, worldview of survival of the fittest, with little if any gray to mitigate it, is colored only by the red lifeblood of the victims of the bigger, the stronger, the smarter, the wilier, who literally and/or figuratively "eat" their victims—overcoming, overwhelming, controlling, oppressing them.

A critical concept in this process, visualizing and identifying the *other* as victim, is key. This concept underlines that, in both life and literature, the cultural/ethnic/racial *other*, whether s/he looks, sounds, or simply is identified as *different* from the perpetrator, is as common a victim as is the *other* based on sex/gender/traditional female roles.

This book focuses on violence towards, or victimization of, the *other*, recognizing the possible multiplicity of *otherness*. The two-part self/*other* perpetrator/victim dynamic can be exacerbated by a self/*other* conflict within the victim him/herself who cannot separate his/her identities. The conflicted character may alienate him/herself within the contexts across biological and social categories and actually participate in his/her own victimization in the process.

The premise behind *Insult to Injury: Violence in Spanish, Hispanic American and Latino Art and Literature* focuses on the visual and literary artistic products of a group of seemingly alike yet divergent societies, with linguistic and cultural ties that reflect those societies' means of control. These representations socialize viewers and/or readers in personal or public situations, establishing ubiquitous hierarchies. French social anthropologist/literary critic/theorist René Girard maintains in *Violence & the Sacred* that "the oldest means of social control is . . . violence." While the incorporated violence itself may not be the overweening theme of any of the works studied, the representation or threat of violence functions in reality in terms that imply its consequences to the viewer or reader. These consequences are discussed in terms of control-directed violence. The underlying message is the necessity to behave according to imposed norms, stated or implied, or suffer those consequences—a convincing leitmotif in works by Spanish, Hispanic American and Latino visual artists and writers in the Spanish language over the ages.

The Body, Subject & Subjected: The Body, Illness, Injury, Treatment & Death in Spanish, Indigenous & Hispanic American Art & Literature

This book addresses the hominid obsession with his/her own body and its functions as a subject, plus the effects of exterior factors to which the body may be subjected, as represented in art and literature of the extended Hispanic world. The first "selfies" were prehistoric negative hand images and human stick figures, followed by stone and ceramic representations of the human figure. Thousands of years later, moving via historic art and literature to contemporary social media, the contemporary term "selfie" was self-generated.

The Body, Subject & Subjected illuminates some "selfies." This collection of critical essays about the fixation on the human self addresses a multi-faceted geographic set of cultures—the Iberian Peninsula to pre-Columbian America and Hispanic America—analyzing such representations from medical, literal and metaphorical perspectives over centuries. Chapter contributions address the representation of the body itself as subject, in both visual and textual manners, and illuminate attempts at control of the environment, of perception, of behavior and of actions, by artists and authors. Other chapters address the body as subjected to circumstance, representing the body as affected by factors such as illness, injury, treatment and death. These myriad effects on the body are interpreted through the brushes of painters and the pens of authors for social and/or personal control purposes.

The essays reveal critics' insights when "selfies" are examined through a focused "lens" over a breadth of cultures. The result, complex and unique, is that what is viewed—the visual art and literature under discussion—becomes a mirror image, indistinguishable from the component viewing apparatus, the "lens."

Index

Fictional characters are listed within single quotes, with the name of the novel/story in brackets. In most cases the character is indexed under the first name e.g. 'Adriana' (Vargas Llosa's *Lituma en los Andes*). Page numbers in italics refer to figures.

abortion, Brazil, 141
abuelas, 156
Action Francaise, 152
'Adelaide' (Cerruto's *Adelaid y la furia*), 220
'Adolfo' (Díaz-Ridgeway's *Tango: Alive on the Skin*), 19, 198, 199, 201–2, 203, 204–7
African art, 36–9, 41, 42, 43, 44–6, 52
African masks, 37, 41, 43, 53
African myths, 38
Agamemnon, 216
'Alejandro' (Díaz-Ridgeway's *Tango: Alive on the Skin*), 18, 21
Alinski, Saul, 156
altepetl, Mexica people, 180, 182, 190, 191, 193, 195–6
American Indians, 167, 170
Anahuac *see* Mexica people
Anaya Flores, Jerónimo, 9
anciana, Limón's *Song of the Hummingbird*, 78, 85–8, 90
'Ándara' (Pérez Galdós' *Nazarín*), 94, 95, 96, 99, 100, 101, 102, 103
Andes
 altiplano, 213, 216, 217, 218, 220, 222
 Cerruto's *Adelaida y la furia*, 222
 Cerruto's *Los buitres*, 218
 Cerruto's *Cerco de penumbras*, 212–13, 215
 Cerruto's *Iphigenia, el zorzal y la muerte*, 216
 Cerruto's works, 177, 212–23
 human sacrifice ritual, 199, 203, 204, 205–7, 208
 myths, 177, 200, 201, 202, 203–4, 206, 210, 212–23
 pishtaco (vampire), 198, 200, 202, 203, 204–5, 209
 rituals, 197–8, 199, 202, 203, 204, 205–7, 208, 209–10
 spirits or monsters, 198, 199, 203, 204, 206
 superstitions, 199, 200, 201, 202, 203, 204, 206, 207, 208, 209
 Vargas Llosa's *Lituma en los Andes*, 197, 198–210
Andrist, Debra D., 227
 (Culinary) Counter-Conquest, 3
 cultural perception, 83
 The Kitchen & Dining Room, 3
 Liberation Theology, 82*n*
 Life to Literature, 79
 Limón's *Song of the Hummingbird*, 78, 87
 rites, rituals and "religious" experiences, 4
androcentrism, 136, 137, 141, 143
Angry *Tias and Abuelas* group, 156
Anointing of the Sick sacrament, 112
'Anselmo, Father' (Limón's *Song of the Hummingbird*), 87, 89
Anthony, Saint, 57
antipolitical populism, 157
Anzaldúa, Gloria, 166
Apollinaire, Guillaume, 35
apus, Vargas Llosa's *Lituma en los Andes*, 203–4, 210*n*
architecture
 Bodegas Marqués de Riscal, 13, 15

Bodegas R. López de Heredia,
    13–14, 15
Bodegas Ysios, 12–13, 15
    defined, 15
Arendt, Hannah, 155, 157
Argentina, Peronism, 155
Ariadne, 203
Aristotle, *Poetics*, 97
Arnheim, Rudolf, 56
Artemis, 216
Asian Americans, 167
Asian tea ceremonies, xi
assimilation schemes, 164–7, 170
Augustine, Saint, 159, 161
Aymara myth, 220
Ayo, Álvaro A., 103
Aztec *anciana*, Limón's *Song of the Hummingbird*, 78, 85–8, 90
Aztec Empire *see* Mexica people

Bacchus, Veláquez's *El Triunfo de Baco*, 11
Barr, Alfred H, Jr., 56
Bataille, Georges, 54, 55
Bateau-Lavoir, 34, 35
Beatitudes, 114
'Beatrice' (Pérez Galdós' *Nazarín*), 94, 95, 96, 99–100, 101, 102, 103
Bellah, Robert, 150
'Belmonte' (Pérez Galdós' *Nazarín*), 96, 97, 101
"beloved community", 81, 152, 160–1, 164–6, 167, 170, 171
Benedict of Norcia, 89–90, 91*n*
'Benito, Father' (Limón's *Song of the Hummingbird*), 85–9, 90
Berceo, Gonzalo de, 9
Berdyaev, Nicholas, 152
Berg, Mary G., 200
Berkowitz, Peter, 74*n*
Bhabha, Homi, 209
'Bianca' (Díaz-Ridgeway's *Tango: Alive on the Skin*), 18
Bianco, Benedetta, 34
Bidney, David, 204
Bilbao Guggenheim, 13
Bills, Garland D., 122
Bingemer, María Clara, 138, 140, 143
Bingo, 144, 145
Birmingham, Alabama, civil rights movement, 159
"Black Legend" stereotype, 90, 91*n*
Black Lives Matter Movement, 168

black magic, 38, 45, 46
Black Power Movement, 164
Black Social Gospel heritage, 152, 158–63
black theology, 164
Blier, Suzanne Preston, 37
Bly, Peter, 103
Bodegas Marqués de Riscal, 13, 15
Bodegas R. López de Heredia, 13–14, 15
Bodegas Ysios, 12–13, 15
Boesky, Ivan, 104*n*
Bolivian Revolution (1952), 216
Borges, Jorge Luis, 217
Boudaille, Georges, 48
Braig, Marianne, 71, 72, 73, 74–5*n*
Brassaï, 53
Brazil, abortion, 141
Bretherton, Luke, 152, 155–8, 160–1, 163, 166, 167, 168–9, 170
Breton, André, 33, 48, 49, 50, 56
Brexit, 71, 72, 74*n*
Brooks, David, 158
'*bruja* (witch)', Vargas Llosa's *Lituma en los Andes*, 203, 204
Buckingham, Susan, 147*n*
Burke, John Francis, xiv, 81, 148*n*, 228

Cabanne, Pierre, 57
Los Cachuchas, 28
Calatrava, Santiago, 12
Callahuaya, 213, 224*n*
The Cambridge Encyclopedia of Anthropology, ix
Canales, Victor, 9
Canals, Ricardo, 34
candomblé, x
Canovan, Margaret, 157
Cantú, Norma, 147*n*
capitalism, 73, 147*n*, 154
Caracalla, Emperor of Rome, 51
Carney, D.R., 83
Carpentier, Alejo, 212, 224*n*
Casagemas, Carles, 47
Casas, Bartolomeo de las, 88, 90, 91*n*
'Casimiro Huarcaya' (Vargas Llosa's *Lituma en los Andes*), 198, 199, 202
Castro, Mark A., 25
Caws, Mary Ann, 56
Cendrars, Blaise, 38
Cerberus, 55

Cerdán, Eduardo, xiv, 3, 79, 233
Cerruto, Óscar
  Adelaida y la furia, 220, 222–3
  Alegría del mar, 221
  Alimento profético, 218
  Altiplano, 223
  altiplano theme, 213, 216, 217, 218, 220, 222
  Aquella noche Ana presintió, 218
  La araña, 221–2
  El aviso, 221, 222
  Los buitres, 217, 218–19, 222
  Cerco de penumbras, 212–23
  El círculo, 214–15, 220
  classical metaphors, 221
  death theme, 213, 215–16, 217, 218
  La estrella de agua, 221
  fatalism, 213, 215
  indigenous myth in the Bolivian Andes, 177, 212–23
  Iphigenia, el zorzal y la muerte, 215–17
  La junta de sangres, 218
  metal theme, 221–2
  Morada de ébano, 218, 221, 222
  Un poco de viento, 217–18, 219
  Retorno con Laura, 217
  El rostro sin lumbre, 218
  wind theme, 215, 217–18, 219, 220, 222
Cervantes, Miguel de, *El Quijote*, 8, 9, 100
Cézanne, Paul, 35, 42
chalchihuitli beads, 180, 185, 194
Chalchihuitlicue (Jade Her Skirt), 179, 180–91, *181*, *182*, *183*, *184*, *185*, 192, *192*, 194–6, *195*
Chan, Edwin, 13
Charro Gorgojo, Manuel Ángel, 6
Chavarro, Jorge, 3, 233–4
Chicano movement, 152, 161, 167, 169
Chichimecs, 186, 194
"children of darkness", 160
"children of light", 160
Christian Democratic movement, Latin America, 152, 153
Christian, Ed, 209
Christianity
  anarchist model, 154
  battle with paganism, 147–8n
  Bodegas Ysios, 13

Holy Spirit, 107, 110, 113, 114–15, 116
Limón's *Song of the Hummingbird*, 87, 88–9
rites and rituals, x
Trinity, 107, 116, 117
wine culture, 7
see also faith; Jesus Christ; Liberation Theology; Old Testament; priests; Roman Catholic Church; sacraments
'el ciego' (*Lazarillo de Tormes*), 9–10
Cité de Vin, Bordeaux, 12
civil religion, 150–1, 157, 161, 169–70
civil rights movement, 158, 159, 160, 164
civil society, 155–6
Clark, Timothy James, 49
climate change, 137–8, 153
Clytemnestra, 216
Coalition of Brazilian Women, 148n
Coatlicue (Serpent Skirt), 179
Coatlinchan, 182, *182*, 185, 195
Codex Florentino, 180, 181, 188, 189, 194
collectivism, 151
Cone, James, 164, 165, 167
Confession sacrament
  Cerruto's *El Círculo*, 214
  Limón's *Song of the Hummingbird*, 86, 89
  Unamuno's *San Manuel Bueno, mártir*, 112
Congo, Vili statuette, 37
consociational democracy, 152, 157, 158, 160–1
consumers, 154, 155
corrida, xi
Cortázar, Julio, 223n
Cortés, Hernán, 86, 88, 90
Coscio, Elizabeth, xiv, 177–8, 228
costumbrista literary movement, 221, 225n
"*Cotidiano*", 136–7
Cowling, Elizabeth, 51
Coyolxauhqui (She of the Jingle Bells), 179
Crespelle, Jean-Paul, 55
Crick, Bernard, 157
Cruz Barcenas, Arturo, 182
Cuba, dances, x
Cubism, 36, 39, 40, 42, 44, 46

cultural intersections, 152, 166–9, 170–1
culture
  approach to God, 124–5
  defined, 84, 123
  and faith, 119, 124, 125, 126, 128, 129, 130, 131
  inculturation, 119, 124, 126–7, 131
  and language, 119, 123, 125–6, 127
  restoration of, 119, 126–31
  Roman Catholic Church, 123–5
  and women, 126–30

Daedalus, 50
Dagen, Philippe, 56
Daix, Pierre, 42, 46
Dalí, Salvador, 8
dance rites, x–xi, 3, 17–22
Davis, Angela, 167
DeLaRosa Burke, Mary Jane, xv, 80–1, 142–7, 227–8
Delevoy, L., 45
'Demetrio Chanca' (Vargas Llosa's *Lituma en los Andes*), 198, 199, 202
democratic populism, 157, 158
demons, religious beliefs, 23
Derain, André, 37, 39
Derby, Lauren M.P., xiii, 234
Deutch, Miriam, 42
Les Deux-Magots, 53, 54
Díaz-Ridgeway, Gwendolyn, xiv, 3, 229
'Dionisio' (Vargas Llosa's *Lituma en los Andes*), 198, 199, 201–2, 203
Dionysus, 203
Dolgin, Stacey L., 100
'Don Manuel' (Unamuno's *San Manuel Bueno, mártir*), 107, 108–14, 115–17
'Don Pedro' (Pérez Galdós' *Nazarín*), 96, 97, 101
'Doña María de Belén' (Limón's *Song of the Hummingbird*), 85–8, 89, 90
Doña Marina, 90, 91n
Dorgelès, Roland, 36
Dorrien, Gary, 164
double consciousness, 162, 165
Du Bois, W.E.B., 162, 165
Dubienne, Laurent, 34, 35
Durán, Diego, 90, 91n, 188, 190

Ecclesiastes, Book of, 7
eco-theology, 138
eco-violence, 81
ecofeminism, 80–1, 136–8, 140, 142, 145–7, 147n
ecological concerns, 81, 136
economic inequality, 160
Elciego town, 13
'Electra' (Díaz-Ridgeway's *Tango: Alive on the Skin*), 17–18, 20, 21
Eliade, Mircea, 38
Elizondo, Virgilio, 122–3, 152, 158, 161–3, 164, 165, 166, 168
Éluard, Paul, 53–4
'Elvira' (Cerruto's *El círculo*), 214, 215, 220
emotions, 168, 169
environmentalism, 147n
Eros (life drive), 40
Escuela Nacional Preparatoria, 28
Espinosa, Patricia, 137–8
Esprit journal, 153, 154
Eucharist sacrament, 7, 112
European Union
  Brexit, 71, 72, 74n
  crises, 71–2
  economic growth, 72
  populism, 71, 72–3
existentialism, 153
exorcism, religious beliefs, 23

Faggioli, Massimo, 151
faith
  and culture, 119, 124, 125, 126, 128, 129, 130, 131
  Hispanic women, 127, 128, 129, 130, 131
  influence on work, 129
  Pérez Galdós' *Nazarín*, 102, 103
  personalism, 151
  prayer of the rosary, 127
  Unamuno's *San Manuel Bueno, mártir*, 106, 107, 108–9, 110, 111, 112, 113, 114, 116
  women in poverty, 139
Fang masks, 37
fascism, 59, 71, 152, 153, 155
Félix, María, 27
feminism
  European American dominance, 167
  race politics, 167
  see also ecofeminism; women

248 | Index

'Fermín' (Cerruto's *Adelaida y la furia*), 220, 222
Fernández de Moratín, Leandro, 94, 104*n*
Ferrier, Jean-Louis, 48
Feu López, Montse, xiii, 234–5
Flam, Jack D., 42
flamenco, xi
Flores, Nicole, 152, 167–9, 170
Foncerrada de Molina, Marta, 181
Fraga, Mike, Limón's *Song of the Hummingbird*, 86–8
France
   personalist communitarianism, 152–5
   Vichy regime, 153
Freud, Sigmund, 40
Fridamania phenomenon, 31
Friesz, Othon, 34
Fuentes, Carlos, 223*n*
Fuertes, Gloria, 10
Fujimori, Alberto, 197

Gaia, 145
García Márquez, Gabriel, 212, 223*n*
Garcia-Rivera, Alejandro, 167
Gargallo, Germaine, 47
Garrow, David, 159, 169
Gasman, Lydia Csató, 48, 51, 52
Gauguin, Paul, 45
Gebara, Ivone, 80–1, 136, 137, 138, 139–41, 142, 143, 144, 145–6
Gehry, Frank O., 13
Genesis, Book of, 143
genocide, 170
George, Francis E., 124, 125, 126
Gillespie, Jeanne, xiii, 78–9, 176, 229
Gilot, Françoise, 40, 51
gitanos, xi
Glaude, Eddie, 170
global warming, 137–8, 153
globalization, 72, 73
God
   "beloved community", 160
   calling of priests, 108, 109–10, 116
   Cerruto's *El círculo*, 214
   cultural approach to, 124–5
   death of, 93
   feminine characteristics of, 138
   Gebara's ecofeminism, 138, 140
   Limón's *Song of the Hummingbird*, 87, 89
   Pérez Galdós' *Nazarín*, 100, 101, 103–4, 105*n*
   revelation through language, 124
   Unamuno's *San Manuel Bueno, mártir*, 107, 108–10, 111, 112–15, 116–17
González, Corky, 161
González Gómes Cásseres, Patricia, xiv, 79, 235
Good Reads, 85–6
Goodman, Nelson, 15
Gorski, Philip, 150, 151, 158
Gotthardt, Alexxa, 29, 30
Greece, crises, 72
Greek mythology, 203, 216
Guadalajara International Book Fair, 70–4
Guadalupe, Our Lady of, 147
   Elizondo's political theology, 162
   Feast Day, 137, 146
   feminine characteristics of God, 138
   interaction with Juan Diego, 167–8
   Nican Mopohua account, 136, 140, 147*n*, 148*n*
   quote to Mexican Indigenous, 136
   women in poverty, 140, 142
Guatemala, US intervention, 28
Guégan, Stéphane, 12
'gypsy' (Pérez Galdós' *Nazarín*), 99

habanera, x
Habegger, Kimberly, xiv, 2–3, 14, 230
Hadid, Zaha, 13–14
Haro town, 13–14
hearing, sense of, 83
Hegel, Georg Wilhelm Friedrich, 28, 93
Hephaestus, 50
hermanas, 156
Herrera, Hayden, 25
Heymann, Emile, 37
Hidalgo, Jacqueline, 152, 164, 167, 169, 170
Las Hijas de María, 142–7
Hinojosa, Rolando, 79
Hispanic family
   importance of, 126–7
   restoration of culture, 126–31
   women's role, 130–1
Hispanic women
   motherhood, 130
   New Mexico, 126–30

religious faith, 127, 128, 129, 130, 131
restoration of culture, 126–31
revitalization of language, 126, 127–8, 131
role in the family, 130–1
Holy Orders, Unamuno's *San Manuel Bueno, mártir*, 107, 108–10, 115, 116
Holy Spirit, Unamuno's *San Manuel Bueno, mártir*, 107, 110, 113, 114–15, 116
huancas, Vargas Llosa's *Lituma en los Andes*, 202–3, 210n
Huayra-Tata god, 220
Huey Tozoztli festival, 180, 188
Huitzilopochtli, 179, 192, 194
huitzitzilin bird, 90
'Huitzitzilin/Hummingbird' (Limón's *Song of the Hummingbird*), 85–8, 89, 90
Hungary, right-wing populist government, 150
Huntington, Samuel, 166

Industrial Areas Foundation (IAF), 156, 157
Ingres, Jean-Auguste-Dominique, 42
'Iphigenia' (Cerruto's *Iphigenia, el zorzal y la Muerte*), 216, 217
ironism, 74n
Isasi-Díaz, Ada María, 167
Isenheim Altarpiece, 57
Isis, 13
ITAP (Illinois) website, 83–4, 91n
Iztaccihuatl volcano, 186, 187

Jacob, Max, 36, 38
Jamaica Bingo, 144
jerez (sherry), 10
Jesus Christ
  Beatitudes, 114
  casting out of demons, 23
  Cerruto's *El círculo*, 214
  choosing of apostles, 108
  and the Church, 107, 110, 115–16
  Directory on the Ministry and Life of Priests, 107, 110
  Elizondo's political theology, 162
  founding figure of Christian Era, 95, 100
  Gebara's ecofeminism, 140
  Incarnation, 111
  Last Supper, 7
  Limón's *Song of the Hummingbird*, 87
  Passion and Death, 111
  Pérez Galdós' *Nazarín*, 95, 96, 97, 101, 102, 103
  perfection of, 107–8, 109
  priesthood's relationship to, 107–8, 110, 112–13, 115–16
  Renan's *The Life of Jesus*, 93
  Sacred Heart, 127
  Unamuno's *San Manuel Bueno, mártir*, 106, 107, 110, 111, 112–14, 115–17
  women in poverty relations with, 137, 139
  Word made flesh, 124
John of the Cross, Saint, 103
Johnson, Lyndon, 163
Juan Diego, Saint, 147n, 148n, 167–8
Jung, Carl, 50

Kahlo, Cristina, 24, 26
Kahlo, Frida
  El accidente, 25
  The Broken Column, 26
  The Bus, 25
  bus accident, 24, 25–6
  childhood polio, 24
  communism, 28–30
  death theme, 31
  diary, 27
  Diego and I, 27
  Diego on My Mind, 27
  Diego y Frida, 26
  final leg amputation, 24, 31
  Frida and the Cesarean, 27
  Fridamania phenomenon, 31
  "fruit" works, 25, 28
  Henry Ford Hospital, 27, 28
  indigenous costumes, 24, 27
  later-life medical issues, 24
  legacy of, 31
  Marxism will give Health to the Sick, 29
  medical history and suffering, 24, 26
  miscarriages & therapeutic abortions, 24, 27–8
  Naturaleza viva, 25
  physical and emotional demons, 4, 23–4, 31
  post-polio syndrome, 24

Kahlo, Frida *(continued)*
  self-exorcism, 4, 23–4, 31
  Self-Portrait with Stalin, 30
  self-portraits, 4, 23–4, 26–7, 28, 30
  social & professional misogyny, 24, 31
  socio-political concerns, 24, 28–30
  still-lifes, 25, 28, 31
  Thinking about Death, 31
  Two Fridas, 26
  El venado herido, 24
  Without Hope, 31
Kant, Immanuel, 28
'Karolyn' (Díaz-Ridgeway's *Tango: Alive on the Skin*), 17–21
Keenan, Sean, 91*n*
Kettenmann, Andrea, 29
Khokholova, Olga, 4–5, 48–9
Kierkegaard, Søren Aabye, 214, 224*n*
King, Martin Luther, Jr., 152, 158–61, 162, 163, 164–5, 166, 168, 169, 170, 171
Kozloff, Max, 41
Kris, Ernst, 50

Laclau, Ernesto, 157
Laguardia town, 12–13
Lake Texcoco, 188, 189, 190, 194, 195
'landlady' (Pérez Galdós' *Nazarín*), 99
Lang, Amélie (Fernande Olivier), 4, 34–6, 40, 59*n*
language
  and culture, 119, 123, 125–6, 127
  and faith, 125
  and identity, 119, 122, 123, 125
  revelation of God, 124
  revitalization of, 119, 126, 127–8, 131
  significance of, 119, 122–3
language death, 119, 121, 131
Larousse, 215
Last Supper, 7
Latin America
  Christian Democratic movement, 152, 153
  colonial period, 161
  emigrants, 154
  mestizaje discourse, 161, 164, 165
  Roman Catholic Church, x, 78, 178
  Spanish conquest of, 161
Latin American Boom, 212, 223*n*, 224*n*

Latino
  New Mexico population, 120
  as traditional term, xi
Latinx communities
  mestizaje, 161
  United States, xi, 152, 156, 158, 161–3, 164, 165, 166–7
Latinx movement, 161
'Lazarillo' (*Lazarillo de Tormes*), 9–10
Le Pen, Marie, 152
Leal, Brigitte, 58–9
Lenin, Vladimir, 28, 30
Leo XIII, Pope, 96, 97
Lévi-Strauss, Claude, 49–50
liberal democracies, 150, 154, 155, 158, 161, 165
liberation movements, 166, 167
Liberation Theology, 80, 82*n*, 136, 141, 153
libertarianism, 151
Limón, Graciela, *Song of the Hummingbird*, 78, 84, 85–90
Literal Publishing, 70, 71
'Lituma' (Vargas Llosa's *Lituma en los Andes*), 20, 198–203, 206, 207–8, 209
Live Science website, 23, 31*n*
living wage, 156
'Llantac' (Vargas Llosa's *Lituma en los Andes*), 199
London Citizens, 156–7, 166
Lord, James, 57
Lorde, Audre, 167
Lotería, 144

Maar, Dora, 4, 53–9
MACC (Mexican American Cultural Center), 163
McCully, Marilyn, 45
Machado, Antonio, 10
madres, 156
madrinas, 144
magic
  as a 'craft', ix
  entertainment aspects of, ix
  Picasso's art, 4–5, 33–4, 38, 45, 46–50, 51–3
  rites, rituals and/or religions, viii–ix, 2
  wine, 14
magic realism, 212, 223–4*n*
Magnificat website, 140, 148*n*

Malinche, 90, 91*n*
Mallén, Enrique, xiii, 4–5, 230
Malraux, André, 45, 53
mambo, x
Man Ray, 54, 58
Marcel, Gabriel, 152
Maritain, Jacques, 152
Marx, Karl, 28, 29
Marxism, 29, 152, 153, 198
Mary, mother of Jesus, 111, 127, 137, 138, 143, 148*n*
Massingale, Bryan, 160
Los matachines, 137, 147–8*n*
Matisse, Henri, 36, 37, 41, 42
Matlacuye volcano, 186, 187
Matrimony sacrament, 112
Maurras, Charles, 152
'mayor' (Pérez Galdós' *Nazarín*), 102
Medina, Nestor, 164, 165, 168
Meneses, Luis, 235–6
'Mercedes' (Vargas Llosa's *Lituma en los Andes*), 198, 199
Mesoamerica, significance of water, 179, 180–1, 185, 186
mestizaje, 161, 162–3, 164, 165, 168
Mexica people
  altepetl, 180, 182, 190, 191, 193, 195–6
  Chalchihuitlicue (Aztec deity), 179, 180–91, *181*, *182*, *183*, *184*, *185*, 192, *192*, 194–6, *195*
  hegemony, 179
  Huey Tozoztli festival, 180, 188
  Huitzilopochtli (Aztec deity), 179, 192, 194
  human sacrifice ritual, 188–9
  Leyenda de los Soles, 191
  Limón's *Song of the Hummingbird*, 86–8
  Nahui Atl, 191, 195
  Nahui ehecatl, 191
  Nahui ocelotl, 191
  Nahui Ollin, 191, 192, *192*, 195
  Nahui quiahuitl, 191
  Quetzalcoatl (Aztec deity), 88, 179, 186, 187, 190, 191, 192
  sculptures, 179–96
  significance of water, 179, 180–1, 185, 186
  Sun Stone, *190*, 191, 192, *192*, 195
  teoicpalli ("divine throne"), 180, 181
  tepictonton, 186, 187–8, *187*, 190

Tlaloc (Aztec deity), 181, 186, 187, 188–9, 191
violence against female bodies, 179
Mexican American Cultural Center (MACC), 163
Mexican Communist Party (PCM), 28
Mexicanidad, 30
Miller, Stephen, xiv, 3, 30–1, 79, 80, 95–6
minimum income policy, 160
modern art, 42
Monte Tlaloc (Tlaloctepetl), 182, *182*, 188, 190, 194, 195
morisca sword dance, 147*n*
Motecuzoma II of Tenochtitlan, 88, 188
Motecuzoma Ilhuicamina, 192
Mounier, Emmanuel, 152–5, 158, 159, 160, 161, 168, 170, 171
Mouton, Norma, xiii, 236
Mucha, Alphonse, 11
Murray, John Courtney, 170
Musée d'Ethnographie du Trocadéro, 39, 42, 44
Museo del Prado, 11
mythic realism, 212, 223
myths
  African, 38
  Andean, 177, 200, 201, 202, 203–4, 206, 210, 212–23
  Aymara myth, 220
  Cerruto's *Los buitres*, 218, 219
  Cerruto's *El círculo*, 215, 220
  Cerruto's *Iphigenia, el zorzal y la muerte*, 215, 216, 217
  Greek mythology, 203, 216
  Vargas Llosa's *Lituma en los Andes*, 200, 201, 202, 203–4, 206, 210

Nahui Atl, 191, 195
Nahui ehecatl, 191
Nahui ocelotl, 191
Nahui Ollin, 191, 192, *192*, 195
Nahui quiahuitl, 191
'narrator' (Pérez Galdós' *Nazarín*), 96, 97, 98, 99, 102
'Nazarín' (Pérez Galdós' *Halma*), 103, 104–5*n*
'Nazarín' (Pérez Galdós' *Nazarín*), 93–5, 96–104
neoliberalism, 72
New Mexico
  culture and language, 123

New Mexico *(continued)*
　dialects of Spanish, 120
　Heritage Language Revitalization Planning Manual, 122
　Hispanic or Latino population, 120
　language shift to English, 121–2
　Mexican immigrants, 120, 121
　prayers of the rosary, 127
　Spanish immigrants, 120
　traditional Spanish language, 119–22
　women, 126–30
New York Times, 71
Nezahualpili, 188
Nican Mopohua, 136, 140, 147*n*, 148*n*
Niebuhr, Reinhold, 159–60, 161, 165, 166
Nietzsche, Friedrich, 93
Nin, Anaïs, 83, 91*n*
nochtli cactus, 194
Nogueira-Godsey, Elaine, 141
Nussbaum, Martha, 168, 169

Oblitas Poblete, Enrique, 213–14
O'Brian, Patrick, 47
Ochpanitzli festival, 180
Odysseus, 59
Old Testament
　Genesis creation story, 143
　prophets, 140, 153
　Tower of Babel story, 125–6
　viniculture discussions, 7
Oliveira, Rosiska Darcy de, 138, 148*n*
Olivier, Fernande, 4, 34–6, 40, 59*n*
onomatopoeia, 83
optical illusions, 83
Orpheus, 49
Ors, Eugeni d', 59
Ortega y Gasset, José, 9
Osiris, 13
Ostria, Yvette, 220
"the other", 19
Otherness, Picasso's *Les trois danseuses*, 49

Pachamama (Mother Earth), 215, 220
Palau i Fabre, Josep, 52
'Paloma' (Limón's *Song of the Hummingbird*), 88, 89
Pantitlan ("Flag Place"), 188, *189*, 190, 194

parables
　defined, 214
　see also Cerruto, Óscar
Parra Sandoval, Nicanor Segundo, 84, 91*n*
Pastor Poppe, Ricardo, 216, 217
patriarchy, 139, 147*n*, 167
Paul, Saint, 114, 115
Paul VI, Pope, 107
Payton, Jason, 81, 236
PCM (Mexican Communist Party), 28
'Pedro Tinoco' (Vargas Llosa's *Lituma en los Andes*), 198, 199
Penrose, Roland, 46–7, 53
Penuel, Arnold M., 200, 203
perception, 83, 84
Le Père Sauvage, 36
Pérez Galdós, Benito
　The Grandfather. Novel in Five Acts, 97
　Halma, 93, 95, 103, 104–5*n*
　Nazarín, 79, 93–5, 96–104
　Realidad. Drama en cinco actos, 97
　Realidad. Novela en cinco jornadas, 97
Peronism, Argentina, 155
personalist communitarianism, 151–5, 158, 161, 170
Peter the Apostle, 97
Pfaff, Juanita Sena, xv, 79–80, 81, 231–2
Picasso, Conchita, 36
Picasso, Pablo
　African art influence, 36–9, 41, 42, 43, 44–6, 52
　art as a shamanistic practice, 38, 44–5
　Atelier avec tête et bras de plâtre, 50–1
　Le baiser, 51
　black magic, 38, 45, 46
　La bouteille du vin, 11
　brothel visits, 40
　Buste d'homme, 59
　Buste et palette, 51, 52–3
　Cubism, 36, 39, 40, 42, 44, 46
　death theme, 46–7, 51–3
　demiurgos figure, 50
　Demoiselle d'Avignon, 41
　Les demoiselles d'Avignon, 39, 40–4, 45–6, 50
　Les demoiselles d'Avignon: nu jaune (Étude), 41

demons, 45, 52
Dora Maar et figure antique, 55
drawing, 40
exorcism, 40, 44, 52, 53
Femme nue aux bras levés, 44
La femme qui pleure, 56–7
La femme qui pleure (Étude) (June 1937), 57
La femme qui pleure (Étude) (May 1937), 56
Figure, 45
Figure de femme debout, 53
German occupation of Paris, 57–9
Guernica, 56
hatchings, 41, 43, 44, 46
Homme debout, 45
intercessors, 39, 44, 53
"Magic Series", 51–3
magical art, 4–5, 33–4, 38, 45, 46–50, 51–3
masks, 37, 41, 43, 53
Musée d'Ethnographie du Trocadéro visit, 39, 42, 44
naturalism, 39–40
Nature morte au buste et à la palette, 51, 53
Nu à la draperie: tête de femme (Étude), 44
Otherness, 49
"Picasso, the Effervescence of Shapes" exhibit, 12
Portrait de Dora Maar pensive, 56
Portrait de femme, 59
Portrait de Max Jacob, 38–9
portrayal of wine, 11, 15
Poupée et femme se noyant, 55–6
primitivism, 34, 39, 42, 44–5, 46, 52
proclivity for superstition, 33
relations with Dora Maar, 4, 53–9
relations with Fernande Olivier, 4, 34–6, 40
sailor guise, 59
self-portraits, 59
shrine at Bateau-Lavoir, 35–6
sketchbooks, 40
"sorcery", 38, 40, 44
La statuaire (La femme sculpteur), 51, 52, 53
still lifes, 12, 52
studio, 34, 35
surrealist period, 48, 50
Tête de bélier, 51–2

Tête de Dora Maar, 53
Tête de femme, 57–9
tribal fetishism, 41
Les trois danseuses, 46–50, 51
windows motif, 47, 52, 53
wood carving, 45
Picasso, Paulo, 50
Pichot, Ramon, 46–7, 48, 51
pishtaco (vampire), Vargas Llosa's Lituma en los Andes, 198, 200, 202, 203, 204–5, 209
Plato, 97
pluralism, 153, 154, 155, 157, 158, 171
Poland, right-wing populist government, 150
polkas, xi
Pontifical Council for Culture, 123, 127–8, 130–1
Popocatepetl volcano, 186, 187
populism, 71, 72–3, 150, 157, 158
post-colonial theory, 209
power politics, 159, 160
priests
  administering of sacraments, 107–8, 109, 110, 112–13, 116
  call of God, 108, 109–10, 116
  cassocks, 104n
  Catechism of the Catholic Church, 107–8, 109, 113, 115–16
  chastity vow, 87, 101, 115, 116
  Directory on the Ministry and Life of Priests, 107, 110
  function and goals of, 107–8
  Limón's Song of the Hummingbird, 78, 85–9, 90
  as ministers of Jesus Christ, 107–8, 110, 112–13, 115–16
  obedience vow, 101, 115–16
  Pérez Galdós' Nazarín, 93–5, 96–104
  poverty vow, 101, 115, 116
  Presbyterorum Ordinis, 107, 114
  representation in literature, 78, 79–80, 84, 85–9, 90, 93–5, 96–104, 106–7, 108–17
  rites and rituals, 79–80
  Unamuno's San Manuel Bueno, mártir, 79–80, 106–7, 108–17
  vocation of priesthood, 106–7, 108, 109–10
  vows, 87, 101, 115–16
  see also faith

Primeros memoriales, 180, *184*, 185–6, *185*, *187*
primitive arts, 41
"primitive" carvings, 38
primitivism, Picasso's style, 34, 39, 42, 44–5, 46, 52
Prometheus, 50
protest strategies, 159–60, 161, 163, 165, 169
Pugliese, Osvaldo, 21
Pyramid of the Moon, 182, *183*

Qollahuayas, 224n
Els Quatre Gats, 34
Quetzalcoatl (Aztec deity), 88, 179, 186, 187, 190, 191, 192
quinceañera, x

racism, 28, 70, 160, 167
Radford, Benjamin, 23, 31n
rationality, 151
Rawls, John, 168
Rebaza-Soraluz, Luis, 200, 210
Reconciliation sacrament, 112
relational ethics, Flores' works, 152, 167–9, 170
religion
  defined, viii
  Limón's *Song of the Hummingbird*, 87
  "magical" aspects of, viii–ix, 2
  see also Christianity; faith; Jesus Christ; Liberation Theology; Old Testament; priests; Roman Catholic Church; sacraments
religious nationalism, 151, 155, 159, 169
Renan, Ernst, 93
'reporter' (Pérez Galdós' *Nazarín*), 96, 98, 99, 102
resurrection, Gebara's ecofeminism, 139–40
La Révolution surréaliste, 48, 50
Richardson, John, 59
Righter, William, 207
Rioja wine area, 12–14
rites
  Christianity, x
  dance, x–xi, 3, 17–22
  defined, viii
  "magical" aspects of, viii–ix, 2
  priests, 79–80
  wine-tasting/drinking, xi, 2–3, 6–15

"rites of passage", x
rituals
  Andes, 197–8, 199, 202, 203, 204, 205–7, 208, 209–10
  defined, viii
  human sacrifice ritual, 188–9, 199, 203, 204, 205–7, 208
  "magical" aspects of, viii–ix, 2
  priests, 79–80
  Vargas Llosa's *Lituma en los Andes*, 197–8, 199, 202, 203, 204, 205–7, 208, 209–10
  wine-tasting/drinking, xi, 2–3, 6–15
Rivelois, Jean, 71, 72–3, 75n
Rivera, Diego, 24, 25, 26, 27, 29–30, 31
Rivera Rodas, Óscar, 218, 219, 220
Rocha, Sheila, Limón's *Song of the Hummingbird*, 85–8
Roman Catholic Church
  Ad Gentes Divinitus, 128
  androcentrism, 137, 141
  caring for creation and saving creation, 138
  Catechism of the Catholic Church, 107–8, 109, 113
  Cerruto's *El círculo*, 214, 215
  confession of sins, 214
  definition of culture, 123
  DeLaRosa Burke's experience in Texas, 142–7
  diversity of, 124
  dominance in Hispanic worlds, x, 78, 178
  Gaudium et Spes, 129, 163
  imitatio Christi, 96, 97, 100, 104, 105n
  importance of culture, 123–5
  Limón's *Song of the Hummingbird*, 78, 85–9, 90
  Pérez Galdós' *Nazarín*, 93–5, 96–104
  Pontifical Council for Culture, 123, 127–8, 130–1
  Presbyterorum Ordinis, 107, 114
  present day problems, 136
  priests' cassocks, 104n
  representation in literature, 78, 79–80, 85–9, 90, 93–5, 96–104
  rites and rituals, x, 79–80
  Sacred Heart, 127
  el santo entierro/the Holy Burial, 144

La Semana Santa (Holy Week), 120, 127, 129
Unamuno's *San Manuel Bueno, mártir*, 79–80, 106–7, 108–17
US Catholic Worker movement, 153, 154
virginity issue, 142, 143
women's role, 80–1, 136–47
see also faith; Jesus Christ; Liberation Theology; Old Testament; priests; sacraments
Roman Curia, 123
Romanticism, 221, 225*n*
Rorty, Richard, 70, 74, 74*n*
Rubin, William S., 40, 50
Ruiz, Juan, Arcipreste de Hita, 9
rumba, x

Sabartés, Jaime, 56
sacraments
  administered by priests, 107–8, 109, 110, 112–13, 116
  Anointing of the Sick, 112
  Confession, 86, 89, 112, 214
  Eucharist, 7, 112
  Holy Orders, 107, 108–10, 115, 116
  Matrimony, 112
  Reconciliation, 112
Sacred Heart, 127
Sahagún, Fray Bernardino de, 190, 196
  Codex Florentino, 180, 181, 188, 189, 194
  Primeros memoriales, 180, *184*, 185–6, *185*, 187
Salk, Jonas, 24
Salmon, André, 38
Salon d'Automne, 35
Salum, Rose Mary, xiii, xiv, 5, 79, 81, 232
salvation, Gebara's ecofeminism, 139–40
Santería syncretic rites, x
Schapiro, Meyer, 41, 51
Schwartz, Paul Waldo, 44
'Sebastián' (Díaz-Ridgeway's *Tango: Alive on the Skin*), 20–1, 22
Seckel, Hélène, 46
secular humanism, 151, 169
secularism, 151, 152, 155
secularity, 155, 170
secularization, 130, 155

Selma, Alabama
  civil rights movement, 159
  voter rights campaign, 161
La Semana Santa (Holy Week), 120, 127, 129
Sendero Luminoso (Shining Path), 178*n*
Vargas Llosa's *Lituma en los Andes*, 20, 177, 198–9, 200–1, 202, 206, 207, 208, 209
sensory perception, 83, 84
separatist schemes, 152, 164, 165–7
Sepúlveda, Juan Ginés de, 88
Shakespeare, William, 94, 104*n*, 218
shamanism, 38, 44–5
Sharp, Michelle, xiv, 3, 237
Shelby, Tommie, 167
sherry (*jerez*), 10
Shining Path *see Sendero Luminoso* (Shining Path)
Shiva, 145
sight, sense of, 83
Silver, Kenneth Eric, 47
sins
  confession of, 214
  Limón's *Song of the Hummingbird*, 87–8
slavery, 88, 165, 170
smell, sense of, 83
Smith, Kenneth, 160
social justice, 139, 146, 151, 168
Socrates, 97, 159
sodality, 137, 142, 145, 148*n*
Sorj, Bila, 138, 148*n*
Sorolla y Bastida, Joaquín, 11, 15
Spain
  crises, 72
  wine culture, 7–8, 12–15
"Spanglish", 121
Spanish Civil War (1936–1939), 28, 55, 56
Spanish language (Standard dialect), 121, 122, 127
Spanish language (traditional dialect)
  decline of, 119–22
  dialects of, 120
  generational divide, 121
  as the home language, 120–1
  New Mexico, 119–22
  origins of, 120
  revitalization and maintenance of, 80, 119, 126, 127–8, 131
  stigma of, 119

256 | Index

SPP-TAP (California) website, 83–4
Stalin, Joseph, 30
Stalinism, 30
statism, 151
Stein, Gertrude, 36–7, 44
Steinberg, Leo, 45
'Stirmsson' (Vargas Llosa's *Lituma en los Andes*), 199, 202–3, 208, 209
Storni, Alfonsina, *Hombre pequeñito*, 84–5
Strecher, Matthew, 224*n*
Sun, Haiqing, xiv, 79, 177, 208, 233
Sunyer, Joaquim, 35
superstitions, Vargas Llosa's *Lituma en los Andes*, 199, 200, 201, 202, 203, 204, 206, 207, 208, 209
Surrealism, 48, 50, 54

tango, x, xi, 3, 17–22
taste, sense of, 83
tauromaquia, xi
tea ceremonies, xi
Tecomate [Gourd] Stone, 182
Templo Mayor, Tenochtitlan, 179, 192
Tenochtitlan, 179, 188, *190*, 192, 194, *195*, 196
Teocalli (Divine House), 192, *193*, 194, 195–6
teoicpalli ("divine throne"), 180, 181
Teotihuacan, 181, 182, *184*, 185–6, 187, 190–1, 195
Tepepulco, *184*
Tepetzinco ("Little Mountain"), 188, 190, 194
tepictonton, 186, 187–8, *187*, 190
Teresa of Ávila, Saint, 103
terrucos, 200, 201, 210*n*
'Tetla' (Limón's *Song of the Hummingbird*), 88, 89
Texas
  Angry *Tias and Abuelas*, 156
  DeLaRosa Burke's experience in ministry, 142–7
  Latinx congregations, 156
Tezcatlipoca, 179, 191, 192
Thanatos (death drive), 40
'thief' (Pérez Galdós' *Nazarín*), 95, 103
Thomas à Kempis, 93
Thomas Aquinas, Saint, 112, 159
tias, 156
Tlaloc (Aztec deity), 181, 186, 187, 188–9, 191

"Tlaloc" sculpture, 182
Tlalocan, 180, 181
Tlaloctepetl (Monte Tlaloc), 182, *182*, 188, 190, 194, 195
Tlaltecuhtli (Earth Ruler), 179, 191, 192
Tlaxcala, 187
Tlazoteotl, 180
Toltec Empire, 186
'Tomás Carreño' (Vargas Llosa's *Lituma en los Andes*), 198, 199, 208
Tonalámatl Aubin, 180, *181*
Tonantzín, 145
Totila, Goth King, 90
touch, sense of, 83
Tower of Babel story, 125–6
Trinity, Unamuno's *San Manuel Bueno, mártir*, 107, 116, 117
trompe l'oeil, 83
Trotsky, Leon, 29, 30
Trotskyism, 30
Trump, Donald, 150, 170
Tucker, Michael, 38, 42
Turkey, accession to EU, 72

Ulibarri, Sabine, 122, 125
Ulysses, 59
Umberger, Emily, 186, 192, *195*
Unamuno, Miguel de, *San Manuel Bueno, mártir*, 79–80, 106–7, 108–17
Unger, Miles J., 36, 40, 46
United States
  African American communities, 152, 158–61, 162, 164–5, 166–7, 168
  American Indians, 167, 170
  Black Lives Matter Movement, 168
  Black Power Movement, 164
  Catholic Worker movement, 153, 154
  Chinese Exclusion Act, 170
  civil religion, 151
  Civil Rights Act (1964), 159
  civil rights movement, 158, 159, 160, 164
  community alliances, 167
  Great Society programs, 163
  IAF organizations, 157
  intervention in Guatemala, 28
  Latinx communities, xi, 152, 156, 158, 161–3, 164, 165, 166–7

Mexican Americans, 80–1, 142–7, 161–2, 163
"Poor People's Campaign", 161
populism, 71, 72
Trump's Presidency, 150
voter rights campaign, 161
Voting Rights Act (1965), 159
see also New Mexico; Texas
"unity-in-diversity", 151, 152, 169, 170–1

Valeriano, Antonio, 148*n*
Valladolid debate (1550), 88
Vallentin, Antonina, 43
Vanguardia movement, 223*n*
Vargas Llosa, Mario
  experience of the Andean world, 197
  García Márquez's *Cien años de soledad*, 212
  Latin American Boom, 223*n*, 224*n*
  Lituma en los Andes, 177, 197–210
  Nobel Prize in Literature, 224*n*
  Planeta Prize, 197
  presidential election (1990), 197
  Quién mató a Palomino Molero, 198
Vega, Lope de, 8
Veláquez, Diego de, 11, 15
El Vía Crucis, 127
'Vicente' (Cerruto's *El círculo*), 214, 215, 220
Vickery, John, 204
Vietnam War, 83
Vili statuette, 37
vinificación, xi, 2–3, 6–15
virginity, 142, 143
Vlaminck, Maurice de, 37, 42

waltzes, xi
water, importance in Mesoamerica, 179, 180–1, 185, 186
West, Cornel, 167, 170
white supremacy, 70
Wikipedia, ix, 74*n*, 91*n*, 223*n*, 224*n*, 225*n*
wine
  abuse of, 6, 7
  aging, 10
  architecture, 12–14
  artistic self-expression, 7–15
  famous quotes, 8–9
  humanity's nourishment and health, 6, 7
  intoxicating effects, 7
  literary texts, 9–10, 14
  "magical" essence of, 14
  moderate consumption of, 8
  paintings, 11–12, 15
  profane perspective of, 7
  prohibition of, 7
  sacred perspective of, 7
  secular celebrations, 7
  vital perspective of, 6, 7
wine tourism, 12
wine-tasting/drinking rites & rituals, xi, 2–3, 6–15
wineries
  Bodegas Marqués de Riscal, 13, 15
  Bodegas R. López de Heredia, 13–14, 15
  Bodegas Ysios, 12–13, 15
Winters, Edward, 15
Wolin, Sheldon, 157
women
  in Brazil, 14–17, 138–42
  Church role, 80–1, 136–47
  climate change, 137–8
  creating the kingdom of God on earth, 141–2, 147
  dialog experience, 140–1, 142, 147
  different values from men, 138
  experience of theology, 137
  global warming, 137–8
  as "nurturers", 138
  as political organizers, 156
  in poverty, 136–7, 138–42, 146–7
  race politics, 167
  suffering, 139
  survival experience, 138–40, 141–2, 146–7
  see also ecofeminism; feminism; Hispanic women

Xochiquetzal, 191

Yang, Andrew, 160
Yoruba, *Santería* syncretic rites, x

Zepp, Ira, 160
'Zintle' (Limón's *Song of the Hummingbird*), 87, 89